SMALL STATES IN EUROPE

Small States in Europe
Challenges and Opportunities

Edited by

ROBERT STEINMETZ
Ministry of Foreign Affairs of Luxembourg

and

ANDERS WIVEL
University of Copenhagen, Denmark

ASHGATE

© Robert Steinmetz and Anders Wivel 2010

All rights reserved. No part of this publication may be reproduced, stored in a retrieval system or transmitted in any form or by any means, electronic, mechanical, photocopying, recording or otherwise without the prior permission of the publisher.

Robert Steinmetz and Anders Wivel have asserted their right under the Copyright, Designs and Patents Act, 1988, to be identified as the editors of this work.

Published by
Ashgate Publishing Limited
Wey Court East
Union Road
Farnham
Surrey, GU9 7PT
England

Ashgate Publishing Company
Suite 420
101 Cherry Street
Burlington
VT 05401-4405
USA

www.ashgate.com

British Library Cataloguing in Publication Data
Small states in Europe : challenges and opportunities.
  1. States, Small. 2. European Union countries--Foreign relations--21st century.
  I. Steinmetz, Robert. II. Wivel, Anders.
  327.4'00905-dc22

Library of Congress Cataloging-in-Publication Data
Steinmetz, Robert.
  Small states in Europe : challenges and opportunities / by Robert Steinmetz and Anders Wivel.
     p. cm.
  Includes bibliographical references and index.
  ISBN 978-0-7546-7782-6 (hbk) -- ISBN 978-0-7546-9530-1 (ebk) 1. States, Small--Europe. 2. State governments--Europe. 3. European Union--Membership. I. Wivel, Anders. II. Title.
  JC365.S74 2009
  320.94--dc22

2009037640

ISBN 9780754677826 (hbk)
ISBN 9780754695301 (ebk)

Printed and bound in Great Britain by
TJ International Ltd, Padstow, Cornwall

Contents

List of Tables *vii*
List of Contributors *ix*
Preface: About the Resilience of Small States *xi*
    Mario Hirsch
Acknowledgements *xvii*

PART I   SMALL STATES IN EUROPE: DEFINING THE ISSUES AT STAKE

1 Introduction   3
   Robert Steinmetz and Anders Wivel

2 From Small State to Smart State: Devising a Strategy for Influence in the European Union   15
   Anders Wivel

3 Small State Diplomacy Compared to Sub-State Diplomacy: More of the Same or Different?   31
   David Criekemans and Manuel Duran

4 Small States and the European Security and Defence Policy   47
   Clive Archer

PART II   THE CHALLENGES AND OPPORTUNITIES OF SMALL EUROPEAN STATES

5 Small States and Innovation   65
   Rainer Kattel, Tarmo Kalvet and Tiina Randma-Liiv

6 Small States, Power, International Change and the Impact of Uncertainty   87
   Toms Rostoks

7 The Fluid Nature of Smallness: Regulation of the International System and the Challenges and Opportunities of Small States   103
   Plamen Pantev

PART III THE EXPERIENCE OF SMALL STATES WITH THE EUROPEAN UNION

8   In a League of its Own? The Netherlands as a Middle-Sized EU Member State   117
    Jan Rood

9   The Foreign Policy of Luxembourg   131
    Jean-Marie Frentz

10 Slovakia and the Czech Republic in the European Integration Process: Birds of a Feather Flying Apart?   147
    Mats Braun

11 Cyprus, Small-Powerhood and the EU's Principles and Values   161
    Costas Melakopides

12 Neutrality Inside and Outside the EU: A Comparison of Austrian and Swiss Security Policies After the Cold War   181
    Jean-Marc Rickli

13 The Icelandic Crash and its Consequences: A Small State without Economic and Political Shelter   199
    Baldur Thorhallsson

PART IV CONCLUSION

14 Conclusion   217
    Robert Steinmetz and Anders Wivel

Index   *227*

List of Tables

4.1	Numbers in Armed Forces ('000s), 2001 and 2007	49
4.2	Forces in ESDP Operations, 2007	51

List of Contributors

Clive Archer is Emeritus Professor of Politics at Manchester Metropolitan University.

Mats Braun is Researcher at the Institute of International Relations, Prague.

David Criekemans is Research Coordinator and Senior Researcher at the Flemish Centre for International Policy (FCIP) and Postdoctoral Researcher at the Research Group 'Diplomacy and Geopolitics' at the Faculty of Political and Social Sciences, University of Antwerp. He is also an Assistant Professor in Belgian and Comparative Foreign Policy at the University of Antwerp, and an Assistant Professor in 'Geopolitics' at the Royal Military Academy in Brussels.

Manuel Duran is Researcher at the Research Group 'Diplomacy and Geopolitics' at the Faculty of Political and Social Sciences, University of Antwerp, on a project for the Research Foundation-Flanders (project number G.0270.09N).

Jean-Marie Frentz is Associate Research Fellow at the Luxembourg Institute for European and International Studies.

Mario Hirsch is Director of the Institut Pierre Werner in Luxembourg, a trinational cultural institute set up and financed by France, Germany and Luxembourg. He is a former Lecturer at Sciences-Po Strasbourg, Political Adviser and Editor of the Luxembourg weekly 'd'Lëtzebuerger Land'.

Tarmo Kalvet is Senior Research Fellow in Innovation Policy at the Institute of Public Administration, Tallinn University of Technology.

Rainer Kattel is Professor of Technology Governance and Innovation Policy at the Institute of Public Administration, Tallinn University of Technology.

Costas Melakopides is Associate Professor of International Relations at the University of Cyprus and Director of the Cyprus Institute for Mediterranean, European and International Studies (KIMEDE), Nicosia.

Plamen Pantev is Professor of International Relations and International Law at Sofia University St. Kliment Ohridsky, founder and Director of the Institute for Security and International Studies (ISIS), Sofia.

Tiina Randma-Liiv is Professor of Public Administration and Policy at the Institute of Public Administration, Tallinn University of Technology.

Jean-Marc Rickli is President of the Geneva University Strategic Studies Group and Adjunct Professor at Webster University, Geneva.

Jan Rood is Head of Strategic Research at the Clingendael Institute, The Hague and Professor of European Integration at the University of Utrecht.

Toms Rostoks is Assistant Professor at the Faculty of Social Sciences, University of Latvia, Riga.

Robert Steinmetz is Press Officer and Personal Assistant to the Minister of Foreign Affairs of the Grand Duchy of Luxembourg.

Baldur Thorhallsson is Jean Monnet Professor of Political Science and Chair of the Institute of International Affairs and the Centre for Small-State Studies at the University of Iceland.

Anders Wivel is Associate Professor of International Relations in the Department of Political Science, University of Copenhagen.

Preface
About the Resilience of Small States

Mario Hirsch

The contributions to this volume are the outcome of an international conference on 'Small States Inside and Outside the European Union', which took place on 16 and 17 May 2008 in Schengen, Luxembourg. This gathering, bringing together some 30 scholars from most small and smaller European states, was convened jointly by the Luxembourg Institute for European and International Studies (LIEIS) and the Institut Pierre Werner, Luxembourg (IPW).

The meeting place and its 'genius loci' is not only a symbol of one of the great achievements of European integration. Schengen, which is without any doubt the best-known village in the world, perfectly illustrates the very special status enjoyed by Luxembourg in Europe.

Napoleon said 'a country's foreign policy is dictated by its geography'. A small state with powerful neighbours, Luxembourg has learnt to its detriment that the balance of power can have devastating effects for the midget between. Its economic success is inseparable from its openness to the world. Having joined the European adventure as a founding member, it benefits from an intimate knowledge of the Community machinery's internal workings. This has enabled it to repeatedly leave its mark on the majority of projects advancing the integration process: it was a Luxembourg presidency that in 1985 oversaw the adoption of the Single European Act, the linchpin in the resurgence of the integration process in the 1980s, and, in 1991, it was another Luxembourg presidency that launched the intergovernmental conference that was later to be concluded in Maastricht.

Luxembourg statesmen like Pierre Werner, Gaston Thorn, Jacques Santer and Jean-Claude Juncker have played a decisive role in some of the more remarkable breakthroughs in the history of European integration. As early as 1970, Pierre Werner was the author of the 'Werner Plan' – the roadmap to the common currency. Both Gaston Thorn and Jacques Santer were presidents of the European Commission. Since the introduction of the euro currency, Jean-Claude Juncker has chaired the Eurogroup. The decisive influence exerted by these politicians in European affairs is not only a result of their strong personalities, but also of the longevity of Luxembourg politicians. The country enjoys a remarkable degree of political stability: coalition governments complete their term as a rule, and politicians stay in office longer than elsewhere. Jean-Claude Juncker has been minister in various capacities since 1982 and he is the longest serving prime minister in the

European club, occupying this position since 1995. This inevitably contributes to Luxembourg's clout in Europe. Unlike its bigger partners, a small country cannot afford the luxury of changing its key political personnel continuously.

The vast experience of Luxembourg politicians in European integration highlights one of the notable features and assets of small countries engaged in international cooperation. Small states are effective and can be successful, provided that they are capable of setting aside their own immediate interests in favour of the common interest. Luxembourg has become a genuine champion in the role of 'honest broker' and it is known as staunch supporter of the 'méthode communautaire', based on the same idea, which has proven to be the best shield for smaller member countries against the relentless attempts by their larger partners to call the shots and to impose their domineering views and, of course, their selfish national interests.

On institutional matters, Luxembourg always used to act together with its two Benelux partners. The concerted action of these three countries, illustrated by the famous 'Benelux memoranda', has hitherto played a decisive role in charting the course of European integration whilst preserving the basic philosophy of the founding treaties and the key concept of 'égalité statutaire'.

One can, of course, be cynical and relativise the merits of small countries and their contribution to the integration process, as was the French journalist, Luc Rosenzweig, when he commented, with reference to Luxembourg, on the idea that smaller member states tend to be more successful at the helm of the EU than their larger counterparts: 'The praise of small nations for a "successful" presidency is based on how zealously the "little countries" implement the ideas of the "big countries", rather than for having brought their specific concerns or ideas to the European level' (*Le Monde*, 27 March 1997). Instrumentalisation is a common feature in international relations, especially in the case of small countries, but it doesn't invalidate our thesis that under certain circumstances they can enjoy considerable freedom of manoeuvre, provided they get their act together and are capable of seizing the opportunity.

Luxembourg remains largely a good pupil in the European class, although, according to recent Eurobarometer surveys, it has lost some of the aura of a model pupil. A certain dose of realism and a keen awareness of the country's intrinsic vulnerability have taken over of late. This is a new development in a country that has had to face the fact that, as far as European integration is concerned, idealism and self-sacrifice do not always pay. This change of mood became manifest when the July 2005 referendum on the Constitutional treaty was passed with a surprisingly low approval rate (56 percent in favour, 44 percent against).

Over the years, Luxembourg has also learned to defend its own interests in a Europe that looks more and more like a 'free-for-all' enterprise, but it is doing this with a greater amount of restraint than others and on a restricted number of issues, largely preserving its role as honest broker. In its almost 60 year history of participation in the integration process, the country, invoking the vital national interests at stake, has made use of its veto power only twice. This is in stark contrast to the behaviour of larger countries, which make use of this instrument in a relentless, shameless and uninhibited way. The Orwellian dictum 'some animals are more equal than others' seems to apply perfectly to the European integration process.

The resilience of small states is always relative. It depends on the circumstances, in particular on the interests of the big powers. The recent clampdown on tax havens perfectly illustrates how fast the fortune of small states such as Luxembourg, Switzerland, Liechtenstein, Austria, Belgium and a few others can change. This is in fact an excellent case study on the resilience of small states. In this preface, we can only provide a rough sketch of the telling developments in this particular area.

For decades, these small states were able to withstand considerable pressure from larger states in fiscal matters until they had to give in to the combined pressure of the European Union, the OECD, fiscal authorities from France, Germany and the United States and ultimately the G20, following its meeting in London in early April 2009. This gathering proclaimed 'the beginning of the end of tax havens', according to the British Prime Minister, Gordon Brown.

It is not remarkable that these countries had ultimately no choice but to give in to considerable pressures to comply with the 'internationally agreed tax standards', which, according to Angel Gurria, the OECD's secretary general, were set by the OECD 'in order to strengthen the integrity and transparency of the international financial system'.

What is more remarkable is that they had been able to get away with 'non-cooperative' behaviour for so long. In the case of Luxembourg, resistance to EU-wide rules for common fiscal treatment of savings goes back to 1989, when the first attempt was made to introduce such a scheme via a draft directive. In this particular case, Luxembourg was helped by the fact that, within the EU, decisions regarding fiscal matters require unanimity. Luxembourg was therefore able to exercise its veto to fend off such initiatives, which were considered to run counter to its vital interests. (The financial sector contributes more than one third of the country's GDP, makes for almost 40 percent of tax revenues and employs more than 10 percent of its work force.) It did so twice (in 1989 and in 1994).

In addition, Luxembourg could also benefit from the fact that it was not the only member state to disagree with fiscal harmonisation. Over the years, it could count on various allies and was never isolated on this issue. Even during the final showdown, which occurred in the year 2000 at the European Council meeting in Santa Maria da Feira, Luxembourg was once more able to buy time. Thanks to the support of Austria and Belgium, it managed to secure a compromise regarding the compulsory introduction of an automatic system of information exchange between national fiscal authorities that was favoured by a majority of member states. Instead, by way of compromise, an alternative system of a withholding tax was implemented for a transitional period, ending in 2015. The main advantage of the withholding tax system is its anonymity which preserves the strict banking secrecy system cherished by Luxembourg and like-minded countries such as Austria, Belgium and Switzerland (at the request of Luxembourg the Feira compromise was also binding for Switzerland and other well-known tax havens) while assuaging the countries concerns about tax evasion/fraud by sharing tax revenues with them. However, this compromise did not stop attempts at the EU level by partner countries to bring Luxembourg and its allies to heel by obliging them to improve their cooperation in matters of serious tax fraud.

With the creation of the 'Financial Action Task Force' (FATF) in 1989 under the auspices of the OECD, whose role became even more important after '9/11', those EU countries who had not given up the hope that they might eventually succeed in obliging the three renitent countries to join their cause in fighting money laundering, made relentless use of this new, unexpected leverage. Their secret hope was to blur the lines between tax evasion and tax avoidance. While the former, consisting in not declaring taxable income, is considered a crime in most jurisdictions, tax avoidance is deemed quite acceptable in tax havens, because it amounts to use of tax-efficient arrangements and exploiting loopholes in the legislations to minimise the overall level of tax paid, a common practice known as fiscal engineering.

Since the beginning of the financial crisis in 2008, tax havens have come under siege because governments, confronted with heavy public deficits, were more eager than ever to root out and track down every taxpayer's dues to finance their ambitious spending and bailout programmes. It was inevitable that they became increasingly concerned with tax havens and banking secrecy.

During 2008 and early 2009, a 'name and shame' campaign was launched by senior politicians in both France and Germany. This was highly unusual in the, usually polite, relations between EU members. President Sarkozy, SPD chairman Franz Müntefering and German Minister of Finance Peer Steinbrück used strong words in public. Müntefering publicly regretted the end of the times when one could send troops to settle the issue and Steinbrück made reference to the times when the US cavalry could intimidate the Indians. This kind of verbal threat was perceived as highly insulting in both Switzerland and Luxembourg. Especially in Luxembourg, this reminded people of 1940, when the country was invaded, occupied and annexed by Nazi Germany.

The 'name and shame' campaign culminated in a statement made at the G20 meeting in London. This announced that from then on, renegade countries would not only face naming and shaming, but also sanctions. The G20 published a list drawn up by the OECD Secretariat, made up of three sub-lists. The first, the so-called 'white' list, was made up of countries that the OECD judged to have implemented their tax standards. It included Argentina, Russia, the United Kingdom, the United States and most Western European countries, including the Channel Islands. At the other end, there was a 'black' list of countries that were not even committed to opening their banking systems to outside regulators. This list included Costa Rica, the Labuan Island in Malaysia, the Philippines and Uruguay. This 'black' list was eventually dropped when the countries on this list pledged to comply.

The real problem was the so-called 'grey' list made up of countries that had agreed to adopt disclosure standards, but had not yet implemented them. This grey list comprised European tax havens such as Monaco, Liechtenstein and Switzerland as well as the EU members Luxembourg, Austria and Belgium. Since none of the countries on that list was consulted prior to its publication, the published list produced quite a public outcry.

Luxembourg's Prime Minister and Minister of Finance, Jean-Claude Juncker responded forcefully, describing the list as 'fatuous'. He stated: 'I think that the treatment given to some countries is a bit incomprehensible' and went on by expressing his surprise that several US states with tax-friendly laws were not put on either list by saying that 'if Luxembourg was placed on any international list of offshore financial centres, then Delaware, Nevada and Wyoming should also be named and shamed as tax havens' (*The Independent*, 4 April 2009). Other commentators were quick to point out that the absence of UK dependencies, notably the Channel Islands and the Isle of Man, as well as China's Special Administrative Regions, Hong Kong and Macao, from the OECD's black and grey lists was ample evidence of double standards.

But these protests were to no avail. The countries on the infamous 'grey' list got the message that the only way out was to implement as quickly as possible the internationally agreed tax standards. In that respect, the OECD established a threshold. If a country wants to be removed from the 'grey' list, it had better conclude, as a gesture of good will, at least 12 bilateral fiscal treaties (so-called 'double taxation agreements') that allow for some exchange of information in tax evasion cases.

Austria, Belgium and Luxembourg speeded things up and accepted the idea that they have to loosen their banking secrecy to allow information exchange with foreign tax authorities when specific cases of tax evasion are suspected and documented. It should be noted that the OECD requirements fall short of automatic exchange of tax data as envisaged within the EU after 2015, which means that banking secrecy is not dead as yet. The generalisation of automatic exchange, if it is going to be introduced, will administer the fatal blow to banking secrecy as we know it.

Within four months, Luxembourg concluded no less than 15 double taxation agreements, thus living up to OECD requirements. As a reward, on 8 June 2009, it was the first country to be removed from the 'grey' list. In doing so, the OECD publicly certified that the country is now considered to co-operate sufficiently in tax evasion cases. In a public statement it welcomed Luxembourg's 'swift implementation' of its standards.

This case study is quite revealing. It shows that, ultimately, small states have no real chance to escape concerted international pressure. Their resilience is on the wane. At best, they can play for time, but the moment of truth is bound to come sooner or later. In this particular case, political tolerance for non-compliance is heading rapidly towards zero. One has, of course, to give due consideration to the special circumstances of the financial crisis. This dimension is highlighted in a recent IMF paper arguing that 'tax distortions are likely to have encouraged excessive leveraging and other financial market problems evident in the crisis' (*The Guardian*, 23 June 2009). The resilience of small states such as Luxembourg and Switzerland was undermined by the unusual pressure exerted on them by the OECD and the G20, relying on highly unusual intimidation tactics like naming and shaming. This is of course a special case, unlikely to occur in other domains of international relations, but it is quite striking.

International relations (IR) as an academic discipline traditionally uses a two-pronged approach to analyse the smaller actors in the international field. One approach, based on power components as determining factors of the behaviour of states in their interaction with others and the international system, gives little credit to the freedom of manoeuvre and plays down the clout of smaller entities in the system. Small states tend to be portrayed as mere pawns, which are easily disposed of and instrumentalised in the power games of their larger counterparts. The privileged status of large states implies that other, smaller, actors have no choice but to take into consideration and interiorise the great powers' interests and that they should avoid challenging them.

This reductionist view has been corrected thanks to the emergence of studies devoted to the behaviour of smaller states. Most of these studies, based on case studies, have been the work of scholars from smaller states. One of the more interesting consequences is the conclusion that small does not necessarily mean weak, depending, of course, on circumstances: geography, the international environment and specific issues. These studies also drew attention to the importance of, often neglected, factors that are not power-related such as social cohesion, neo-corporatist arrangements and consensus on foreign policy issues, which are typical features of small states and which considerably enhance their bargaining position on the international scene.

This preface does not intend to rewrite IR theory, nor does it intend to be a thorough reappraisal of the position of small states *vis-à-vis* the international system. Its scope is much more limited. While it wholeheartedly subscribes to the second approach, it contents itself with some insights into the resilience of a certain category of small states operating within the particular context of Europe, the European Union and the OECD. This preface has taken a closer look at one specific case study, sketched as a kind of reality test for the resilience of those smaller states particularly exposed in this field. The remaining chapters in this book will analyse further case studies.

Acknowledgements

This book would not have been possible without the generous support and professional assistance of the Luxembourg Institute for European and International Studies (LIEIS). In particular, we would like to thank the Director of the Institute, Dr. Armand Clesse, for organising the conference held in Schengen, Luxembourg, in May 2008 and for backing the book throughout the editing process. Also, we would like to thank the Institut Pierre Werner (IPW) and its Director Mario Hirsch for participating in and contributing to the financing of the conference in Schengen. The conference became the starting point for this book project, and many of the arguments appearing in the book were first presented at the conference. In addition, we would like to thank the Department of Political Science, University of Copenhagen, and the Danish Social Science Research Council for economic support.

We owe special thanks to Anemone Thomas, Head of Publications and Planning at LIEIS. Anemone's skilful and professional handling of all the administrative procedures related to the editing process has been invaluable.

Last but not least, we would like to thank the contributors to this volume. It has been a pleasure to work with all of them, and we have learned a lot about the opportunities and challenges of small European states. Hopefully, the readers will feel the same way.

Luxembourg and Copenhagen, 6 January 2009

Robert Steinmetz and Anders Wivel

PART I
Small States in Europe: Defining the Issues at Stake

Chapter 1
Introduction

Robert Steinmetz and Anders Wivel[1]

The aim of this book is to identify the most important challenges and opportunities influencing small state foreign policy-making in Europe today and to explore how small European states have responded to these challenges and opportunities. We seek to identify the most important factors that influence small state foreign policy in Europe and discuss the costs and benefits of each different foreign policy strategy. In essence, the book seeks to answer four general questions about small states in Europe: What are the major opportunities and challenges facing small state foreign policy in Europe today? How have Europe's small states responded to these opportunities and challenges? Why did small states respond the way they did? What are the costs and benefits of the most important small state foreign policy strategies in Europe today?

Small states in Europe have seen their geopolitical environment and, in many cases, their political and administrative structures, fundamentally changed over the past decades. The end of the Cold War in 1989 and the ensuing collapse of the Soviet Union in 1991, the intensification of the European integration process in the early 1990s, the consecutive enlargements of the European Union in 1995, 2004 and 2007, as well as the ongoing process of globalisation have all transformed the nature of the foreign policy challenges in Europe. At the same time, these changes in the external environment of Europe's small states have served as an important cause of domestic political adaptation (cf. Hanf and Soetendorp 1998). The societies in small states in Central and Eastern Europe reinvented themselves as a consequence of the revolutions following the Cold War. The newly constructed small states that succeeded the Soviet Union, Yugoslavia and Czechoslovakia, faced a particular set of challenges, while at the same time their establishment helped to transform the geopolitics of Europe. Small states in Western Europe have seen domestic restructuring as well, often adapting more rapidly to global economic and technological trends than the European great powers.

Even though the literature on small states – and particularly the literature on small states in Europe – has been growing rapidly since the end of the Cold War, there have been few attempts to go beyond single country studies and provide an

---

1 A first draft of this chapter was presented at the panel 'Small States in a Globalized World: Challenges and Opportunities' at the CISS ISA Millennium Conference, Potsdam, Germany, 13-15 June 2009. We would like to thank all participants in the discussion at this occasion and in particular our discussant Sabina Kajnc for useful suggestions.

overview of the general pattern of challenges, opportunities and strategies. Now, as in the past, the study of small states is plagued by a lack of cumulative insights and coherent debate. There is no agreement on how we should define a small state, what similarities we would expect to find in their foreign policies, or how small states influence international relations (Antola and Lehtimäki 2001: 13-20; Knudsen 2002: 182-5; Archer and Nugent 2002: 2-5).

This book takes one step in the direction of providing a more coherent picture of small states in Europe by including a number of analyses of small states and the challenges they face in contemporary European politics. In order to focus our analyses and facilitate comparisons, we delimit our study of small state foreign policy in Europe in three important ways. First, we understand foreign policy as 'the sum of official external relations conducted by an independent actor (usually a state) in international relations' (Hill 2002: 3). Thus, official policy, as stated by actors representing the government in various public sources (such as official statements and speeches), are our primary focus in this volume. Second, we focus on small state policies towards the European Union (EU). Thus, rather than analysing all aspects of small state foreign policy in Europe, the contributors to this volume zoom in on how small states relate to developments in the EU. Finally, we focus on foreign policy output rather than foreign policy process. The contributors to this volume describe and explain policy positions, but they tell us only little about how policy is made or how policy-making in the EU is changing administrative procedures at the national level.[2]

The aim of the remaining part of this chapter is fourfold. First, based on a survey of the small state literature, we define what we mean by a 'small state'. Second, we explain why the study of small states is important, in particular in a European context. Third, we outline the two fundamental approaches for small state foreign policy in Europe. Finally, we offer a brief introduction to the rest of the book.

What is a Small State?

'Should small states be categorised along geographic, demographic or economic lines, or do institutions, resources, and power hold the key?', ask Smith, Pace and Lee in a recent discussion of small states (Smith, Pace and Lee 2005). Discussions about small states – both in practical politics and in academic debates – suffer from a number of ambiguities. To be sure, ongoing debate and lack of consensus on how to define 'small state' is not a problem per se. Despite the fogginess of the 'small state' concept, few people question that small states exist and that they share

---

2 Important studies of small state foreign policy in the context of the EU include among others Gstöhl (2002), Ingebritsen (1998), Larsen (2005), Mouritzen and Wivel (2005), Petersen (1998) and Tonra (2001). Manners and Whitman (2000) include both small and big member states in the EU in their study.

a number of common challenges (Christmas-Møller 1983; cf. Knudsen 2002). Moreover, consensus on how to define key concepts is more often the exception rather than the rule in the study of international relations. The lack of consensus over how to define key concepts such as the balance of power, security or even great powers has not – and should not – stop us from studying these important aspects of world politics (cf. Amstrup 1976). However, it does necessitate a brief discussion of how we define 'small state' for the purposes of this book and why we make this choice.

Typically small states are defined in terms of capabilities, i.e. the possession of – or rather the lack of – power resources in absolute or relative terms. Generally, capabilities are measured by reference to proxies such as population size, GDP, military expenditure etc. Three benefits follow from defining 'small state' in terms of capabilities. First, if we are to analyse the economic, administrative or military opportunities and limitations of a specific state, indications of absolute and relative capability are important, because they inform us of the absolute and relative limitations in these states' capacity to handle different types of challenges. Second, an absolute and universal threshold between big and small states of e.g. a population size of 15 million people or a GDP of 500 billion Euros has the benefit of creating a clear and easily applicable definition of small states. The same can be said of a relative definition defining great powers as the top-10 in the world, or the top-5 in Europe – for example measured by reference to population size, GDP or military expenditure – and the rest as small states.[3] Third, there is a vast amount of literature on both specific great powers and on the international system in general, which starts from a power possession definition.[4] Using power possession as the point of departure for studies on small states would facilitate the integration of the study of great powers and small states with potential benefits for the study of foreign policy and international relations in general, e.g. through comparative studies of the challenges and opportunities for different types of states.

However, the power possession definition of small states has at least two important limitations. First, power is difficult to measure and its effects are almost impossible to distinguish from the calculations and perceptions of policy makers. Thus, the cut-off point between big and small states is rarely self-evident, and accordingly there is no consensus on what constitutes a small state in term of power possession. In contrast, the notion 'small state' is typically used to denote at least three different types of states: micro states, small states in the developed

---

3 Alternatively inspiration could be taken from the power indexes of the (realist) international relations literature, which seeks to combine a number of variables, e.g. population size, GDP and military expenditure in order to evaluate the aggregate power of states (e.g. Schweller 1998; Wohlforth 1999).

4 Most often these studies begin from a neorealist understanding of international relations. For the most prominent statement of neorealism, see Waltz (1979).

world and small states in the third world (Hey 2003: 2).[5] Adding to the confusion, none of these categories are clear-cut, nor is there any agreement on how to define them. Micro states are sometimes defined as states with a population with less than 1 million inhabitants (Anckar 2004: 208), but at other times the threshold is set higher, e.g. 1.5 million inhabitants (Naseer Mohamed 2002: 1) or lower, e.g. 300,000 (Plischke 1977: 21) or 100,000 (Neumann and Gstöhl 2006: 6) or alternatively a micro state is simply viewed as characterised by 'a size so diminutive as to invite comment' (Warrington 1998: 102). Likewise, small states in the developed world have been defined using a number of different – often incompatible – criteria leading to confusion over how to know a small state when we see one. Thus, Väyrynen in a survey on the small state concept identifies two axes for defining small states (Väyrynen 1971). One axis focuses on whether the defining criteria for small states are objective, e.g. size of GDP or population, or subjective, e.g. the perceptions of domestic or foreign elites. The other axis focuses on whether the defining criteria are endogenous, i.e. internal characteristics of a country, or exogenous, i.e. the country's relations with other states. As noted by Archer and Nugent, this typology remains relevant for the study of small states in Europe today (Archer and Nugent 2002: 2-3). Adding to the complexity, small states in the third world usually have much larger populations than what we term small states in the developed world, because 'population size is taken as a proxy of a range of other economic characteristics – all of which are deemed to bestow particular vulnerabilities on small states' (Heron 2008: 246). Thus, in his now classical study *The Inequality of States*, David Vital studies small states with 'a) a population of 10-15 million in the case of economically advanced countries and b) a population of 20-30 million in the case of underdeveloped countries' (Vital 1967: 8).

Vital's attempt at a dual definition of small states in order to grasp the complexity resulting from very different historical, economic and political contexts of different types of small states discloses a second limitation of defining small states in accordance with their possession of material power: concepts like 'small state' and 'great power' often make most sense within a specific spatio-temporal context. The challenges and opportunities of small states in Europe have been transformed over time and today the challenges and opportunities of small states in Europe are very different from those faced by small states in Africa, Asia or Latin America.

Acknowledging this limitation, as well as the difficulties of measuring power and its consequences, we define a small state as the weak part in an asymmetric relationship (cf. Mouritzen and Wivel 2005). According to this definition a state may be weak in one relation, but simultaneously powerful in another. For instance, Romania is a great power in its relations with Moldova but a small state in its relations with Russia, and Sweden is a small state in the European Union

---

5 In addition, the conceptual borderline between micro state, small state and 'middle power' is usually blurred and arbitrary (cf. Neumann and Gstöhl 2006: 4-7).

but a great power in relation to the Baltic countries. Thus, we argue that being a small state is tied to a specific spatio-temporal context and that this context, rather than general characteristics of the state, defined by indicators such as its absolute population size or size of GDP relative to other states, is decisive for both the nature of challenges and opportunities and the small states' answer to these challenges and opportunities.

What does it mean to be the weak part in an asymmetrical relationship? Small states are those states which are 'stuck with the [...] power configuration and its institutional expression, no matter what their specific relation to it is' (Mouritzen and Wivel 2005: 4). For instance, in the Euro-Atlantic area the United States, Germany, France and Great Britain are considered great powers, because they are all able to change the conditions for policy-making in the area through their actions: Should the United States choose to move all of its troops from the European continent or to leave NATO, or should France choose to leave the EU or fundamentally change its policy within the EU, this would radically change these institutions and therefore conditions for policy-making in the region, but if Denmark left NATO or Austria fundamentally changed its policy within the EU, the consequences would mainly be felt by these small states themselves. Therefore, they cannot credibly threaten to leave, transform or destroy the institutional structures. For this reason they are expected to face a different set of challenges than the great powers.

In essence, our definition of small states is relational: smallness is defined through the relation between the state and its external environment. This definition deviates from the most commonly used definitions which tend to focus on the absolute or relative power of the state. Thus, following Mouritzen and Wivel, we shift the focus from the power that states *possess* to the power that they *exercise* (Mouritzen and Wivel 2005).[6] From this point of departure, the authors of this book use the concept of small states as a 'focusing device' directing us towards interesting research puzzles stemming from 'the experience of power disparity and the manner of coping with it' (Knudsen 1996b: 5; cf. Gärtner 1993: 303; Rickli 2008; Thorhallsson and Wivel 2006; Wivel 2005: 395). Thus, '[s]mallness is, in this conception, a comparative and not an absolute idea' (Hanf and Soetendorp 1998: 4). This brings to our attention a particular set of policy problems and foreign policy dilemmas and allows us to distinguish between issue areas, where the notion of small state is relevant, and issue areas, where it is not.

Why are Small States Important?

Small states are largely neglected in the study of international relations (cf. Neumann and Gstöhl 2006). The growth of International Relations (IR) as an academic discipline coincided with the Cold War, which led many researchers

---

6 Mouritzen and Wivel prefer 'non-pole powers' to signal that their study is not based on what is usually understood as small state theory (Mouritzen and Wivel 2005: 3-4)

to focus on other issues. Superpower rivalry meant that most research efforts, not least in the United States, were focused on understanding and explaining the foreign and security policy of great powers and the problems they faced. The global character of the divides between East and West and North and South meant that theoretical IR debates often focused on the character of the international system and its general implications.[7] In addition, early research efforts in the study of small states in the 1960s and 1970s failed to create a common research agenda – let alone a shared theoretical starting point. As noted in early assessments of the literature, there was 'an astonishing lack of cumulation' (Amstrup 1976: 178), and accordingly the study of small states in international relations was characterised by 'coexistence without interdependence' (Christmas-Møller 1983: 40).

The present world order has resulted in a renewed interest in how small states respond to international challenges, and which role they play in international security and organisations. There are three reasons why studying small states is important in understanding contemporary international relations in general and European politics in particular. First, the unipolar character of the present world order means that all states except the United States are now small states in the sense that 'they are *not* in command of power resources sufficient to pursue dominant power politics' (Kelstrup 1993: 162).[8] The challenges and dilemmas traditionally faced by small states are now faced by most states in the international system. Therefore, the study of small states may serve as a source of information for all states on the consequences of being the weak part in an asymmetric relationship.

Second, small states today play a much more active role in international relations than in previous historical epochs (cf. Hey 2003; Knudsen 1996a; Løvold 2004). In economic affairs, small states have taken a leading role in reforming their societies within the context of a globalised world. Not necessarily because they have been more innovative than the larger states, but because the consequences of globalisation have materialised earlier and in a harsher form in small states than in larger ones. In security affairs, rather than just being consumers of security – the traditional role of small states in the past when the military defence of national territory dominated the security agenda and their survival could only be guaranteed by the great powers – small states now actively contribute to the production of security in various issue areas. As small states more actively seek to gain influence over international affairs, we need to know more about how and why they do it if we are to understand international relations. As summed up by Keohane, '[i]f Lilliputians can tie up Gulliver, or make him do their fighting for them, they must be studied as carefully as the Giant' (Keohane 1969: 310).

---

7 Among the most important examples are the theoretical debates about Kenneth Waltz's neorealist theory (Waltz 1979) and Immanuel Wallerstein's world systems (Wallerstein 2000).

8 Kelstrup explicitly discusses European states, but his argument is relevant for states outside Europe as well.

Third, small states make up the vast majority of states in the international system and in international organisations such as the UN, OECD, NATO and EU. Even those scholars, who argue that the unipolar order is drawing to a close, find that it is replaced by only a handful of great powers (e.g. Buzan 2004). Also, at the regional level in Europe, small states constitute a large majority of states (Thorhallsson and Wivel 2006). Neglecting at least 90 percent of all states in favour of studying a few great powers is highly problematic if we wish to understand international affairs (Neumann and Gstöhl 2006: 28).

Studying small states in Europe may prove to be particularly illuminating, because small states in this region play a more active role in international affairs than small states in any other region in the world. As the most heavily institutionalised and thoroughly globalised region in the world, small states in Europe now face some of the challenges and enjoy some of the opportunities that small states in other parts of the world may face in the future.

Small States in European Policy-Making: From Hiding to Binding

Small states seek to further their interests by trying to preserve as much autonomy as possible while influencing the actions of the great powers upon which their security and survival ultimately depend. They seek to expand their influence over the great powers mainly through international organisations, but this participation typically reduces their own political autonomy (Goetschel 1998: 17). The stronger the institutions, the greater the potential costs and benefits of participating and the more intense this autonomy/influence dilemma becomes. Costs and benefits are likely to arise continuously as the institutionalisation process becomes still more binding and encompasses ever more areas. A state facing this 'autonomy/influence dilemma' needs to strike a balance between (i) surrendering autonomy, and risking entrapment in a process that leads to more dependency as institutions are strengthened, and (ii) preserving autonomy, and thereby running the risk of abandonment, i.e. forgoing the chance to influence other states and other gains stemming from institutionalisation.[9]

Until the Second World War, small states valued autonomy over influence. Striving to survive in a world, where military conquest was seen as a useful and legitimate means to political power and prestige for the great powers, small states pursued a hiding strategy aiming to stay out of trouble by staying out of sight (cf. Wallace 1999). Aiming primarily to ensure their own short-term military security and survival, small states followed pragmatic policies, responding to the agenda set by near-by great powers and external developments, rather than formulating and pursuing their own strategic goals. As permanent security consumers,

---

9 For discussions of this dilemma focusing on the development of EU institutions, see Kelstrup (1993), Petersen (1998) and Wivel (2005). For an analysis of how the dilemma is affected by NATO and EU membership, see Mouritzen and Wivel (2005).

they had little to offer to the great powers and, therefore, also a limited room for manoeuvre, when pursuing strategic goals beyond security and survival. By focusing on autonomy in economic affairs and neutrality in security affairs, they quietly conducted their own affairs hoping not to become entangled in the quarrels of the great powers. For most European small states, the vulnerability of the hiding strategy became apparent during the two world wars. In addition, growing economic and security interdependence during the Cold War made it increasingly costly to follow this strategy.

For these reasons most West European states turned towards a more ambitious strategy: binding. Whereas the primary aim of the hiding strategy is to stay out of trouble, the primary aim of the binding strategy is to prevent trouble from occurring at all by creating and strengthening the governance of international affairs through international rules. Binding entails a formalisation of international affairs and therefore a development away from the raw power politics of international anarchy and towards a rule-based international society. Thus, states following a binding strategy seek to strengthen multilateral institutions in order to delimit the action space of the great powers: all members of international institutions are usually subject to the same rules and face the same sanctions, if they break the rules, and at the very least great powers need to justify breaking the rules if they do so (cf. Neumann and Gstöhl 2006: 19-21).

Today, binding is the preferred strategy of most European small states. All European small states are members of the UN and a significant number are members of NATO as well. In general, small states have worked to strengthen international society by creating a rule-based international realm.[10] This is also true of European integration, although there are significant variations (Mouritzen and Wivel 2005). The Benelux countries were founding members of the European Coal and Steel Community in 1951 and the European Economic Community in 1957, and Belgium, in particular, has consistently played an active role in the strengthening of EU institutions, albeit partly for different reasons (Jones 2005). The Nordic states – often characterised as 'reluctant Europeans' or 'the other European Community' – preferred to cooperate through the UN during the Cold War. They explored alternatives to EU membership and did not give up their attempt to create a Nordic customs union until 1970. The first Nordic country, Denmark, joined the European Community as late as 1973. Finland and Sweden only joined in 1995, and even today Norway and Iceland remain outside the EU. Moreover, the behaviour of the Nordic states has varied once inside the EU. Denmark and – to an increasing degree – Sweden have been unenthusiastic about further institutionalisation, whereas Finland has participated eagerly and even promoted a more active role for the EU in relation to North-West Russia. Greece – much like Denmark, and more recently Sweden – has preferred membership, but at the same time tried to limit negative consequences for national autonomy. Switzerland has remained outside the EU altogether despite the important potential for economic

---

10   For a discussion of why this is the case, see Chapter 1 in the present volume.

gains through membership (cf. Gstöhl 2002) and has, in contrast to other non-pole states in the region, pursued a foreign policy strategy emphasising non-membership of international organisations.[11] For most of the history of European integration, Central and Eastern European small states were barred from entering, because of their location in the Soviet sphere of interest during the Cold War. As soon as the Cold War ended, they flocked to the EU applying for membership, but once inside, their policies towards European Union politics started to diverge considerably.[12]

The contributors to this volume explore different expressions of the binding strategy in order to bring us one step closer to a more systematic understanding of when, how and why small states choose one type of binding over another. Accordingly, the conclusion of the book brings together the results of the analytical chapters in order to map the various types of binding and identify the most important explanatory factors behind them.

The Structure of the Book

The overall aim of this book is to offer an accessible, coherent and informative analysis of the contemporary and future foreign policy challenges facing the small states in Europe. In particular, we emphasise the implications of institutional change at the European level for the smaller states and explain how the foreign and European policies of small states in the region are affected by the EU. We specifically aim to identify both the challenges and the opportunities of small European states and to discuss the costs and benefits of the foreign policies pursued by small states in Europe. The authors of the book focus on the present and on the recent past (since the end of the Cold War). Authors include references to the more distant past only where it is relevant to understanding the challenges, opportunities and politics of the present.

---

11   The Swiss example shows that, even for small states, there has always been some room of manoeuvre when deciding foreign policy strategies. Like other small European states, Switzerland is 'a small state surrounded by much larger nations', and it 'had no national resources worth mentioning' (except salt and water) and like other small European states, its primary foreign policy objectives have traditionally been to 'stay out of wars between the surrounding states and secure trans-border trade' (Goetschel, Bernath and Schwarz 2005: 14). Yet, in contrast to the experience of most of Europe's small states, it avoided direct involvement in the Second World War. This was largely attributed to a policy of armed neutrality, which was subsequently seen as a cornerstone of Swiss foreign policy. However, the meaning of neutrality has changed in response to changing international conditions and events. On Swiss neutrality today, see Jean-Marc Rickli's contribution to this volume. On Swiss foreign policy more generally, including its policy towards Europe, see Goetschel, Bernath and Schwarz (2005).

12   Cf. Mats Braun's analysis of Slovakia and the Czech Republic in the present volume.

In order to fulfil this aim and to answer the four questions posed at the beginning of this introductory chapter, the book is divided into four main parts. The first part identifies the issues at stake by discussing the definition of small states shared by all authors of this volume and presenting the basic research questions and rationale for the book (this chapter). It continues by debating how small states may take advantage of the EU's organisational structure in order to maximise influence (Chapter 2) and how the evolving nature of diplomacy is both challenging small states and providing new opportunities (Chapter 3) before turning to the issue of security policy and how we may utilise different strands of international relations theory in order to understand the policies of small states within the EU's European Security and Defence Policy (Chapter 4). The second part focuses on particular challenges and opportunities of small states in Europe, and how these challenges affect the power and influence of small European states. The issues analysed include innovation (Chapter 5), the changing nature of power (Chapter 6) and regulation of the international system (Chapter 7). The third part zooms in on the particular experiences of small states within the EU. It analyses the experiences of the Netherlands (Chapter 8), Luxembourg (Chapter 9), Slovakia and the Czech Republic (Chapter 10) and Cyprus (Chapter 11) before turning to a comparison of Austrian and Swiss security policies after the Cold War (Chapter 12) and the political consequences of Iceland's economic crash (Chapter 13). The final part of this book sums up the analysis and concludes the book with a number of lessons for small state strategy inside and outside the EU (Chapter 14).

References

Amstrup, N. 1976. The Perennial Problem of Small States: A Survey of Research Efforts. *Cooperation and Conflict*, 11(3), 163-82.
Anckar, D. 2004. Regime Choices in Microstates: The Cultural Constraint. *Commonwealth and Comparative Politics*, 42(2), 206-23.
Antola, E. and Lehtimäki, M. 2001. *Small States in the EU*. Turku: Jean Monnet Centre of Excellence.
Archer, C. and Nugent, N. 2002. Introduction: Small States and the European Union. *Current Politics and Economics of Europe*, 11(1), 1-10.
Buzan, B. 2004. *The United States and the Great Powers*. Cambridge: Polity.
Christmas-Møller, W. 1983. Some Thoughts on the Scientific Applicability of the Small State Concept: A Research History and a Discussion, in *Small States in Europe and Dependence*, edited by O. Höll. Wien: Wilhelm Braumüller, 35-53.
Gärtner, H. 1993. Small States and Security Integration. *Coexistence*, 30, 303-12.
Goetschel, L. 1998. The Foreign and Security Policy Interests of Small States in Today's Europe, in *Small States Inside and Outside the European Union*, edited by L. Goetschel. Dordrecht: Kluwer Academic Publishers, 13-31.

Goetschel, L., Bernath, M. and Schwarz, D. 2005. *Swiss Foreign Policy.* London: Routledge.
Gstöhl, S. 2002. *Reluctant Europeans.* Boulder: Lynne Rienner.
Hanf, K. and Soetendorp, B. 1998. *Adapting to European Integration: Small States and the European Union.* London and New York: Longman.
Heron, T. 2008. Small States and the Politics of Multilateral Trade Liberalization. *The Round Table*, 97, 243-57.
Hey, J.A.K. 2003. Introducing Small State Foreign Policy, in *Small States in World Politics*, edited by J.A.K. Hey. Boulder: Lynne Rienner, 1-11.
Hill, C. 2002. *The Changing Politics of Foreign Policy.* Houndmills: Palgrave Macmillan.
Ingebritsen, C. 1998. *The Nordic Countries and European Unity.* Ithaca: Cornell University Press.
Jones, E. 2005. The Benelux Countries: Identity and Self-Interest, in *The Member States of the European Union*, edited by S. Bulmer and C. Lequesne. Oxford: Oxford University Press, 164-84.
Kelstrup, M. 1993. Small States and European Political Integration: Reflections on Theory and Strategy, in *The Nordic Countries and the EC*, edited by I.D. Petersen and T. Tiilikainen. Copenhagen: Copenhagen Political Studies Press, 136-62.
Keohane, R.O. 1969. Lilliputians' Dilemma: Small States in International Politics. *International Organization*, 23(2), 291-310.
Knudsen, O.F. 1996a. Introduction, in *Small States and the Security Challenge in the New Europe,* edited by W. Bauwens, A. Clesse and O.F. Knudsen. London: Brassey's, xv-xxiii.
Knudsen, O.F. 1996b. Analysing Small-State Security: The Role of External Factors, in *Small States and the Security Challenge in the New Europe*, edited by W. Bauwens, A. Clesse and O.F. Knudsen. London: Brassey's, 3-20.
Knudsen, O.F. 2002. Small States, Latent and Extant: Towards a General Perspective. *Journal of International Relations and Development*, 5(2), 182-98.
Larsen, H. 2005. *Analysing the Foreign Policy of Small States in the EU.* Houndmills: Palgrave Macmillan.
Løvold, A. 2004. Småstatsproblematikken i internasjonal politikk. *Internasjonal Politikk*, 62(1), 7-31.
Manners, I. and Whitman, R. 2000. *The Foreign Policies of European Union Member States.* Manchester and New York: Manchester University Press.
Mouritzen, H. and Wivel, A. 2005. *The Geopolitics of Euro-Atlantic Integration.* London: Routledge.
Naseer Mohamed, A. 2002. The Diplomacy of Micro-States. *Clingendael Discussion Papers in Diplomacy*, 78. The Hague: Netherlands Institute of International Relations Clingendael.
Neumann, I.B. and Gstöhl, S. 2006. Introduction: Lilliputians in Gulliver's World?, in *Small States in International Relations*, edited by C. Ingebritsen,

I.B. Neumann, S. Gstöhl and J. Beyer. Seattle: University of Washington Press, 3-36.
Petersen, N. 1998. National Strategies in the Integration Dilemma: An Adaptation Approach. *Journal of Common Market Studies*, 36(1), 33-54.
Plischke, E. 1977. *Microstates in World Affairs*. Washington, DC: American Enterprise Institute for Public Policy Research.
Rickli, J.-M. 2008. European Small States' Military Policies after the Cold War: From Territorial to Niche Strategies. *Cambridge Review of International Affairs*, 21(3), 307-25.
Schweller, R.L. 1998. *Deadly Imbalances*. New York: Columbia University Press.
Smith, N., Pace, M. and Lee, D. 2005. Size Matters: Small States and International Studies. *International Studies Perspectives*, 6(3), 395-7.
Thorhallsson, B. and Wivel, A. 2006. Small States in the European Union: What Do We Know and What Would We Like to Know? *Cambridge Review of International Affairs*, 19(4), 651-68.
Tonra, B. 2001. *The Europeanization of National Foreign Policy: Dutch, Danish and Irish Foreign Policy in the European Union.* Aldershot: Ashgate.
Väyrynen, R. 1971. On the Definition and Measurement of Small Power Status. *Cooperation and Conflict*, 6, 91-102.
Vital, D. 1967. *The Inequality of States: A Study of the Small Power in International Relations.* Oxford: Clarendon Press.
Wallace, W. 1999. Small European States and European Policy-Making: Strategies, Roles, Possibilities, in *Between Autonomy and Influence: Small States and the European Union*, edited by W. Wallace, B. Jacobsson, S. Kux, S.S. Andersen, T. Notermans, F. Sejersted, and K. Hagen. Arena Report, 1/99. Oslo: Arena, 11-26.
Wallerstein, I.M. 2000. *The Essential Wallerstein*. New York: The New Press.
Waltz, K.N. 1979. *Theory of International Politics*. New York: McGraw-Hill.
Warrington, E. 1998. Introduction: Gulliver and Lilliput in a New World Order: the Impact of External Relations on the Domestic Policies and Institutions of Micro-States. *Public Administration and Development*, 18, 101-5.
Wivel, A. 2005. The Security Challenge of Small EU Member States: Interests, Identity and the Development of the EU as a Security Actor. *Journal of Common Market Studies*, 43(2), 393-412.
Wohlforth, W.C. 1999. The Stability of a Unipolar World. *International Security*, 24(1), 5-41.

Chapter 2

From Small State to Smart State: Devising a Strategy for Influence in the European Union

Anders Wivel[1]

Introduction

How do small states maximise influence in the European Union? Accepting that in international relations 'the strong do what they have the power to do and the weak accept what they have to accept' (Thucydides [1954] 1972: 302), small states have traditionally played only a marginal role in the decisive decisions in international affairs, whether inside or outside international organisations. In the nineteenth century, the Congress of Vienna recognised the special role of the United Kingdom, Prussia, Austria, France and Russia, and for almost a century the great powers set the rules of the game by meeting 'in concert on a regular basis in order to discuss questions of concern, and to draw up agreements and treaties' (Neumann and Gstöhl 2006: 5). Small states were those states that were not great powers, i.e. the states left to obey the rules of the game, because they were too weak to be taken seriously when the rules were negotiated.

The opportunities and challenges of European small states in the twenty-first century are markedly different from those of the nineteenth century. Most importantly, the vast majority of European small states need not fear military invasion for the foreseeable future. This has changed the foreign policy room of manoeuvre considerably as European small states need no longer to fear that policies provoking or irritating the strong will lead to military subjugation or extinction.

A small state is by definition the weaker part in an asymmetric relationship.[2] Traditionally small European states have pursued two strategies when coping with this weakness: hiding and binding (Wallace 1999). Small states following a hiding

---

1 A first draft of this chapter was presented at the conference 'Small States Inside and Outside the European Union' hosted by the Luxembourg Institute for European and International Studies, 16 and 17 May 2008 in Kochhaus, Schengen, Luxembourg. I would like to thank the participants in this conference and Caroline Grøn for a number of useful comments on an earlier draft.

2 For a discussion of this definition, see Chapter 1 of the present volume.

strategy aim to stay out of trouble by staying out of sight. They quietly conduct their own affairs hoping not to get entangled in the quarrels of the great powers. The vulnerability of the hiding strategy became apparent during the two world wars, and growing interdependence during the Cold War made it increasingly costly to follow this strategy. The second strategy is binding. The binding strategy is more ambitious than the hiding strategy. Whereas the primary aim of the hiding strategy is to stay out of trouble, the primary aim of the binding strategy is to prevent trouble from occurring at all by creating and strengthening the governance of international affairs by international rules and institutions. As noted by Wallace, '[w]ithout institutional constraints, large states may concert their interests at the expense of smaller states around their borders, or pursue regional hegemony at small state expense' (Wallace 1999: 11).[3] The binding strategy has been the fundamental strategy of small European states since the end of the Cold War, and the European Union may be seen as the most important example of its success.

Still, power asymmetry and its effects do not end with institutionalisation. In the European Union, small states are at the same time more dependent on European integration than the great powers and less able to influence the outcome of treaty negotiations. Typically, they are unable to defend themselves militarily against their more powerful neighbours, and their economies are more dependent on trade because of their small domestic markets. Thus, the lowering of barriers to free-trade and, more broadly, cooperation on economic and security affairs in the European Union is beneficial for small states. However, at the same time small states are vulnerable in negotiations, because they benefit relatively more from institutionalisation and integration than the great powers and are most often unable to 'go-it-alone' (cf. Gruber 2000).

Despite these obstacles small states have played and continue to play an active role in the development of the European Union. Small states played an important role in the initial phase of the European integration project. The Benelux Customs Union (from 1948) and the Benelux Economic Union (from 1960) served as important sources of inspiration and testing ground for the subsequent developments of the European integration project (Maes and Verdun 2005: 332), and the Benelux states played an active and influential role in the formative years of the European Community through their own initiatives (cf. Dosenrode 1993; Jones 2008; Milward 1992). More recently, small states have played an important role in the Lisbon process, the development of EU's security policy and the enlargement of the European Union. In addition, a number of Presidents of the Commission and influential Commissioners have been from small states (Archer and Nugent 2002: 6) and small states have often jumped at the opportunity to play an active role when holding the presidency of the Council (Thorhallsson and Wivel 2006).

---

3   For a more thorough discussion of these two strategies, see Chapter 1 of the present volume.

How do small states get as much influence as possible out of their activity? This chapter argues that even though the formal institutional development of the EU creates new challenges, small states are in a good position to take advantage of the informal aspects of the European integration process. In particular, small states will benefit from a so-called 'smart state' strategy allowing them to play a more active and influential role in European policy-making. The argument proceeds in to steps. First, I describe and discuss three types of characteristics of the European Union and their implications for small EU member states. Second, I discuss how small states may navigate in this institutional environment in order to maximise their influence.

The European Union as an Organisation: Small States and 'Rational', 'Natural' and 'Open' Aspects of European Integration

The optimal strategy of a state depends on its own capabilities as well as its external environment. For a small state navigating the institutional settings of the European Union, the nature of the organisational structure of the institutions is pivotal for assessing the costs and benefits of its strategic choices. Taking Scott as my point of departure, I distinguish between three ideal type organisational structures: rational, natural and open systems (Scott 2003).[4] Scott discusses different theoretical perspectives on organisations, whose members are typically individuals. I do not use the three perspectives as competing or mutually excluding theoretical perspectives. Instead, I use his distinction between rational, natural and open organisations to describe and discuss empirical aspects of the European Union and their implications for small member states. Each ideal type organisational structure allows me to focus on one particular aspect of the European Union as an organisation and its consequences for small states. Thus, in essence, I use the three perspectives as 'different coloured lenses: if you put one of them in front of your eyes, you will see things differently. Some aspects of the world will look the same in some lenses, for example shapes, but many other features, such as light and shade of colour, will look very different, so different in fact that they seem to show alternative worlds' (Smith 2007: 11; cf. Sterling-Folker 2006). To Smith, the different coloured lenses allow us to see different theoretical constructions of international relations. However, in this chapter I use the lenses' analogy in a very different way, i.e. as a method for singling out different empirical aspects of the EU. Seeing the world of small states in the European Union through these three lenses allows me to identify challenges and opportunities of small states and to discuss, which strategies may allow them to maximise influence.

---

4   I do not intend to imply that Scott would accept my characterisation of these three perspectives as 'ideal types'. Rather, he uses the distinction as point of departure for organising his discussion of literature on organisations, and he seems to view them more as different stages in the development of this literature than ideal types, see Scott (2003).

Small States and the Rational Aspects of the European Union

Rational 'organisations are instruments designed to attain specified goals' (Scott 2003: 33) populated by 'purposeful and coordinated agents' (Scott 2003: 34). The agents choose between different policy options by a set of clear criteria based on their policy preferences. Formal organisational structures are central to decision-making in rational organisations. Formal rules regulate and standardise expectations, thereby making it more predictable. Also, formal rules institutionalise and legitimise inequalities, thereby awarding different roles to different actors (Scott 2003: 35-6). For instance, even though all member states have one vote in the United Nations General Assembly, the five great powers with permanent membership of the United Nations Security Council are allowed to prevent the adoption of a proposal by vetoing it. Thus, institutional structures award them a special role compared to other UN member states. Formal inequality is also found in the European Union. In the Council of the European Union, the number of votes that each state is allocated is based primarily on the state's population size relative to other member states.[5] Thus, bigger states have more weight than small states.

Looking at the EU, through the theoretical lens of rational organisations, the formal structures of the EU are decisive for small state influence. By binding the European great powers, the institutional arrangement has two consequences for small states regarding their influence within the European Union: 1) they level the playing field: making traditional power capabilities (i.e. military power) less important; 2) they make the use of power more visible, because of the formalisation of what is agreed by the members to be acceptable behaviour (cf. Neumann and Gstöhl 2006: 20).

However, at the same time we see three changes in the formal channels of influence for small states in EU institutions challenging small state influence in the European Union after the implementation of the Lisbon Treaty: the change of voting methods in the Council of Ministers, changes in the presidency of the Council and changes in the composition of the European Commission.

First, voting methods in the Council of Ministers matter for small state influence because no policy or legislative decision can be taken without the agreement of the Council of Ministers. Unanimity voting and simple majority voting – the two traditional voting methods – favour small EU member states. The unanimity voting method requires the approval or acquiescence of all members of the Council. Thus, in principle small member states and big member states have the same opportunity to prevent proposals from being adopted. Likewise, the simple-majority voting method favours small states, because each state has the same weight regardless of their size. However, it mainly applies to some procedural matters in a very limited number of policy areas (Lewis 2003; Westlake and Galloway 2004). The Lisbon Treaty continues the strengthening of the qualified-majority voting method that now applies to most

---

5   As noted by Brown, 'the most common yardstick by which magnitude is measured is that of populations' (Brown 2000: 13).

policy areas and has largely replaced unanimity and simple majority voting. Qualified majority voting favours the bigger member states. The weighing of the votes means that it is easier for the big states to build a winning coalition by qualified majority voting than it is for the smaller states and that it is impossible to form a blocking minority without the participation of big member states. The Lisbon Treaty further strengthens qualified majority voting by increasing the number of areas where it will apply. Moreover, the Lisbon Treaty changes the voting system, striking a compromise between big and small EU member states: from 2014 onwards a qualified majority will require that decisions are supported by 55 percent of the member states and that these states represent at the same time 65 percent of the EU population.

Second, changes in the presidency of the Council following from the Lisbon Treaty are likely to challenge the formal influence of small EU member states. The six-month rotating presidency will continue except for the Foreign Affairs Council which will be chaired by the High Representative for Foreign Affairs and Security Policy. Most importantly, according to the Treaty, the chairing of the European Council by the head of government or state of the member state holding the six-month EU presidency will be replaced by a President of the European Council, elected by qualified majority by the members of the European Council. The role of the President will be to chair and coordinate the work of the European Council. The President is elected for two and a half years and may be re-elected once. This development is problematic for small states, because the rotating presidency may be used to increase their influence and prestige and, furthermore, rotation signals the equality of all EU member states.

Third, changes in the European Commission challenges the formal channels of influence for small states. At present, each member state nominates one member of the Commission. According to the Lisbon Treaty this will change from 2014 onwards, when only two-thirds of the member states will nominate a Commissioner. This development challenges the influence of the small EU member states, because they will not always have a Commissioner in the future. This is, of course, also the case for big EU member states, but big member states are better able to compensate, because of their larger resources. As noted by Thorhallsson, the big EU member states are better able to exert their influence on the Commission, because in contrast to the small administration of small EU member states '[l]arge administrations have enough information and resources available to challenge the Commission's position and they tend to do so on all occasions' (Thorhallsson [2000] 2006: 224). In addition small member states do not have the same voting power in the Council of Ministers as the big EU member states. Thus, they can not compensate as easily for the loss of a Commissioner.

Small States and 'Natural' Aspects of the European Union

Natural organisations are collectivities, i.e. 'they are, fundamentally, social groups attempting to adapt and survive in their particular circumstances' (Scott 2003: 57). Focusing on the 'natural' aspects of organisations, we 'do not deny the existence of highly formalised structures [...], but [we] do question their importance, in particular, their impact on participants' (Scott 2003: 59). Informal structures – dependent on actor characteristics and relations between actors – are just as important as formal structures, and accordingly we are to focus on the practices of states rather than the formal institutional set-up.

Viewed through the 'natural organisation' lens, the most important aspects of the European Union are not the formal treaties, Presidency conclusions, Commission regulations and Council directives, but instead the practices of the EU members. For this reason, the challenges to small state influence, identified when looking through the 'rational organisation' lens above, appear less severe.

Instead, the organisational culture and norms of the Council are pivotal. Two norms that are central to the culture of the Council stand out. First, actors in the Council expect themselves and each other to appeal to the 'European project'; i.e. the greater good of Europe understood as the continuation and furthering of the European integration project rather than narrow self-interest when negotiating (Adler-Nissen 2009; cf. Lewis 2006). Second, decision-making by consensus rather than voting is a fundamental norm in the Council (Hayes-Renshaw 2006; Wallace 2005: 61). The consensus culture in the Council means that the voting method is of little importance in many cases, and a vote takes place in only about 15 percent of cases where the qualified majority voting applies (Wallace and Hayes-Renshaw 2003). As a result, the impact of qualified majority voting on small state influence should not be overstated. Moreover, even when they have the possibility small states only rarely veto or threaten to veto decisions (Heisenberg 2005: 77). As argued by Lewis, this means that 'arguments matter' if they are formulated powerfully within the 'European project' discourse and therefore small states may punch above their weight even in the Council (Lewis 2006: 287).

Similarly, the current system of the EU presidency is less appealing in practice than it seems when looking at the formal rules. Even though small states have often attempted to use the presidency of the Council as a stepping stone for increased influence, and sometimes with success, their ability to set an independent agenda under the system with a shift in presidency every six months should not be exaggerated. Thus, the ability of a small state to promote its own agenda when holding the presidency may be severely limited by unexpected events beyond its control at the national, European and international level (Tallberg 2003). Even if this is not the case, some estimates show that 80-90 percent of issues appearing on a presidency's agenda are predetermined (Bengtsson 2002). Moreover, it could be argued that the issues left to the rotating presidency under the Lisbon Treaty model are actually 'low politics' issues that small states have a realistic chance of influencing, whereas the issues now taken over by the new Council President and the High Representative for Foreign Affairs and Security Policy are typical 'high politics' issues, which have so far been dominated by the big member states.

Finally, the loss of the right to nominate a Commissioner to every Commission may not spell the end of small state influence on the Commission, because of the practices already developed by small states to overcome their deficit in traditional power capabilities. As shown by Thorhallsson, small states are not able to lobby the Commission to the same extent as big EU member states, but they may compensate 'by developing a special relationship with officials of the Commission and by exercising their influence within its advisory committee system' (Thorhallsson [2000] 2006: 224). Thus, the relatively small number of officials dealing with a relatively limited number of issues allows officials from small states to establish a relatively close relationship with officials working on the same issues in the Commission. Looking through the 'natural organisation' lens, small states may even wish to give up their own Commissioner in order to maintain a strong Commission: if the big EU member states are not guaranteed the right to nominate a Commissioner, then the European Commission risks being marginalised, because big EU members will direct their diplomatic resources to other fora.

Therefore, the formal safeguards of small state influence are less important when viewed through the 'natural organisation' lens. Formal voting weights matter less if influence depends on devising convincing arguments appealing to the 'European project' in a system dominated by a norm of consensus. Likewise, the right to nominate a Commissioner becomes less important if the real road to influence is the development of informal ties between officials at the national and EU levels, and the right to hold the presidency becomes less important, if the agenda is more or less decided before the presidency.

Viewed through the 'natural organisation' lens the most important challenges to small state influence in the European Union are informal. Two major challenges are of particular importance. First, the past decade has witnessed a resurgence of intergovernmentalism as a legitimate state strategy. One important effect has been to undermine the central position of the Commission in EU policy-making (Kurpas et al. 2008: 31; Peterson 2008: 763). This is a problem for small states which have traditionally viewed the Commission as protector of common interest against power politics (Baechler 1998) and therefore the 'small states' best friend' (Geurts 1998; Antola and Lehtimäki 2001: 28-9). Second, the practices of ad hoc cooperation developed among the big EU member states challenge small state influence. Ad hoc cooperation between France and Germany has been particularly important during the history of EU integration. In addition, unofficial communication and negotiation among the European great powers have played an important role in EU security policy as the 'big member states are especially known to negotiate amongst themselves before going to the Council table' (Gegout 2002: 331-2; cf. Keukeleire 2001). Over the years, and in particular since the establishment of the contact group for the Balkans, France, the United Kingdom, Germany and Italy have cooperated among themselves and with the United States in order to coordinate policies and agree on a common position if possible. Thus, the most discernible pattern regarding small states and European security is the '*extent to which the smaller states were excluded from the ad hoc decision-making processes and military action*' (Duke 2001: 41, emphasis in original). Even when big member states disagree – as in the case of the Iraq War – the institutions fail to provide a forum for coordination or even consultation.

Small States and 'Open' Aspects of the European Union

Open organisations are '*complex* and *loosely coupled* systems' (Scott 2003: 83). Open organisations 'are capable of self-maintenance on the basis of throughput of resources from the environment' (Scott 2003: 84). Their boundaries are permeable and difficult to identify with any precision. Thus, viewed through the 'open organisation' lens, '[t]he organisation is a coalition of groups and interests, each attempting to obtain something from the collectivity by interacting with others, and each with its own preferences and objectives' (Pfeiffer and Salancik 1978: 36, quoted in Scott 2003: 88).

In regard to the European Union, the 'open organisation' perspective shows us a 'stakeholder Europe'. The character of European integration and the challenges and opportunities of small states within the European Union are not only influenced by formal structures and social practices, but also by the many and very different actors trying to influence the European Union at multiple levels. Looking through the 'open organisation' lens, 'Europe is developing unique forms of political organisation neither by replicating the state form at a higher level, nor by annulling the old order, but by mixing a continuity of sovereignty with new forms' (Buzan and Wæver 2003: 352).

A large number of European stakeholders are non-governmental, sub- or transnational actors (Greenwood 2007; Mazey and Richardson 1993). Many large business firms target both the national and EU levels when lobbying for their special interests either on their own or through larger groups and organisations representing their interests. Nationally-based interest groups, representing e.g. environmental or consumer interests, also seek to influence the EU system, either on their own or via larger European interest groups. Also, sub-national levels of government may occasionally communicate their concerns directly to the Commission rather than through their national government. External stakeholders are not only situated within Europe. Business firms and interests groups outside the EU may also try to further their interests. Other stakeholders are institutional: politicians in the European Parliament and civil servants of the various EU institutions may further the specific interests of their institutions as well as certain norms associated with European integration.

Non-governmental actors may be very influential in the issue areas that they target, but the most influential stakeholders when it comes to the general direction of the EU remain the governments representing EU member states. Three countries play a special role in the development of the EU: France, Germany and the United Kingdom (cf. Mouritzen and Wivel 2005). Germany and France constitute the engine driving the integration process through a series of grand bargains. Their combined – and to a large extent complementary (Pedersen 1998; 2002) – capabilities and their central locations on the continent allows them to decide the fate of continued European integration. The United Kingdom is Europe's strongest military power. Developing a genuine European security actor without the United Kingdom would be impossible. In addition, governmental stakeholders outside the European Union, most importantly the United States in security affairs, influence decision-making, both directly and indirectly.

Looking through the 'open organisation' lens, the pluralist nature of 'stakeholder Europe' creates both challenges and opportunities for small states. On the one hand, the limited resources of small states are challenged not only by big EU member states but also by a number of other actors inside and outside EU institutions. On the other hand, multiple actors also create multiple opportunities of coalition building, when managing the challenges posed by the development of both the formal aspects and social practices of EU integration.

A Smart State Strategy for Maximising Small State Influence

Which strategy may help small states to maximise their influence in the European Union? The analysis so far has identified three types of characteristics of the European Union and its current development:

- Rational characteristics: Small state influence is protected by formal EU institutions making traditional power capabilities less important and by codifying what is deemed acceptable behaviour within the EU, but recent developments in the voting methods in the Council of Ministers, changes in the presidency of the Council and changes in the composition of the Commission challenge the formal influence of small EU member states.
- Natural characteristics: Small state influence is protected by the consensus culture of EU decision-making and the informal relationships between officials at the national and EU levels. At the same time, their influence is undermined by the increasing legitimacy of intergovernmentalism and ad hoc cooperation between big EU member states. Still, small states may further their influence by appealing to the 'European project'.
- Open characteristics: The pluralist nature of 'stakeholder Europe' creates multiple opportunities for coalition-building but at the same time states with limited power resources are challenged by a number of actors inside and outside EU institutions.

The 'rational' characteristics of the EU suggest that the binding strategy has served small EU member states well in the past, but that recent developments challenge its continued effectiveness. An important implication of the 'natural' and 'open' characteristics is that the binding strategy has only limited value in a system with many different actors seeking influence through both formal and informal channels and with deeply ingrained social practices sometimes by-passing the rules and regulations of formal institutions. In this institutional environment strengthening the institutional binding of the great powers may prove to be counterproductive, because they have ample opportunity to move their communication and negotiations outside the formal institutional settings and to team up with a variety of different actors in order to obtain their goals if they are dissatisfied with the formal channels of influence.

Moreover, formalisation may also entail costs for the small states. First, formalisation institutionalises inequality. Formal inequality is the price paid by small states in exchange for institutionalisation. Few great powers will allow themselves to be tied down by formal rules and institutions unless they get some institutional safeguards against being dominated by the small states, which will usually outnumber them but have far fewer capabilities. At worst, formal institutionalisation will lock small states into their traditional role of 'rule-taker' rather than 'rule-maker'. It will put the individual small state in a position of permanent relative weakness *vis-à-vis* the bigger member states of the organisation. Second, formalisation limits innovation (cf. Scott 2003: 37). Small states are relatively weak when measured on material power capabilities such as population, military spending and personnel, territorial size and GDP. This is often why they are defined as small (cf. Thorhallsson and Wivel 2006), but measured on 'soft' or 'normative' parameters they may do significantly better as exemplified by the success of the Scandinavian countries in promoting particular sets of norms in regard to global environmental politics, conflict resolution and global welfare (Ingebritsen 2002). Thus, small states may thrive in an institutional environment rewarding innovation.

Fortunately, the European Union creates new possibilities for small member states in realising their normative power potential. The exercise of military power between EU member states is out of the question, and therefore small European states need not fear the military threat of the regional great powers. In contrast to the nineteenth century, small member states need not accept concert-style rule by the European great powers. Rather, the institutional environment created by EU integration encourages the creation of a large number of mutually overlapping 'concerts' in different issue areas with small states and many other actors playing an active role through formal and informal channels of influence.

In order to maximise influence in this institutional environment small states will benefit from acting as smart states (Arter 2000; Joenniemi 1998; Wivel 2005). A smart state strategy has three fundamental aspects (cf. Wivel 2009: 29-30). The first aspect concerns the political substance of the strategy. The political substance of the strategy must present (part of) the solution to a problem recognised by all or most of the relevant political actors. Small member states do not have sufficient resources and political clout to pursue a political agenda, which is radically different from the major actors let alone in opposition. Thus, political initiatives from small EU member states should avoid being in conflict with existing EU initiatives or political proposals from any of the big EU member states. Ideally, they should be presented as specific contributions to a general development, not as a change of policy or an attempt to slow it down.

The second aspect concerns the form of the strategy. Small states do not have sufficient resources to pursue a broad political agenda with many different goals. Therefore, they must focus their resources and signal their willingness to negotiate and compromise on issues that are not deemed to be of vital importance. Small states need to choose issues where influence is a real possibility, and for them this most often means sticking to 'low politics', i.e. economic, cultural and climate issues, rather than high politics, i.e. military security.

The third aspect concerns the role of the small state itself. In order to maximise its own influence the small state must aim to position itself as an 'honest broker' acting independently of any of the big EU member states' interests. Thus, the small state needs to work within the dominant discourse of the Union and at the same time avoid being identified too closely with any particular actor's interests. In addition, for the small state to succeed as an honest broker it needs to allocate sufficient resources to play an active role on the European stage and to focus on issues where it has a comparative advantage, i.e. particular technical or administrative capabilities. Also, initiatives need to be focused on the long-term and well prepared.

Weakness facilitates a role as an honest broker focused on compromise (Elgström 2003; cf. Arter 2000). Whereas big EU member states have interests in most policy areas and are generally expected to take advantage of their powerful positions to advance their own national interests (Bengtsson, Elgström and Tallberg 2004), small states are sometimes seen as more efficient as mediators, because they are too weak to pursue their own interests without taking into account the position of others (Bjurulf 2001). Thus, using a smart state strategy, small states may use their lack of power to gain influence over selected issues, because it enables them to be viewed by competing great powers as 'honest brokers' able to promote the general interest of the Union (cf. Antola and Lehtimäki 2001: 38; Arter 2000: 679).[6]

In essence, traditional small state strategies accept the weakness of small states as the point of departure for strategies aiming at 'damage control', i.e. limiting the negative consequences of the lack of traditional power resources either by preserving autonomy (through hiding) or limiting the actions of the great powers (through binding). A smart state strategy uses the weakness of small states as

---

6   These characteristics of a smart state strategy are all present in the Finnish Northern Dimension Initiative, which involves a number of soft security measures to enhance cooperation and stability in the north-eastern part of Europe accepted as official EU policy in 1998. The Finnish initiative was carefully planned and lobbied over a long period of time, and despite initial scepticism, Finland successfully built a viable coalition after convincing the big EU member states that they need not fear the consequences of the new initiative (cf. Arter 2000). Another example is Denmark's and Sweden's successful attempt to influence the enlargement of the European Union with central and eastern European countries, which resulted in negotiations with a larger number of applicant countries than initially favoured by the big member states (Friis 1998). Other small states have successfully employed aspects of the smart state strategy, e.g. in regard to environmental policy-making (cf. Liefferink and Andersen 1998).

a resource for influence. The weakness of small states means that they are not viewed as rivals by the great powers and therefore might be allowed more freedom of action when launching policy initiatives, building coalitions and acting as mediators.

Conclusion

Despite their weakness in material capabilities, small states may act as policy entrepreneurs and maximise their influence in the European Union by employing a smart state strategy. Pursuing a smart state strategy – with highly focused goals and means ordered sharply in accordance with preferences, political initiatives presented as examples of the common interest of member states, and a role for small states as mediators – will allow small EU member states to take advantage of the unique combination of 'rational', 'natural' and 'open' aspects of the European Union, and therefore to maximise their influence.

References

Adler-Nissen, R. 2009. *The Diplomacy of Opting Out*. Copenhagen: University of Copenhagen.
Antola, E. and Lehtimäki. M. 2001. *Small States in the EU*. Turku: Jean Monnet Centre of Excellence.
Archer, C. and Nugent, N. 2002. Introduction: Small States and the European Union. *Current Politics and Economics of Europe*, 11(1), 1-10.
Arter, D. 2000. Small State Influence within the EU: The Case of Finland's Northern Dimension Initiative. *Journal of Common Market Studies*, 38(5), 677-97.
Baechler, G. 1998. Conclusions: Future Relevance and Priorities of Small States, in *Small States Inside and Outside the European Union*, edited by L. Goetschel. Dordrecht: Kluwer Academic Publishers, 267-83.
Bengtsson, R. 2002. Soft Security and the Presidency. *Cooperation and Conflict*, 37(2), 212-18.
Bengtsson, R., Elgström, O. and Tallberg, J. 2004. Silencer or Amplifier? The European Union Presidency and the Nordic Countries. *Scandinavian Political Studies*, 27(3), 311-34.
Bjurulf, B. 2001. How did Sweden Manage the European Union? *ZEI Discussion Paper*, No. C96, 2001. Bonn: Zentrum für Europäische Integrationsforschung.
Brown, J. 2000. *Small States in the European Institutions*. Turku: Jean Monnet Centre of Excellence.
Buzan, B. and Wæver, O. 2003. *Regions and Powers*. Cambridge: Cambridge University Press.

Dosenrode, S.Z.V. 1993. *Westeuropäische Kleinstaaten in der EG und EPZ*. Zürich: Verlag Rüegger.
Duke, S.W. 2001. Small States and European Security, in *Small States and Alliances*, edited by E. Reiter and H. Gärtner. Heidelberg: Physica-Verlag, 39-50.
Elgström, O. 2003. Introduction, in *European Union Council Presidencies: A Comparative Perspective*, edited by O. Elgström. London: Routledge, 1-17.
Friis, L. 1998. EU Enlargement and the Luxembourg Summit: A Case Study in Agenda Setting, in *Explaining European Integration*, edited by A. Wivel. Copenhagen: Copenhagen Political Studies Press, 56-77.
Gegout, C. 2002. The Quint: Acknowledging the Existence of a Big Four-US Directoire at the Heart of the European Union's Foreign Policy Decision-Making Process. *Journal of Common Market Studies*, 40(2), 331-44.
Geurts, C. 1998. The European Commission: A Natural Ally of Small States in the EU Institutional Framework?, in *Small States inside and outside the European Union*, edited by L. Goetschel. Dordrecht: Kluwer Academic Publishers, 49-64.
Greenwood, J. 2007. *Representing Interests in the European Union*. Second Edition. Houndmills: Macmillan.
Gruber, L. 2000. *Ruling the World*. Princeton, New Jersey: Princeton University Press.
Hayes-Renshaw, F. 2006. The Council of Ministers, in *The Institutions of the European Union*, edited by J. Peterson and M. Shackleton. Second Edition. Oxford: Oxford University Press, 60-80.
Heisenberg, D. 2005. The Institution of 'Consensus' in the European Union: Formal Versus Informal Decision Making in the Council. *European Journal of Political Research*, 44, 65-90.
Ingebritsen, C. 2002. Norm Entrepreneurs: Scandinavia's Role in World Politics. *Cooperation and Conflict*, 37(1), 11-23.
Joenniemi, P. 1998. From Small to Smart: Reflections on the Concept of Small States. *Irish Studies in International Affairs*, 9, 61-62.
Jones, E. 2008. *Economic Adjustment and Political Transformation in Small States*. Oxford: Oxford University Press.
Keukeleire, S. 2001. Directorates in the CFSP/CESDP of the European Union: A Plea for 'Restricted Crisis Management Groups'. *European Foreign Affairs Review*, 6, 75-101.
Kurpas, S., Grøn, C. and Kaczynski, P. 2008. *The European Commission After Enlargement: Does More Add Up to Less?* Brussels: CEPS.
Lewis, J. 2003. The Council of the European Union, in *European Union Politics*, edited by M. Cini. Oxford: Oxford University Press, 148-65.
Lewis, J. 2006. National Interests: Coreper, in *The Institutions of the European Union*, edited by J. Peterson and M. Shackleton. Second Edition. Oxford: Oxford University Press, 272-91.

Liefferink, D. and Andersen, M.S. 1998. Strategies of the 'Green' Member States in EU Environmental Policy-Making. *Journal of European Public Policy*, 5(2), 254-70.

Maes, I. and Verdun, A. 2005. Small States and the Creation of EMU: Belgium and the Netherlands, Pace-setters and Gate-keepers. *Journal of Common Market Studies*, 43(2), 327-48.

Mazey, S. and Richardson, J. 1993. *Lobbying in the European Community*. Oxford: Oxford University Press.

Milward, A.S. 1992. *The European Rescue of the Nation-State*. London: Routledge.

Mouritzen, H. and Wivel, A. 2005. *The Geopolitics of Euro-Atlantic Integration*. London: Routledge.

Neumann, I.B. and Gstöhl, S. 2006. Introduction: Lilliputians in Gulliver's World?, in *Small States in International Relations*, edited by C. Ingebritsen, I.B. Neumann, S. Gstöhl and J. Beyer. Seattle: University of Washington Press, 3-36.

Pedersen, T. 1998. *Germany, France and the Integration of Europe: A Realist Interpretation*. London: Pinter.

Pedersen, T. 2002. Cooperative Hegemony: Power, Ideas and Institutions in Regional Integration. *Review of International Studies*, 28(4), 677-96.

Peterson, J. 2008. Enlargement, Reform and the Commission: Weathering a Perfect Storm? *Journal of European Public Policy*, 15(5), 761-80.

Scott, W.R. 2003. *Organizations: Rational, Natural, and Open Systems*. Upper Saddle River: Prentice-Hall.

Smith, S. 2007. Introduction: Diversity and Disciplinarity in International Relations Theory, in *International Relations Theories: Discipline and Diversity*, edited by T. Dunne, M. Kurki and S. Smith. Oxford: Oxford University Press, 1-12.

Sterling-Folker, J. (ed.) 2006. *Making Sense of International Relations Theory*. Boulder: Lynne Rienner Publishers.

Tallberg, J. 2003. *European Governance and Supranational Institutions: Making States Comply*. London: Routledge.

Thorhallsson, B. [2000] 2006. The Role of Small States in the European Union, in *Small States in International Relations*, edited by C. Ingebritsen, I.B. Neumann, S. Gstöhl and J. Beyer. Seattle: University of Washington Press, 218-27.

Thorhallsson, B. and Wivel, A. 2006. Small States in the European Union: What Do We Know and What Would We Like to Know? *Cambridge Review of International Affairs*, 19(4), 651-68.

Thucydides [1954] 1972. *History of the Peloponnesian War*. London and New York: Penguin Books.

Wallace, H. 2005. An Institutional Anatomy and Five Policy Modes, in *Policy-Making in the European Union*, edited by H. Wallace, W. Wallace and M.A. Pollack. Fifth Edition. Oxford: Oxford University Press, 49-90.

Wallace, H. and Hayes-Renshaw, F. 2003. *Reforming the Council: A Work in Progress*. Stockholm: Swedish Institute for European Policy Studies. Available at: http://www.sieps.se/en/publications/rapporter/reforming-the-council-a-work-in-progress.html [accessed: 28 July 2009].

Wallace, W. 1999. Small European States and European Policy-Making: Strategies, Roles, Possibilities, in *Between Autonomy and Influence: Small States and the European Union*, edited by W. Wallace, B. Jacobsson, S. Kux, S.S. Andersen, T. Notermans, F. Sejersted, and K. Hagen. Arena Report, No. 1/99. Oslo: Arena, 11-26.

Westlake, M. and Galloway, D. 2004. *The Council of the European Union*. Third Edition. London: John Harper Publishing.

Wivel, A. 2005. The Security Challenge of Small EU Member States: Interests, Identity and the Development of the EU as a Security Actor. *Journal of Common Market Studies*, 43(2), 393-412.

Wivel, A. 2009. Hvad har klimaet nogensinde gjort for Danmark? En midtvejsevaluering af dansk klimapolitik som udenrigspolitisk strategi. *Politik*, 12(1), 27-35.

Chapter 3

Small State Diplomacy Compared to Sub-State Diplomacy: More of the Same or Different?

David Criekemans and Manuel Duran

In the international system, all states are equal, but some are more equal than others. Small states find themselves at the lower end of the 'international pecking order'. They have to try to find *niches* so as to make a difference in their diplomacy compared to the greater powers. These niches can, for instance, be realised through setting specific topics on the international agenda. Small states also possibly rely more on structural or ad hoc-multilateral frameworks and/or alliances, so as to augment their voice in the international arena. Last but not least, small states will sometimes also utilise specific 'diplomatic' instruments, more closely tailored to their 'soft power'-character. As a result of their great dependency on the external environment and their sensitivity and vulnerability to external changes, the question of cooperation with other small states and in the international arena becomes an important one (Jazbec 2001: 56). Usually, international institutions are the best friends of small states (Väyrynen 1996). Such a tendency is not always the case when one studies the foreign policy of 'big' states.

A similar asymmetric relationship can be explored when comparing small states to sub-state entities. During the last decades, the phenomenon of 'sub-state diplomacy' has grown quite substantially. Regions with constitutional powers such as Québec, Flanders, Wallonia, Catalonia, Scotland, Bavaria, etc. are more and more active on the world scene on their own merits. Sometimes they develop a foreign policy parallel, complementary or in conflict to the external policies developed by their own 'central' governments. The 'diplomatic' instruments which these non-central governments have developed have become more and more refined over the years. Some sub-state entities, such as Flanders and Wallonia are able to conclude treaties, not only with other regions but also with classical states. A host of regions such as Flanders, Wallonia, Catalonia, Québec, and others have developed a small diplomatic network of political representatives abroad. Furthermore, sub-state entities conclude political declarations of intent, cultural agreements, transnational contracts, cooperation agreements, ententes, etc. Furthermore, they heavily rely on more informal policy instruments such as public diplomacy and the development of specific international policy networks.

This chapter explores the differences and similarities between small state diplomacy and sub-state diplomacy. Is sub-state diplomacy more of the same compared to small state diplomacy, or is it different? If both focus on 'soft power'-issues, where does the difference lie? Can one compare it to the difference between small and great powers in the international system? To what extent is the boundary between 'small state diplomacy' and 'sub-state diplomacy' diluting? First, we will examine the traditional relation between small state diplomacy versus great power diplomacy. Second, we will zoom in to the specific nature of sub-state diplomacy. Third, we will examine the degree of distinction between the diplomatic activities of small states and those of sub-state entities. Finally, we ask the *so what?-question*; what consequences or opportunities does sub-state diplomacy entail or offer to small states?

The Traditional Comparison: Small State Diplomacy Versus Great Power Diplomacy

A good starting point for analysing the specific issue of small state diplomacy is to take a closer look at the way small states relate to great powers. Before we start analysing, it is imperative to underline that in this chapter, just as in every contribution in this book, 'being a small state' is being tied to a specific spatio-temporal context, not to a general characteristic of the state. Thus, a 'small state' should not be defined by indicators such as its absolute population size or size of GDP relative to other states. Instead, a small state is defined by *being the weak part in an asymmetric relationship*.

Traditionally, especially in an International Relations (IR) perspective, the difference between small and great states was drawn in terms of capabilities. Morgenthau (1972: 129-30) puts it like this: 'A Great Power is a state which is able to have its will against a small state...which in turn is not able to have its will against a Great Power.' This harsh statement, expressed in full Cold War, is still widely accepted by IR scholars. Present-day neo-realists still tend to begin their analyses of powers great and small with an examination of *relative* capabilities, and some of them even end there (Neumann and Gstöhl 2006: 18). The relationship between small and great powers is thus primarily an asymmetric one between a strong and a weak international actor. After all, small states just do not possess the political, economic or military resources the great and middle powers have at their disposal to influence world affairs. This especially runs true with regard to rather traditional security matters. Only great and some middle power states are capable of developing a full-fledged military apparatus and intelligence services.

From this rationale, when studying small state diplomacy, one tends to emphasise the importance of bandwagoning or balancing as the main international strategies for small states. This approach, while certainly having its merits, tends to oversimplify the actual reality of small state diplomacy by reducing its role to a merely, sometimes even passive, reaction to the policies of the great and middle powers. The *active* role small states can play internationally is underexposed or even totally ignored by this approach. We believe this underexposure is undeserved, because small states do play an active role, be it some more active than others and in doing so are even influencing the theories and practices of present day diplomacy *tout court*.

Bottom line is that small states have to carefully analyse their priorities and evaluate their options in order to choose an international strategy that not only suits their interests, but that also takes into account their means and assets. In doing so they will try to minimise their limitations and weaknesses *vis-à-vis* great and even middle powers,[1] in an effort to escape the relatively speaking weaker geopolitical and geo-economic variables with which they are endowed. Thus, in setting up their foreign policy, as well as their diplomatic apparatus and practice, small states are often guided by these limitations. Strategies have to be developed so as to compensate for these or to reverse them into an asset. Alan Henrikson roughly summarises the following six categories of small state diplomacy (Henrikson 1998):

1. *Quiet diplomacy*, when a small state takes shelter under the umbrella of a larger country;
2. *Protest diplomacy*, a confrontational stance to draw international attention;
3. *Group diplomacy*, when small states align with others in a regional or ideology-based group;
4. *Niche diplomacy*, when small states enhance their international position by specialising in a certain policy domain;
5. *Enterprise diplomacy*, a highly aggressive and entrepreneurial activity that 'steals' international advantages; and finally
6. *Regulatory diplomacy*.

These six categories become particularly relevant if we stop taking (power) capabilities as a starting point for analysing small state diplomacy instead of the role of institutions and relations (Neumann and Gstöhl 2006: 19-25).

Small states favour – for obvious reasons – the institutionalisation of rules and norms, in the form of international law, international regimes and international institutions. They regard these not only as a means to moderate the greater powers, but also as a forum to set their own international agenda and look for allies in setting this agenda. This explains the importance which smaller states attach to their sometimes oversized (when taken into account their limited size) representations in New York, Geneva or Brussels. These are the places where the international agenda is set and where they have to be present in order to influence it.

---

[1] On middle powers, read: Carsten Holbraad (1984). *Middle Powers in International Politics*. London: Macmillan.

Perhaps even more important is to examine the various forms of interstate relations. Not only do we observe an ever-growing degree of global interdependence, but also different forms of regional integration, where greater and smaller powers are integrated in larger intergovernmental (MERCOSUR, ASEAN, CIS) or even (pseudo)transnational entities (EU). These intergovernmental or transnational entities are favoured by small nations since they regard these as a means to confine the power of the greater states, while at the same time enhancing their own influence. After all, every member state, small and great alike, has to abide to the same rules and principles.

Parallel to this contextual environment, small states also have developed a whole range of techniques or instruments to play the diplomatic game. Examples of these are the practice of 'associative diplomacy', when small states make a foreign policy *démarche* together. For example, in 1972, Jamaica, Guyana, Trinidad and Tobago and Barbados decided together to establish diplomatic relations with Cuba (Sanders 1989: 420). Next to the system of resident ambassadors, they can opt for non-resident ambassadors who don't reside within the country to which they are accredited, but live in a nearby country. Other options are the maintenance of consulates and other offices abroad like tourism offices or economic bureaus. An alternative method of representation is unilateral representation, in which one country maintains a resident mission in another, but the latter does not reciprocate in kind. The country that does not maintain a resident mission is able to deal with the government of the other through the resident mission of the latter (Naseer Mohamed 2002: 20). Joint representation by using shared embassies is another means to overcome the lack of resources, just as using the missions to the United Nations is to overcome the problem of non-representation. New modes of diplomacy, like virtual embassies or e-diplomacy, seem too recent to be already judged on their merit. It should also be stated that small states more and more rely on the cost effective instruments of nation-branding and public diplomacy (Batora 2005).

To conclude, in comparison to great power diplomacy, the diplomatic activities of small states are – relatively speaking – focussed on making a difference in specific functional dossiers, often together with others. Far less than great powers can they rely on more systemic and regulatory mechanisms in international affairs to 'push through' their own political and economic agenda.

Zooming into the Specific Nature of Sub-state Diplomacy

Over the last few decades, the international state system has increasingly been faced with other players entering in the global arena. Next to transnational corporations, NGOs, transnational civil society and international organisations, subnational (or sub-state) entities are coming more often to the fore. The reasons for this are twofold: on the one hand important modifications have occurred on both national and international levels, while on the other hand important economic developments within subnational entities also have taken place (Keating 1999: 1). 'Paradiplomacy' can be defined as 'the foreign policy of non-central governments' (Aldecoa and Keating 1999), a term which is not always accepted with enthusiasm in parts of the academic community. According to some critics, the term seems to suggest an artificial separation between 'centralised diplomacy' and the 'diplomatic practice of sub-state entities', which is not always the case. Hence the prefix 'para' (cf. parallel) is contested; the diplomacy of sub-state entities might also in some cases be part of a multi-level endeavor of central and non-central entities who together join diplomatic forces on the international scene.

The topic of sub-state diplomacy is a recent field of research. Although there is a high increase in the number of publications, it suffers from a lack of balance (Criekemans 2007). *Initially* most of the studies concentrated on the problem of the distribution of responsibilities between central and regional governments. This resulted in a vast corpus of literature on the legal and internal political framework within which sub-state entities develop their own foreign policy.[2] A steadily increasing amount of empirical literature tries to gain insight into the phenomenon of sub-state diplomacy in an inductive manner, mostly by means of case studies, e.g. Catalonia (Scotoni 1998; Scotoni 2006); Québec (Paquin 2001); the Basque Country (Lecours and Moreno 2006); Flanders (Criekemans 2006a; Criekemans 2006b), etc. A *second group of scholarship* is also case-oriented, but in a comparative fashion. Here the domestic influence on the territorial division of power is studied from the bottom up. Comparative studies often focus on the way in which domestic situations influence the territorial division of power and hence also search for solutions to be active on the international scene. In this context, the variable of 'nationalism' sometimes is also put forward as an understudied one (see Paquin 2004). Finally, a *third group of empirical scholarship* starts from an IR perspective. Sub-state diplomacy is situated in ever changing international surroundings, or from the top down; the context of a changing or turbulent world order which creates a new situation with which the national diplomatic apparatus has to try to deal, for instance via adapting the foreign policy machinery (see Hocking 1993; Hocking 1999). One of the challenges in the academic study of sub-state diplomacy is to *gather comparable data* on the institutional mechanisms,

---

2   Also the judicial framework for 'para-diplomatic' activities in federal countries has been carefully mapped, both by students of law and political science. As a culmination of this process, we can for instance refer to the book edited by Majeed, Watts and Brown, titled *Distribution of Powers & Responsibilities in Federal Countries*, published by the Canadian Forum of Federations and the International Association of Centers for Federal Studies (see Majeed, Watts and Brown 2005). Also both organisations recently published an interesting booklet called *Dialogues on Foreign Relations in Federal Countries* (see Blindenbacher and Pasma 2007), which provides additional information regarding the foreign policy-position 'sub-state' or 'federated' entities enjoy in different countries. Most recently, the Forum of Federations published a book titled *Foreign Relations in Federal Countries*, which offers in-depth analyses of a number of European countries, the US, India, etc. (Michelmann 2009).

the diplomatic instruments and the organisational structures which non-central governments utilise so as to develop a foreign policy, parallel, complementary or conflictual to those of their central state colleagues. Gathering such data can help us to better evaluate the nature and width of sub-state diplomacy, and in a second move also to be able to appraise the relation between sub-state and small state diplomacy.

Sub-state diplomatic practices can be divided into four clusters of activities:

1. Horizontal cooperation;
2. Vertical cooperation;
3. Promotion of interests;
4. The use of innovative policy instruments.

By *horizontal cooperation* we refer to all forms of cross-border and interregional cooperation between regions, often in the form of bilateral or multilateral cooperation with neighbouring regions, but just as much in a European context (e.g. EUREGION). *Vertical cooperation* expresses the way in which regions participate in and design the foreign policy of the federal state. Germany does pioneering work in the way in which the representatives of the governments of the *Länder* delineate the foreign policy of the Federal Republic in the *Bundesrat* (Hrbek 2007). The most striking form of interest promotion of subnational entities is their own network of representatives or offices abroad. Sub-state entities rely on a whole range of innovative policy tools like public diplomacy, informal networking, city diplomacy and an integrated international cultural policy. The phenomenon has gained importance in so much as the growing presence of sub-state entities on the international stage has become a structural element of the international political system. A certain normalisation of the phenomenon is taking place, sometimes even to the extent that boundaries between state and sub-state diplomacy have become somewhat blurred (Manojlovic and Thorheim 2007: 23).

From an historical point of view, one could state that currently a 'third wave' is developing in sub-state diplomacy, especially in Europe (Criekemans, Duran and Melissen 2008: 389). The *first wave* manifested itself from the 1980s onwards: a growing number of non-central governments tried to attract foreign direct investment through own initiatives or to use culture and identity as a lever to place oneself on the international map. Such initiatives often were of an ad-hoc nature, there was only a minor integration of all the external activities that were generated. The *second wave* in the 1990s was characterised by the creation, within the sub-state entities of certain (European) countries, of a judicially grounded set of instruments for their own (parallel as well as complementary) diplomatic activities. These instruments were supplemented by the gradual development of a 'separate' foreign policy-apparatus (administration or policy-body) which started to horizontally coordinate the external activities of the different administrations in certain regions. The current *third wave* is characterised by steps in the direction of a 'verticalisation' of the organisational structure of the administration or department of external/foreign affairs, a strategic reorientation of the geopolitical and functional priorities and attempts to integrate the external instruments for a sub-state foreign policy into a well performing whole.

In this process, some regions are manifestly more active than others. Parallel to the dichotomy great versus small states, we can observe a similar distinction between active and rather passive regions. Already in 1990 Ivo Duchacek stated that the activities of non-central governments in the field of international relations diverge quite strongly, both in form, intensity and frequency (Duchacek 1990). Some 'paradiplomatic' actions developed by federated entities are technical in nature, some are economically motivated. Other interventions want to stress the unique culture and identity, and finally there are interventions which are politically motivated. Whereas (power) capabilities set great states apart from small states, it is primarily the combination of institutional possibilities and political will that sets the active and passive regions apart. Let us explore this distinction somewhat further in the following paragraphs.

The Belgian regions Flanders and Wallonia can be considered to be textbook examples of regions that developed a substantial foreign policy, based on both constitutional competences and political will. In 1993 the Belgian state was reformed, which resulted in awarding formal *treaty-making power* and *political representation* abroad to the 'Regions and Communities' within the country (Clement et al. 1993: 33-45). The principle *in foro interno, in foro externo* entails that the Belgian 'federated entities' or 'regions' have to manage their (still growing number of) competencies – not only in day-to-day domestic policy, but also on a permanent basis in the foreign policy-dossiers which touch upon their 'internal' material competencies (Lagasse 2002). *In concreto*, this meant the Belgian regions possess a formal treaty making power, not only with other regions, but even with other states. Furthermore, the Belgian federated entities also have a right to send their own representatives abroad, i.e. to bilateral posts, to other regions/areas and to international organisations (e.g. the European Union or intergovernmental multilateral organisations). Both Flanders and Wallonia have indeed used these rights by developing a vast network of political representations abroad (next to the numerous economic and tourist representations). Flanders now has ten bilateral and two multilateral representations, while Wallonia possesses 15 bilateral and two multilateral representations (Duran and Criekemans 2008: 261). Both regions signed dozens of treaties, both exclusive and mixed treaties. Thus, looking at the institutional possibilities and political will of these Belgian federated entities, one could conclude that they come very close to what traditional states can do in their respective foreign policies.

When one compares the Belgian federated entities with other regions with constitutional power, one can observe a marked contrast. Most regions are perhaps somewhat 'jealous' of the vast external powers of the Belgian Regions and Communities. Others such as Québec and Bavaria come close to the Belgian model since they also have forms of treaty-making power, but most others only have instruments at their disposal such as political declarations of intent, cultural treaties, or they rather invest in developing their own international policy networks. In absence of more formal instruments of foreign policy, some regions such as Catalonia or even Scotland have seriously invested in flexible mechanisms of cooperation. First, they invest more often in the development of policy-networks. In this way, they try to do agenda-setting, to bring together specific know-how and actors within different policy domains and to learn from other regions with similar or different experiences. 'The Four Motors of Europe' is a good example for such a regional policy-network. It brings together four highly industrialised regions in Europe: Catalonia, Baden-Württemberg, Rhône-Alpes and Lombardy. They cooperate in a long-term relationship in the fields of science, research, education, environment, culture and other sectors. The purpose of this relationship is to provide a unification force within Europe as well as increasing the potential for economic growth within the four regions. Other well-known regional policy-networks include REGLEG (Regions with Legislative Powers), the Assembly of European Regions, the Conference of Peripheral Maritime Regions, Flanders DC (Flanders District of Creativity) and so on. Second, a lot of regions prefer bilateral and cross-border cooperation over multilateral cooperation. Catalonia[3] for instance has developed a very elaborate cross-border policy over the years, focused on the Pyrenees region. Since 1983 they work together with Aragon, Navarre, the Basque region (Spain), Languedoc-Roussillon, Midi-Pyrénées, Aquitaine (France) and the small country of Andorra in the Working Community of the Pyrenees in the fields of tourism, cultural dialogue and environmental policy (Bizoux 2006: 75). Parallel to this *Comunitat de Treball dels Pirineus*, Catalonia is also active in the EUREGION Pyrénées-Méditerranée, thus doubling its own activities in the region. The same goes for the German Land of Bavaria, which is involved in a lot of cross-border projects with other German, Swiss and Austrian regions and the small country of Liechtenstein through the *Bodensee Konferenz* and the *Arbeitsgemeinschaft Alpenländer*. Finally, a growing number of regions have, compared to small states, devoted relatively more attention to public diplomacy. This last diplomatic instrument has both a domestic and foreign component. Domestic public diplomacy in its narrow sense is only focused on providing a platform for foreign policy, but in a broader sense it could very well be more used as an instrument for regional awareness and identity. Foreign public diplomacy means that one actively tries to inform the international audience about the economic, cultural and political developments (Criekemans 2008b).

In the absence of 'hard power', regions seem to embrace 'soft power' with passion. Public diplomacy is an interesting instrument to do so (e.g. Huijgh and Melissen 2008). If both small states and sub-state entities are focusing on 'soft power'-issues, where does the difference then lie? The answer seems to be that

---

3   Nevertheless, it is true that Catalonia also has become interested in being represented in UNESCO, following the example of the Belgian regions and Québec. However, these initiatives remain limited compared to the bilateral and cross-border initiatives within their overall sub-state diplomacy.

regions don't *have* to cover the whole range of policy domains (they are *but* sub-state entities), so they can choose at will these domains where they excel. To a certain extent, this provides sub-state entities with an advantage over small states. On the other hand, some sub-state entities such as Québec, Catalonia and even Scotland can play a very 'elaborate' role on the international stage: they are even active in policy-domains that were once thought to be the exclusive domain of states (migration, security, etc.) (Paquin 2007).

Indeed, to make matters even more complicated, there are also those who claim that the most 'advanced' examples of sub-state diplomacy constitute in essence really a preparation for independence. In that case, one no longer uses the term 'paradiplomacy' to label those specific sub-state diplomatic activities, but rather the term 'protodiplomacy'. Look for instance at Catalonia; the diplomatic activities of the Catalan government are often mentioned in the national political debate as arguments that 'Barcelona' can do a 'much better job' than 'Madrid'. Even in Scotland, similar patterns can be detected. Slovenia could be seen as a case which has successfully transcended from 'sub-state diplomacy' into 'small state diplomacy'. Inherently, some politicians within sub-state regions feel that their governments should aim 'higher' and move up a place in the international pecking order. It would, however, be a mistake to 'catalogue' every example of sub-state diplomacy as an attempt at 'secession'. In most cases, sub-state diplomatic activity is generated as the result of a combination of factors: a more complex international environment endowed with problems which can only be solved via a multi-level approach, a regional government which is interested in the world and also which is trying to develop the necessary diplomatic tools. In this way, regions hope to 'gain access' and recuperate some of the influence which they lost as a result of 'globalisation'.

The Blurring of the Distinction in the Diplomatic Activities of Small States Versus those of Sub-state Entities

Whereas some 10 to 15 years ago, it was still possible to make a clear distinction between the diplomatic activities emanating from central versus non-central (or sub-state) governments, that line has today become much more blurred. Such a process can be empirically illustrated by looking at different dimensions (Criekemans 2008a):

- *How regions with legislative powers define their respective 'foreign policy'.* Clear evidence exists of ever more all-encompassing conceptualisations and operationalisations. The 'foreign affairs' of regions with legislative powers sometimes closely emulates the activities of central governments and becomes ever more sophisticated as time goes by.
- *How 'diplomatic' instruments are utilised.* One can state that without any doubt the picture of early twenty first century 'paradiplomacy' has become

quite diverse and lively: extra (political and other) representations abroad are opened and planned, even more cooperation agreements with third parties are concluded, and the domain of multilateral policy is no longer the monopoly of the central states. However, in contrast to the situation with small states, international institutions are not always the 'best friends' of regions: *at a policy-level* they might accept the input of the regions (financial contributions, policy-relevant know-how), but *at the political level* only states are accepted as full-fledged members. One also notices that regions are very active in developing formal and informal networks that try to tackle specific needs/problems in very diverse policy areas. Moreover, it seems that they are more eager to invest in additional, new forms of diplomacy like for example in 'public diplomacy'. The conclusion in our opinion is that paradiplomacy and diplomacy have become enmeshed.

- *What is the character of the representations abroad?* One notices that the external projection of many regions with legislative power has many facets: political, economical, cultural, educational and even such 'hard dossiers' such as immigration. Although the foreign networks of regions are still very modest in comparison to their respective central governments, they nevertheless do important work so as to further expand and deepen the existing cooperation with third parties *beyond the level of the classical diplomatic relations*.

All of the trends that have been detected ultimately pose *the question whether the implicit distinction between paradiplomacy and diplomacy can still be upheld*. On the one hand, the above analysis shows that sub-state diplomacy clearly emulates the diplomacy of that of small states. In this sense the dynamics between small states and sub-states are distinctly different when compared to the relationship between small and great powers. On the other hand, it is obvious that small states have an international legal position and embeddedness, which is stronger compared to that of sub-state entities. In that sense the dynamics between small states and sub-state entities are similar when compared to the relationship between small and great powers. However, the Belgian Communities and Regions constitute the exception to the rule. Thanks to their right to (1) conclude treaties with third parties (other regions and even states) and (2) send out their own 'diplomatic' representatives abroad, they come awfully close to what small states are able to do in international affairs.

The boundaries between 'diplomacy' and 'paradiplomacy' are watering down. In our opinion this opens up wholly new and exciting avenues in future comparative research, not only from a purely academic, but also from a more policy-oriented perspective. *From an academic point of view*, a route to explore is how the traditional study of small state foreign policy and diplomacy could be 'opened up' to take into account the changing nature of the external environment, the international rules and the entrance of relatively new actors such as sub-state entities on the global and regional scene. *From a policy-relevant point of view*, the relevant questions are: to what extent can regions in their foreign policy and diplomatic activities learn from small states, and vice versa? Small states inside and outside the EU are confronted by a host of internal and external dynamics. Being able to define these challenges and the related problems can be a first step as to figure out how these can be utilised as an advantage.

So What? What Consequences and Opportunities does the Rise of Sub-state Diplomacy Entail or Offer to Small States?

When looking at the above mentioned evolution of sub-state diplomacy in Europe, one can ask the so what?-question. What consequences and opportunities does this entail or offer to small states? The answer might seem quite simple: it all depends on the small states themselves. The international political environment has become more complex, yet are small states willing to accept that sub-state diplomacy today constitutes a new reality? Some small states – quite like middle-sized or big states – seem reluctant to deal with regional authorities. The reasons for this reluctance can be manifold. They might be afraid to offend the central government. This was very clear in the case of the Netherlands who initially hesitated to do business with the Flemish government out of fear to go against the will of the Belgian central authorities. They might also have been afraid to stir up some nationalist movements within their own boundaries. Or they simply weren't convinced of the benefits to engage in diplomatic relations with sub-state entities.

Nevertheless, it is our opinion that small states could benefit from, and seize a lot of opportunities in, embracing and engaging in the dynamics of sub-state diplomacy. To illustrate the benefits for small nations, we can take the example of the EUREGION La Grande Région. This 'Great Region' is one of the Interreg IV-programmes aimed at promoting and enhancing the cross-border cooperation between the Belgian Walloon region, the Belgian Francophone and Germanophone communities, the German *Länder* of Saarland and Rheinland-Pfalz, the French department of Lorraine *and* the state of Luxembourg. A whole range of cooperation programmes are initiated in this Grande Région in the fields of cross-border exchange of workers, but also in the transnational cooperation regarding drug prevention, policing and emergency services. Seen from the position of the state of Luxembourg, engaging in this network has further placed this small state on the map. It has further strengthened Luxembourg as a place to work and has offered opportunities to find solutions to very concrete problems in the area of security. If Luxembourg had refused such a cooperation with mostly regions neighbouring its borders, it would have missed some unique opportunities to 'do business' and to offer solutions to some very real problems with which its population is being confronted on a daily basis. The same kind of cooperation scheme exists, for instance, between the Czech Republic and the German *Land* of Bavaria. They have a longstanding tradition of cross-border cooperation, going back to the heydays of the Cold War, of encompassing exchange of police officials, educational cooperation, and so on. Moreover, engaging in diplomatic activities with subnational entities might prove a very pragmatic way to enter into contacts with the respective central governments.

Small states have to understand that, from a multi-level perspective, subnational entities are often the first and most apt partners in cooperation. To embrace this idea might open new windows of opportunities to them. After all, subnational governments are but one of the many possible international partners next to multinational corporations, NGO's, international organisations, cities with international ambitions and even individuals. One might thus even claim that 'dealing with subnational entities' forms an integral part of a well understood international policy in a globalising world.

This brings us to a final thought. Of course, the rise of sub-state diplomacy does not constitute the only challenge with which the diplomacies of small states in Europe today are being confronted. On the other end, at the European level, can we now also detect new developments which will affect the position of the national diplomacies: the gradual development of a *European External Action Service* (EEAS), the nucleus of a new 'European diplomacy'. Together with the rise of sub-state diplomacy, this transnational diplomacy-in-the-making form the two most fundamental challenges with which small state diplomacy is being confronted. Perhaps this second trend constitutes an even more existential challenge to the diplomacy of small states. It is then not difficult to make the case that today Europe constitutes the laboratory for new forms of diplomacy, a diplomacy which is no longer based on states as such but on a close cooperation between the European, the national and the sub-state level. It is probable that from this process, a new 'division of tasks' will unfold between the diplomacies of the different policy-levels. The coming years will be very interesting, indeed, especially when watching how the small states in Europe will cope with all of these trends and how they will try to adapt and re-invent their international 'actor-ness'.

References

Aldecoa, F. and Keating, M. (eds) 1999. *Paradiplomacy in Action: The Foreign Relations of Subnational Governments*. London: Frank Cass.

Batora, J. 2005. Public Diplomacy in Small and Medium-sized States: Norway and Canada. *Clingendael Discussion Papers in Diplomacy*, 97. The Hague: Netherlands Institute of International Relations Clingendael.

Bizoux, A. 2006. *Catalogne: L'Émergence d'une Politique Extérieure*. Strasbourg: L'Harmattan.

Blindenbacher, R. and Pasma, C. 2007. *Dialogues on Foreign Relations in Federal Countries*. Global Dialogue on Federalism Series, No. 5. Canada: McGill-Queen's University Press.

Clement, J., D'Hondt, H., Van Crombrugge, J and Vanderveeren, C. 1993. *Het Sint-Michielsakkoord en Zijn Achtergronden*. Antwerp: Maklu.

Criekemans, D. 2006a. *How Subnational Entities Try to Develop Their Own 'Paradiplomacy': The Case of Flanders (1993–2005)*. Proceedings of the International Conference 'Challenges for Foreign Ministries: Managing Diplomatic Networks and Optimising Value', Geneva, 31 May-2 June 2006.

Criekemans, D. 2006b. *Culture, Communications and Subnational Actors: The Flemish Experience*. Proceedings of the International Conference 'Polycentric Governance? Subnational Actors and Foreign Policy in an Age of Globalisation', organised by the Norman Paterson School of International Affairs, the Canadian Institute for International Affairs and the Belgian Royal Institute of International Affairs, Ottawa, Canada, 6-7 June 2006.

Criekemans, D. 2007. *Researching Sub-State Diplomacy: The Road Ahead*. Paper presented at the First The Hague Diplomacy Conference on Crossroads of Diplomacy. The Hague: Netherlands Institute of International Relations Clingendael and The Hague Journal of Diplomacy, 21-22 June 2007.

Criekemans, D. 2008a. *Are the Boundaries Between Paradiplomacy and Diplomacy Watering Down? Preliminary Findings and Hypotheses from a Comparative Study of Some Regions with Legislative Power and Small States*. Paper presented at the Second Global International Studies Conference 'What Keeps Us Apart, What Keeps Us Together? International Order, Justice and Value', Ljubljana, University of Ljubljana, 23-26 July 2008.

Criekemans, D. 2008b. *Het Vlaams Buitenlands Beleid Sinds 1993: Evolutie en Evaluatie van de Instrumenten en het Gevoerde Beleid in een Vergelijkende Internationale Context*. Colloquium Vijftien jaar Vlaams buitenlands beleid: terugblik en toekomstperspectief, Brussel, Vlaams Parlement, 20 October 2008.

Criekemans, D., Duran, M. and Melissen, J. 2008. Vlaanderen en Catalonië: Voorhoedelopers in Europese Sub-statelijke Diplomatie. *Internationale Spectator*, 62(7/8), 389-94.

Duchacek, I. 1990. Perforated Sovereignties: Towards a Typology of New Actors in International Relations, in *Federalism and International Relations: The Role of Subnational Units*, edited by H.J. Michelmann and P. Soldatos. Oxford: Clarendon Press, 1-34.

Duran, M., Criekemans, D. and Melissen, J. (eds) 2008. *Een Vergelijkend Onderzoek naar en Bestedingsanalyse van het Buitenlands Beleid en de Diplomatieke Representatie van Regio's met Wetgevende Bevoegdheid en Kleine Staten*. Antwerp: Vlaams Steunpunt Buitenlands Beleid.

Henrikson, A. 1998. *Diplomacy and Small States in Today's World*. 12th Dr. Eric Williams Memorial Lecture.

Hocking, B. 1993. *Localizing Foreign Policy. Non-Central Governments and Multilayered Diplomacy*. New York: St. Martin's Press.

Hocking, B. 1999. Regionalism: An International Relations Perspective, in *Paradiplomacy in Action: The Foreign Relations of Subnational Governments*, edited by F. Aldecoa and M. Keating. London: Frank Cass, 90-111.

Hrbek, R. 2007. Germany: Cooperation with the Länder, in *Dialogues on Foreign Relations in Federal Countries*, edited by R. Blindenbacher and C. Pasma. Montréal: Forum des Fédérations, 24-6.

Huijgh, E. and Melissen, J. 2008. *De publieksdiplomatie van Québec*. Antwerp: Vlaams Steunpunt Buitenlands Beleid & Nederlands Instituut voor Internationale Betrekkingen 'Clingendael'/Diplomatic Studies Programme.

Jazbec, M. 2001. *The Diplomacy of New Small States: The Case of Slovenia with Some Comparison from the Baltics*. Aldershot: Ashgate.

Keating, M. 1999. Regions and International Affairs: Motives, Opportunities and Strategies, in *Paradiplomacy in Action: The Foreign Relations of Subnational Governments*, edited by F. Aldecoa and M. Keating. London: Frank Cass, 1-17.

Lagasse, N. 2002. The Role of the Regions in Belgium's Foreign Relations. *Federations*, 2(2), 13-14.

Lecours, A. and Moreno, L. 2006. Paradiplomacy and Stateless Nations: A Reference to the Basque Country. *Unidad de Politicas Comparadas (CSIC), Working Paper*, 01-06. Concordia University and Spanish National Research Council (CSIC). Available at: http://www.iesam.csic.es/doctrab2/dt-0106.htm [accessed: 28 July 2009].

Majeed, A., Watts, R. and Brown, D. 2005. *Distribution of Powers and Responsibilities in Federal Countries*. Global Dialogue on Federalism Series, No. 2. Canada: McGill Queen's University Press.

Manojlovic, M. and Thorheim, C.H. 2007. Crossroads of Diplomacy: New Challenges, New Solutions. *Clingendael Diplomacy Papers*, 13. The Hague: Netherlands Institute of International Relations Clingendael.

Michelmann, H. 2009. *Foreign Relations in Federal Countries*. A Global Dialogue on Federalism Series, No. 5. Canada: McGill Queen's University Press.

Morgenthau, H.J. 1972. *Politics Among Nations: The Struggle for Power and Peace*. New York: Knopf.

Naseer Mohamed, A. 2002. The Diplomacy of Micro-States. *Clingendael Discussion Papers in Diplomacy*, 78. The Hague: Netherlands Institute of International Relations Clingendael.

Neumann, I.B. and Gstöhl, S. 2006. Lilliputians in Gulliver's World? in *Small States in International Relations*, edited by C. Ingebritsen, I. Neumann, S. Gstöhl and J. Beyer. Seattle and Reykjavik: University of Washington Press and University of Iceland Press, 3-36.

Paquin, S. 2001. Les Relations Internationales du Québec et l'Unité Nationale: Le Prolongement International des Conflits Internes? *Bulletin d'Histoire Politique (Dossier Thématique – Les Nouvelles Relations Internationales: Le Québec en Comparaison)*, 10(1), 85-98.

Paquin, S. 2004. La Paradiplomatie Identitaire: Le Québec, La Catalogne et La Flandre en Relations Internationales. *Politique et Sociétés* (Montréal), 23(2-3), 203-37.

Paquin, S. 2007. *Politique Internationale et Défense au Canada et au Québec*. Montréal: Presses de l'Université de Montréal.

Sanders, R. 1989. The Relevance and Function of Diplomacy in the International Politics of Small Caribbean States. *The Round Table*, 78(312), 413-24.

Scotoni, P. 1998. *The Four Dimensions of the Catalan Model.* Paper presented at the Conference 'Regional Identities in Europe', University of Sunderland's Centre for European Studies, 12 October 1998.

Scotoni, P. 2006. *Mare Balticum: How the 'Baltic Sea Policy' of the Catalan Government was Conceived and Began to be Implemented.* Barcelona: Secretaria de Relaciones Internacionales.

Väyrynen, R. 2006. Small States: Persisting Despite Doubts, in *The National Security of Small States in a Changing World*, edited by E. Inbar. London: Frank Cass, 41-75.

Chapter 4
Small States and the European Security and Defence Policy

Clive Archer

Introduction

This chapter examines the contribution made by small states within the European Security and Defence Policy (ESDP) of the European Union (EU) and why they commit themselves to actions within this policy. A brief outline of the ESDP is provided, followed by an account of the engagement of the small EU member states in the policy. An assessment will then be made of their contribution and of their reasons for their level of involvement in ESDP. Small states are of interest in terms of the ESDP as they make up the dominant majority of EU – and thus ESDP – countries and, without their defence participation, the military side of the ESDP would consist of large state activity, reflecting the interests of just those states. Furthermore, a number of them have made particular contributions to the development of the ESDP and also the variation between the contributions by the small states seems to depend on a number of factors, only one being their comparative size.

Background to the ESDP

The foundation of the ESDP can be seen in the 1992 Maastricht Treaty. Until then, defence and security matters in Western Europe had been dealt with either by national governments and/or by the North Atlantic Treaty Organisation (NATO). The Western European Union (WEU) had offered an occasional forum on defence matters for West European members of NATO, as well as providing an Article 5 duty of collective defence for its members. The Atlanticist members of the EU (the United Kingdom, Denmark and the Netherlands) had been reluctant to have any mention of defence as an EU area of activity, preferring it as a NATO preserve.

The changes to the ESDP in the Treaty of Amsterdam of 1997 reflected security developments since the Maastricht Treaty. In particular, the conflict in former-Yugoslavia demonstrated that robust action, even within the European continent, by outside forces could enforce a settlement. At the instigation of two non-NATO states – Finland and Sweden – the treaty took over the 'Petersberg tasks' from the WEU. These were mostly humanitarian and rescue tasks, peace-keeping, and using combat forces in crisis management, including peace-making. That last element reflected one of the lessons taken by the EU states from former-Yugoslavia: peace-keeping was often not enough in such conflicts, and combat forces might well be needed to ensure that a settlement was adhered to by all sides. The WEU was integrated into the EU, with the exception of its Article 5 activities, those of collective defence. This meant that the EU could deal with the 'softer', less war-fighting aspects of security, leaving the 'harder' defence side to the member states and/or NATO.

However 'soft', the Petersberg tasks had to be given life. This process started with the Franco-British St Malo summit in December 1998, at which both sides recognised that the EU needed to have 'the capacity for autonomous action, backed up by credible military forces, the means to decide to use them, and a readiness to do so, in order to respond to international crises' (Hill and Smith 2000: 243). This was an important recognition that such a force could act outside the context of NATO.

The next step was to build the operational capability of the ESDP. In December 1999, the EU states agreed a Headline Goal with the aim of bringing together up to 60,000 troops to be deployed within 60 days for up to a year. By December 2001 the ESDP was declared operational with the claim that 'the Union is now able to conduct some crisis-management operations' (Annex II to Presidency Conclusions European Council, Laeken, 14-15 December 2001, cited in Rutten 2002: 120). Capabilities were built up on the civilian side with commitments in police forces, support for the rule of law, civil protection and civil administration. Also the remit of ESDP was expanded from the Petersberg tasks by the Brussels European Council in June 2004 which considered that the ESDP 'might also include joint disarmament operations, support for third countries in combating terrorism and security sector reform' (Chaillot Paper 2005: 104). In early 2004 the EU planned to establish nine battle groups, each with about 1,500 soldiers that could deploy beyond the EU's borders. This demonstrated a change from the quantitative approach of the Headline Goals to a more instrumental view of the forces on offer.

The EU Police Mission in Bosnia and Herzegovina (EUPM) was the first operational mission, starting on 1 January 2003. Operation Artemis (June to September 2003) was the first autonomous military operation conducted by the EU and the first outside Europe – in the Democratic Republic of Congo. A variety of operations followed, many in former-Yugoslavia, but others in places as far apart as Aceh, Indonesia, the Palestinian territories, Moldova and Georgia (Council of the European Union 2008). All EU members are part of the ESDP, though, as part of its reservations on the Maastricht Treaty won at the December 1992 Edinburgh Council, Denmark does not participate in the military side of the policy. The December 2002 Berlin-Plus agreement allows non-EU European NATO members to participate in ESDP operations. The 2004 EU enlargement, run almost in parallel with NATO enlargement, saw central and east European states join both organisations.

Table 4.1 Numbers in Armed Forces ('000s), 2001 and 2007

Country	2001	2007	Change 2001-7
France	274	255	-19
Germany	308	246	-62
Italy	230	186	-44
United Kingdom	211	181	-30
Spain	143	149	+6
Poland	206	127	-79
Netherlands	50	46	-4
Sweden	34	24	-10
Austria	35	40	+5
Belgium	39	40	+1
Czech Rep.	54	23	-31
Denmark	21	30	+9
Estonia	4	4	0
Finland	32	29	-3
Greece	159	157	-2
Hungary	34	32	-2
Ireland	10	10	0
Latvia	7	6	-1
Lithuania	12	14	+2
Luxembourg	1	1	0
Portugal	44	43	-1
Slovakia	33	17	-16
Slovenia	8	6	-2

Source: IISS, 2001 and 2008

Small States and European Security

In this book small states are defined as those countries that are the weak part in an asymmetric relationship. What does this mean in the context of the ESDP?[1] Clearly the large states are those without which the ESDP cannot function. The brief history of the ESDP demonstrated that the policy needed a Franco-British input before becoming active and a headcount of troops demonstrates why (see Table 4.1). France clearly makes a major contribution. The UK has provided more troops for EU

---

1 Of the present 27 EU members, Bulgaria and Romania are excluded from consideration as they have only been members since 2007. The remaining 25 states can be divided into three groups: those which are the stronger part in EU military relations, those that are the weaker part, and three states – Greece, Sweden and the Netherlands – which, for reasons explained below, are in between.

operations than in 2007.² Furthermore its diplomatic support for the ESDP has been necessary to allow the policy to develop even when the UK had a major disagreement with France and Germany over Iraq in early 2003.³ Together with France and the United Kingdom, Germany, Italy and Spain have been important players within NATO and internationally. Italy and Spain contributed to the coalition involved in the invasion of Iraq (although Spain pulled out after a change in government) and, together with France, Germany and the United Kingdom, provide sizeable forces for the NATO operation in Afghanistan. Poland also has provided a large number of troops in both Iraq and Afghanistan – just under a thousand for each by 2008 – and has been a key player in extending NATO into east and central Europe. It was very much the Polish lobby in the United States that helped to bring Poland to early membership of NATO in 1999. Given the asymmetry of forces within both NATO and the ESDP, none of these states can be seen as weak. Their relative size is also bolstered by their strategic position: the United Kingdom and France with their world-wide commitments; Germany and Poland in the heart of Europe; Spain with its South American and North African connections and Italy with its importance in the Mediterranean and proximity to the Western Balkans.

Of the other countries,⁴ three are of particular interest as they may be seen as regional powers: Greece, the Netherlands and Sweden. Greece is noticeable for its large armed forces. However, these are directed to Turkey with whom the country has a number of unsettled disputes, not least that over Cyprus. The Netherlands and Sweden are more problematic. The Netherlands is often seen as being a little bit larger than small European states when judged in population terms, though clearly its landmass marks it out as smaller than states such as Finland and Norway. The country is also a former colonial power that had forces in South America and Asia. Nevertheless Table 4.1 shows that, in relation to other countries, the size of the Dutch armed forces is nothing special, and after the end of the Cold War its strategic position is no longer so important. After the Second World War, Sweden's air force was the second largest in Europe and in 2007 it still had 130 combat capable aircraft (IISS 2008: 185). Spain had 181, Poland 103 and the Netherlands 105 (IISS 2008: 152, 144 and 139). Sweden can be seen as a power of some importance in the Baltic Sea region. Nevertheless, its military power has been reduced by cuts in the defence budgets and reforms of the armed forces in recent years, and Swedish military power has been increasingly involved in international operations rather than having one main job, defending Sweden, with a few peace-

---

2   For example over 1,100 in 2005. See IISS 2006: 111.

3   In particular, see the 'Declaration on Strengthening European Cooperation in Security and Defence' by the UK and France, made at Le Touquet, 4 February 2003. See Missiroli, 2003: 36-9.

4   Neither Cyprus nor Malta is included in the list of EU states. Cyprus is a divided island politically and its security interests are tied to that situation. Malta's security concerns are linked primarily to its closeness to North Africa. Bulgaria and Rumania are excluded as they only joined the EU in 2007 and it is too early to judge their position with relation to the ESDP.

keeping operations on the side (see Wedin 2008: 38-55). In the terms of this book, Spain and Poland will not be regarded as small states in security terms. Both the Netherlands and Sweden can be placed at the higher end of small states, though Sweden has a regional strength of some importance.

Contributions to the ESDP

As can be seen from Table 4.2, all EU member states covered by this chapter contributed to ESDP operations by 2008, even if at the most minimal level.

Table 4.2   Forces in ESDP Operations, 2007

Country	2007 Total in peace operations	2007 ESDP operations	ESDP as share of peace operations
France	8,446	1,585*	18.8 +
Germany	7,300	495	6.8
Italy	7,744	402	5.2
United Kingdom	14,646	21**	0.1 +
Spain	2,762	286	10.4
Poland	3,552	553	15.6
Netherlands	1,883	172	9.1
Sweden	998	225	22.5
Austria	1,269	344	27.1
Belgium	1,278	152	11.9
Czech Rep.	1,089	5	0.5
Denmark	1,404	3	0.2
Estonia	332	3	0.9
Finland	895	124	13.9
Greece	1,165	45	3.9
Hungary	1,010	158	15.6
Ireland	852	425	49.9
Latvia	121	2	1.7
Lithuania	238	1	0.4
Luxembourg	35	1	2.9
Portugal	669	49***	7.3 +
Slovakia	530	42	7.9
Slovenia	198	58	29.3

Italics indicate non-NATO countries
*   excluding air force involvement in EUFOR
**   excluding specialist troops
***   plus two helicopters and crews
Source: IISS, 2008

A number of points arise from these figures. All the states contribute to peace operations (whether UN, OSCE, NATO, EU or by coalitions of the willing), with the four large powers making the greatest contribution. In absolute terms, Spain and Poland also make a contribution above those of any of the smaller states.

Of the remaining small countries, a number of elements stand out. There seems almost to be a 'tariff' of 0.01 percent of the population being devoted to peace operations, however defined. A number of countries have contributed above that level: the Netherlands, Denmark, Estonia, Finland and Ireland; while Latvia, Lithuania and Portugal seem to be well under the level. When examining the share of 'peace operations' devoted to ESDP activities, there are a number of variations. Apart from Slovenia, the high contributors can be found among the non-NATO states. This might be expected as they do not have the same pressures to send their forces to NATO operations, especially that in Afghanistan. Furthermore two of the non-NATO member states, Finland and Sweden, were behind including the Petersberg tasks in the Nice Treaty. Had 2005 figures been used, the share of Finnish peace forces devoted to ESDP operations would have been 23.6 percent (IISS 2006: 125), much closer to the 2007 figure for Sweden, but between then and 2007, some troops were moved away from ESDP operations and a sizeable contribution made to UNIFIL II in the Lebanon. The surprising figure is that of Ireland where 4.1 percent of its active armed forces is engaged in ESDP operations, compared with 0.9 percent in the case of Sweden. The high share of Slovenian forces devoted to EU operations can be explained by its troops' involvement in Bosnia-Herzegovina where they have a linguistic advantage.

The below-par contributions seem to be much of a group apart, except for Greece which has had cultural and political reasons for involvement in NATO's KFOR operation in Kosovo, and Luxembourg where perhaps small numbers have determined matters. The three Baltic States have chosen engagement with NATO and the coalition of the willing, as has the Czech Republic. Denmark has been limited by its Edinburgh 'opt-out' of EU defence cooperation.

Before undertaking any analysis that refers to these figures, some notes of caution should be sounded. First, the figures show a response to a certain demand, that for personnel for ESDP operations. The demand itself changed over time as operations came and went and probably the busiest time for the ESDP over the last decade was 2005-6. Secondly, the figures are, by their nature, quantitative. They do not distinguish between observers and combat troops or between specialist troops and those perhaps with little training. Thirdly, some of the figures are very small and shifts of a few troops from one type of operation to another may seem large in percentage terms. Fourthly, the figures are those given in *The Military Balance* which has its own explanatory notes and qualifications (see, for example, IISS 2008: 7-12). Finally, the contribution of small member states to the ESDP cannot just be measured by the troops deployed. For example, Sweden and Finland's advocacy of including the Petersberg tasks in the Treaty of Amsterdam and Sweden's promotion of the ESDP's civilian aspect have added to the policy's development.

The Reasons Why

No EU member state has to commit forces to any ESDP operation and could, like Cyprus and Malta, choose not to. Why then do small member states commit any forces to EU operations and in a number of cases send a greater share of their peace operation troops than does Germany, Italy and the UK? Possible explanations for this behaviour can be found in Realist thinking, especially in alliance theory, and also in the concepts of interests and identities as expressed in Neo-Liberal Institutionalist and Constructivist thought.

Realist writers are concerned with power in international relations and, in seeing how states survive in the international system, place emphasis in particular on military power. States can use their military power to defend their survival, but they can also 'buy in' power by joining an alliance. Snyder's (1997: 4) definition of alliances is that they are 'formal associations of states for the use (or non-use) of military force, in specified circumstances, against states outside their own membership.' The EU may not be seen as a traditional military alliance such as NATO, but it has elements that reflect Snyder's definition. After all, the Petersberg tasks included 'combat forces in crisis management, including peace-making' and were extended in June 2004 to 'include joint disarmament operations, support for third countries in combating terrorism and security sector reform' (Chaillot Paper 75 2005: 104). This points to occasions when military force may be used against states outside the EU's membership. The EU could be regarded as a 'limited alliance' and certainly 'a political alliance' in the words of an official Swedish document (Regeringens proposition 2004: 15).

Within Realist writings, there is a debate over the utility of alliances. Waltz (1979) has seen alliance membership as being key in creating or upsetting the balance of power (Waltz 1979). Walt (1987: 263) considers that states will ally against the most serious threat rather than against the most powerful states, and that the more serious the threat, the less there will be concerns over ideology in any alliance (*ibid.*: 266-8). Mouritzen (1998: 158) sees states bandwagoning with the most dominant power rather than balancing against it, though Snyder (1997: 158) thinks that bandwagoning rarely takes place. The actual contribution of member states to an alliance will rest on how much that state feels it needs the alliance as balanced against any reluctance to cede autonomy by greater alliance involvement (Snyder 1997: 75). Small states in particular may feel that being drawn too close to larger states in the alliance – entrapment – has to be balanced against the fear of abandonment by allies (*ibid.*: 180-81), especially if one's commitment to the alliance is seen as low. Snyder sees systemic influences as being more important than domestic concerns in alliance policy (*ibid.*: 142-3), but small member states of alliance can, and do, 'free-ride' (Snidal 1979: 534), meaning they enjoy the shielding of an alliance without contributing their 'fair' share, in troops, for example.[5]

---

5 For a treatment of these themes in relation to Estonia, see Männik 2008.

What would these views tell us about small states' contributions to ESDP? First, it seems to support the view that states are concerned about threat rather than power. The European Security Strategy, adopted in December 2003, showed that the EU members had identified a number of threats such as terrorism, proliferation of weapons of mass destruction, regional conflicts and organised crime (European Union 2003) that had replaced the more solid and unified power of the Soviet Union. Furthermore a number of these elements – especially regional conflicts, frozen conflicts and failing states – were to be tackled partly by ESDP.

Secondly, for those states concerned with the power balance in Europe, one factor may have been the waning US interest in the region compared with the days of the Cold War. To start with, the US could be seen as the 'winner' of the Cold War and states in Europe might be expected either to bandwagon with it or try to find some balance against it. In the former case, the ESDP would only be operative in cases where the US showed no willingness to be involved. In the latter, it could start to form the basis of an alternative power-centre in Europe to the US. By the start of the 2000s, the power balance in Europe seemed to have shifted again. US attention has moved to the Middle East and the Pacific. However, Russia is still an important regional power with a large military presence and a growing troubled relationship with a number of EU states, especially the Baltic States and former members of the Warsaw Treaty Organisation. As Russia becomes more powerful, will these states seek to balance it or bandwagon with it? If the former, then the EU could be an alternative or at least a supplement to waning US power in Europe. If the answer is the latter, then NATO membership might become an irritant, but ESDP activity that takes troops out of area would even ease relations with Russia.

Furthermore, in Realist terms, the ESDP might be advantageous for small European states when considering whether being in an alliance detracts from their autonomy and the opposite fears of entrapment and abandonment. The ESDP's basically intergovernmentalist nature allows member states to control the size and distribution of their defence resources. However, as the ESDP becomes more active and commitments are sought for the battle groups, then this autonomy may weaken ESDP. As a 'limited alliance', the ESDP is unlikely to entrap states with a larger ally, and by showing their commitment to the EU through ESDP activity, small member states can hope that other members would be less likely to abandon them in times of need.[6]

In reality, the small members of the EU tended to bandwagon with the US after the end of the Cold War and have cautiously sought a balancer for the increasing power of the Russian Federation. Thus the commitments of these states' troops have primarily been to Afghanistan, Kosovo and Iraq, to operations headed by the US and NATO. This is even the case of the EU non-NATO members Sweden and Finland with, respectively, 70 percent and 60 percent of their 'peace' deployments in those three regions. However, the share falls to 42 percent for Austria and to 27

---

6 For a further discussion of this theme see Rickli 2008: 309-10.

percent for Ireland, both of which have a greater strategic distance from Russia. Poland has 61 percent of its deployed forces in these operations, and Lithuania 98 percent, showing them to be loyal providers for NATO and the US (IISS 2008: 137, 144, 167, 176, 178, and 186). However, Sweden and Finland are not covered by the collective security clause of the North Atlantic Treaty and their further commitment to the ESDP can be seen as a substitute bandwagoning. Also Sweden's high profile in the Nordic battle group provides a closer link with the United Kingdom, a key NATO member, in security matters as the battle group will have its operational headquarters in the UK. A similar point can be made for Finland. The best way to bandwagon in the 1990s would have been to join NATO, but both a majority of public opinion and most of the political parties were against this. Nevertheless, EU membership was seen in security terms (Raunio and Tiilikainen 2003: 37). As Hanna Ojanen (2008: 74) described it: '[c]redibility rather than empty words, contributing rather than free-riding, guide the Finnish stand towards the ESDP'. Thus, in the absence of NATO membership, serving in NATO operations and entrapment by Brussels through engagement in ESDP seems welcome in Helsinki.

In other small states, the situation is more complicated. The Czech Republic seems typical in preferring NATO and the transatlantic link to the ESDP in security matters, when a choice has to be made. This is a result of bandwagoning to the West and seeking a balancer against renewed Russian power. However, according to one commentator, the Czech ministry of defence is lukewarm about ESDP commitments and favours the NATO Response Force initiatives adopted after all at the NATO Prague Summit in November 2002. On the other hand the foreign ministry is 'more sensitive to the Czech position as a EU member state' (Khol 2004: 2). Slovakia makes a distinction between overall security issues where ESDP capacities will be built 'in order to ensure their complementarity with the capabilities of NATO and with our interests in NATO', and the EU solidarity clause, the importance of which is limited to providing help to 'states attacked or threatened by terrorist attacks or hit by natural disasters' (Ministry of Defence, Slovakia 2005: 14).

Neo-Liberal Institutionalists (NLI) stress the importance of the endurance of institutions, even for the security of states. They accept that domestic political factors and values are important in moulding institutions and determining their activities (Jackson and Sørensen 1999: 108-26). This happens in two main ways. First, involvement in ESDP leads to Europeanisation whereby domestic decision-makers start to change their preferences as a result of their involvement in the wider project of integration. Secondly, domestic policies affect European policies. As in Denmark, a country can find its activities within ESDP curtailed by domestic requirements. In other cases, governments with a strong emphasis on human rights and the protection of minorities will stress these in their foreign and security policies. International organisations, including alliances, allow smaller states to advocate their ideas more widely. A former Norwegian foreign minister encapsulated this notion thus: 'Participation in a multinational alliance enables the small state to pursue their idealistic visions of equity and world order rather than succumb to ignoble "realism" or escapism of adherence to the principles of sauve qui peut' (Holst 1985: 283). Also, smaller states especially would use institutions and alliances to build trust by being 'loyal allies'. The hope is that this will be reciprocal and that they will receive security assistance when needed (Keohane 1971: 153), especially by staying in the greater power's focus of attention (*ibid.*: 167-8).

The NLI stress is thus on the importance of institutions to small states. Such states 'favour discourses that institutionalise rules and norms, such as international law, international regime and international institutions' (Neumann and Gstöhl 2004). This would 'qualify the power deficit of small states and the policy strategies open to them' (Goetschel 1998: 19). In Rickli's words, '(b)y anchoring states in repetitive interactions and by linking issues together, institutions regularise states' behaviour, making them more predictable and therefore decreasing uncertainty' (Rickli 2005: 5)

An NLI approach to international security sees the ESDP as a forum for small state, in which they are a majority of participants and in which there is no one dominant power. The Petersberg tasks also reflect the actions in the security sector that can be taken by small states, those of crisis management, peace-keeping, and security sector reform. Here such states cannot change the security agenda but they can ameliorate – or even help prevent – some of the worst aspects of insecurity. However, such an institution would be of limited use for small states if it rivalled NATO; better that it complemented the Atlantic Alliance, being active when the US did not wish to be involved.

In Sweden, ESDP has been seen as a means to encourage change in the Swedish Armed Forces, but it is also a forum within which to externalise Swedish values. Wedin (2008: 51) shows how support for ESDP has been portrayed by Swedish governments as being in accordance with the traditional Swedish aims of upholding the UN, international law and multilateralism. In other states, there is also a strong connection between national politics and this Union-level policy, with the opportunity of externalising domestic values being seen in other small states' reasoning for ESDP involvement. In Austria it is recognised, in the context of ESDP, that 'a coordinated approach with partners whose values and interests coincide has become an absolute necessity' (Breitegger 2005). Ireland's defence minister thought that the country's 'participation in ESDP is fully also in accordance with our traditional support for the UN and our obligations as members of the international community of States, to respond to crises, events and humanitarian disasters, wherever they may occur' (O'Dea 2005). A Finnish minister claimed that during his state's presidency of the EU 'informal discussions were held on how the EU can promote a human security agenda through a broad range of instruments at its disposal, including ESDP instruments. Work on mainstreaming of human rights into CFSP, including ESDP, has continued' (Western European Union 2006).

A Constructivist approach to small states in alliances and institutions stresses identity and values, though these elements are not absent in both Realist and

NLI writings. After all, alliances tend to create a shared identity, though Waltz (1979: 166-70) doubts its strength. From an NLI perspective, and as seen above, governments pursue values, especially those of human rights and democracy. Social Constructivism sees states' identities and interests as being not part of any given logic of the anarchical international system. States can create their understandings of the international system and change these understandings. Institutions tend to create fairly stable understandings, but ones that still can be changed (Smith 2001: 244-5).

Ole Wæver (2000: 282) who calls himself a 'pessimistic constructivist' describes the ESDP as being part of a process that helps make the EU into a more meaningful actor. In examining the ESDP's structures, his question is less about the success of operations and more whether the effort and all the talk along the way help to constitute the EU as an international actor and thereby structure narratives more and more systematically with the EU as the primary occupant of the role of 'actor' – responsible, blamable, the one that makes a difference.

The ESDP is thus seen as part of the process of building an identity for the EU, making it more of an actor, and one that advocates certain values. Taking a Constructivist approach towards the utility of the ESDP for member states, one would have to see how the ESDP fits into the European integration story told by the dominant national voices. This leads to an understanding of how each country, or rather its people and politicians, perceive the European integration process and how ESDP appears as part of that story.

Constructivists such as Iver Neumann (2002) also show how particular discourses within a state can be in conflict with the ideas behind European integration. Some small states certainly perceive the ESDP as being part of a 'Europe-building' process and thus give it support. The classic view is that of the Belgian foreign service: 'The ESDP is an integral and essential part of the European unification process' (Federal Public Service Foreign Affairs, Belgium 2008). The ESDP can also be seen by important political groups as cutting across their desire for a more Atlanticist identity in defence matters and this certainly seems the case in the UK Conservative Party as well as in the small states of the Czech Republic, Estonia, Latvia and Lithuania. In the view of the Lithuanian Ministry of Defence (2006: 18): 'A strong transatlantic link between the US and Europe is an essential precondition to the long-term security of Lithuania' and this led to a view of the ESDP that stressed 'the principle of non-duplication of NATO and EU assets and procedures' and coordinating 'force planning and operational planning' with NATO (Lithuanian Ministry of Defence 2006: 18).

In other small states, the ESDP is seen as a means to implement certain values, as seen in the NLI approach. The notion of the EU as an agent for peace dovetailed with Swedish values: 'When the EU works for peace, the Union also talks for us' (Regeringskansliet 2006: 3, cited in Wedin 2008: 41). Also Finland, like Sweden, has seen the ESDP as a means of externalising some of its own values (Prime Minister's Office 2004: 78). A more complicated perspective can be seen in Denmark. Larsen (2008: 81-4) links the position of Denmark in the ESDP to two conflicting political discourses, those of 'non-privileged cooperation' and 'essential cooperation'. The former does not give the EU a significant role in Danish foreign policy, especially in defence policy. The EU is not seen as strengthening Danish security, indeed the building of a European 'super-state' could threaten Denmark's existence. The latter discourse sees the EU as a key actor in security and defending liberal values, but is held to be additional to Denmark's transatlantic security policy. The EU thus forms an essential forum for Denmark's security policy, just as it does for the country's trade policy. These views are likely to surface should the Danish government propose an end to the Danish opt-out of the defence aspect of ESDP. There could be debates within the centre-right of Danish politics between those who see involvement in EU defence as jeopardising Danish commitment to NATO and those who see it as a useful addition to NATO, and those on the left who welcome ESDP as a possible challenger to NATO, as well as those who see it as 'more defence'. These debates will reflect a wider consideration of Denmark's identity in the world.

The Baltic States' commitment to an Atlanticist approach to defence issues has been mentioned as an explanation of their low level of commitment to ESDP activities. This would be seen by Realists as a reflection of their strategic position and thus their need for a balancer to Russia in the form of the US and NATO. However, a Social Constructivist would note that by the early 2000s, Russia had ceased to be seen by sections of the population as the main security threat. Ozalina (2008: 126-7) notes that the wider public and policy-makers perceive internal threats as being more important. In itself this might marginalise the importance of the ESDP but it could lead to a further integration of Latvia into a European security discourse based on the European Security Strategy. Whether that leads to a greater commitment to the ESDP remains to be seen, especially in the light of Russia's action against Georgia, taken in the summer of 2008, and its likely effect of hardening Baltic States' opinion against Russia. This would provide less space for officials within these countries to 'experiment' with the ESDP option contrary to public views on security concerns and the respective defence solutions expressed in the programmes of political parties (Männik 2008: 151).

Conclusions

Small member states have made an important contribution to the ESDP. They have encouraged the EU to take on defence and security tasks and have been active in the development of this policy, especially its civilian side. They have made distinct niche contributions to a number of operations (Rickli 2008: 318-20) and have provided important troop contributions both in specific operations and in the battle groups.

However, there have been variations that need some explanation. Perhaps the most common explanation of a low commitment of forces to the ESDP is that from the Realist stable. Those states closest to Russia still have to face a powerful and uncertain neighbour and want to bring in any outside forces – or promise of such forces – to balance Moscow. The ESDP does not offer such a service; NATO does. Nevertheless, to show that they recognise the duties of EU membership, a contribution is made to ESDP operations, albeit at a very minimal level.

Both Sweden and Finland can be seen to be operating under this logic. However, NATO membership is ruled out by domestic opinion. They nevertheless commit themselves to NATO operations, but also get involved in ESDP operations as a way of building up mutual security within the EU. A further examination of what ministers have said about ESDP also shows that it is seen by Sweden and Finland, together with Ireland and Austria, as a way of underpinning their view of the world, one which is more institutionalised and sympathetic to the existence of small states. There is the hope that the ESDP – while not reversing the asymmetric security situation within small states – may at least ameliorate some of its less desirable aspects. As their domestic views of security changed, the Baltic States also started to consider greater involvement within the ESDP (as in the battle groups), though it is likely that the Georgian escapade will turn their minds back to Realist thoughts.

This chapter thus suggests two important elements in determining the extent of EU small states' commitment to the ESDP. The first is NATO membership: those EU states that are not NATO members seem to make a larger than average commitment to the ESDP, possibly as an indirect form of bandwagoning and certainly as a commitment to the values represented by the ESDP operations. The exceptions here are the two Mediterranean non-NATO states of Cyprus and Malta, neither of which contributes to ESDP. The second element is perceived strategic closeness to Russia. Those states that see their security being overshadowed by Russia are less interested in the ESDP and wish to bandwagon with NATO. It seems that the Czech Republic is more of this view than Hungary and Slovakia. Finally, Denmark is in a class of its own because of its 'opt-out' from the defence aspects of the ESDP. There the issue of the ESDP has been caught up with the domestic debate about the country's relationship to the EU more generally.

As long as the ESDP remains a sort of optional extra for EU security rather than a policy that supports a common defence, then governments will be able to choose their level of commitment with little pressure to achieve a particular level or standard. In this case, involvement will be determined by the preferred discourse of each government, whether it be one of power or values or identity, and will differ from state to state, regardless of size.

References

Breitegger, A. 2005. *CFSP Watch 2005 – Austria*. Available at: http://www.fornet.info/CFSPannualreports2005/CFSP%20Watch%202005%20Austria.pdf [accessed: 21 September 2008].

Chaillot Paper. 2005. *EU Security and Defence – Core Documents 2004, Volume 1*, Chaillot Paper, 75. Paris: Institute for Security Studies.

Council of the European Union. 2008. EU Operation. Available at: http://www.consilium.europa.eu/cms3_fo/showPage.asp?id=268&lang=en&mode=g [accessed: 26 September 2008].

European Union. 2003. *A Secure Europe in a Better World: European Security Strategy*. Available at: http://www.consilium.europa.eu/uedocs/cmsUpload/78367.pdf [accessed: 15 July 2009].

Federal Public Service Foreign Affairs, Belgium. 2008. *Foreign Trade and Development Cooperation Foreign Policy: European Security and Defence Policy (ESDP)*. Available at: http://www.diplomatie.be/en/policy/policynotedetail.asp?TEX TID=49721 [accessed: 21 September 2008].

Goetschel, L. 1998. The Foreign and Security Policy Interests of Small States in Today's Europe, in *Small States Inside and Outside the European Union*, edited by L. Goetschel. Dordrecht: Kluwer Academic Publishers, 13-31.

Hill, C. and Smith, K. (eds) 2000. *European Foreign Policy: Key Documents*. London and New York: Routledge.

Holst, J.J. 1985. Lilliputs and Gulliver: Small States in a Great Power Alliance, in *NATO's Northern Allies: The National Security Policies of Belgium, Denmark, the Netherlands, and Norway*, edited by G. Flynn. London: Croom Helm, 258-86.

International Institute for Strategic Studies (IISS) 2001. *The Military Balance 2001-2*. Oxford: Oxford University Press.

International Institute for Strategic Studies (IISS) 2006. *The Military Balance 2006*. London: Routledge.

International Institute for Strategic Studies (IISS) 2008. *The Military Balance 2008*. London: Routledge.

Jackson, R. and Sørensen, G. 1999. *Introduction to International Relations*. Oxford: Oxford University Press.

Keohane, R. 1971. The Big Influence of Small Allies. *Foreign Policy*, 2, 161-82.

Khol, R. 2004. *The Czech Republic and ESDP in 2004*. Friedrich Ebert Stiftung, Working Papers, 3. Prague: Friedrich Ebert Stiftung.

Larsen, H. 2008. Denmark and the ESDP Opt-Out: A New Way of Doing Nothing? in *New Security Issues in Northern Europe: The Nordic and Baltic States and the ESDP*, edited by C. Archer. London and New York: Routledge, 78-93.

Lithuanian Ministry of Defence. 2006. *White Paper of Lithuanian Defence Policy 2006*. Available at: http://www.kam.lt/index.php/en/35635/ [accessed: 25 September 2008].

Männik, E. 2008. The Role of the ESDP in Estonia's Security Policy, in *New Security Issues in Northern Europe: The Nordic and Baltic States and the ESDP*, edited by C. Archer. London and New York: Routledge, 139-54.

Missiroli, A. (ed.) 2003. *From Copenhagen to Brussels. European Defence: Core Documents, Volume IV*, Chaillot Paper, 67. Paris: Institute for Security Studies.

Mouritzen, H. 1998. Lessons for Alliance Theory, in *Bordering Russia: Theory and Prospects for Europe's Baltic Rim*, edited by H. Mouritzen. Aldershot: Ashgate, 283-94.

Neumann, I.B. 2002. This Little Piggy Stayed at Home: Why Norway is not a Member of the EU, in *European Integration and National Identity: The Challenge of the Nordic States*, edited by L. Hansen and O. Wæver. London and New York: Routledge, 88-129.

Neumann, I.B. and Gstöhl, S. 2004. *Lilliputians in Gulliver's World: Small States in International Relations*. Reykjavik: Centre for Small State Studies, University of Iceland.

Neumann, I.B. and Gstöhl, S. 2006. Introduction: Lilliputians in Gulliver's World? in *Small States in International Relations*, edited by C. Ingebritsen, I.B. Neumann, S. Gstöhl and J. Beyer. Seattle and Reykjavik: University of Washington Press, University of Iceland Press, 1-36.

O'Dea, W. 2005. Speech by Minister Willie O'Dea on Ireland's Future Participation in UN Peace Support Missions, McKee Barracks, 9 February 2006.

Ojanen, H. 2008. Finland and the ESDP. 'Obliquely forwards'? in *New Security Issues in Northern Europe: The Nordic and Baltic States and the ESDP*, edited by C. Archer. London and New York: Routledge, 56-77.

Ozalina, Z. 2008. European Security and Defence Policy: The Latvian Perspective, in *New Security Issues in Northern Europe: The Nordic and Baltic States and the ESDP*, edited by C. Archer. London and New York: Routledge, 15-38.

Prime Minister's Office. 2004. *Finnish Security Defence Policy 2004*. Helsinki: Prime Minister's Office.

Raunio, T. and Tiilikainen, T. 2003. *Finland in the European Union*. London and Portland: Frank Cass.

Regeringens proposition. 2004. *Vårt framtida försvar Prop. 2004/05:5*. Available at: http://www.regeringen.se/content/1/c6/03/04/63/7c2ac515.pdf [accessed: 1 March 2008].

Regeringskansliet. 2006. *Utrikesdeklarationen*. Available at: http://www.regeringen.se/sb/d/3216 [accessed: 1 March 2008].

Rickli, J.-M. 2005. *The European Neutral and Non-aligned States NATO and the ESDP*. Available at: http://www.allacademic.com//meta/p_mla_apa_research_citation/ 0/7/1/1/8/pages71184/p71184-1.php [accessed: 25 September 2008].

Rickli, J.-M. 2008. European Small States' Military Policies After the Cold War: From Territorial to Niche Strategies. *Cambridge Review of International Affairs*, 21(3), 307-25.

Rutten, M. (ed.) 2002. *From Nice to Laeken, European Defence: Core Documents*, Volume II, Chaillot Paper, 51. Paris: Institute for Security Studies.

Slovakian Ministry of Defence. 2005. *Security Strategy of the Slovak Republic*. Available at: http://www.mod.gov.sk/data/files/795.pdf?PHPSESSID=7799bd 323e55716 2dd600f83d36797db [accessed: 26 September 2008].

Smith, S. 2001. Reflectivist and Constructivist Approaches, in *The Globalization of World Politics*, edited by J. Baylis and S. Smith. Oxford: Oxford University Press, 224-49.

Snidal, D. 1979. Public Goods, Property Rights, and Political Organizations. *International Studies Quarterly*, 23 (No 4), 532-66.

Snyder, G. 1997. *Alliance Politics*. Ithaca and London: Cornell University Press.

Walt, S.M. 1987. *The Origins of Alliances*. Ithaca and London: Cornell University Press.

Waltz, K.N. 1979. *The Theory of International Politics*. New York: McGraw-Hill.

Wæver, O. 2000. The EU as a Security Actor: Reflections from a Pessimistic Constructivist on Post-Sovereign Security Orders, in *International Relations Theory and the Politics of European Integration*, edited by M. Kelstrup and M. Williams. Routledge: London and New York, 250-94.

Wedin, L. 2008. Northern Europe and the ESDP: The Case of Sweden, in *New Security Issues in Northern Europe: The Nordic and Baltic States and the ESDP*, edited by C. Archer. London and New York: Routledge, 38-55.

Western European Union, 2006. Assembly of Western European Union, Address by Mr Pertti Torstila, Secretary of State at the Ministry for Foreign Affairs, Representing the EU Finnish Presidency, Paris, 18 December 2006. Available at: http://www.eu2006.fi/news_and_documents/speeches/vko51/en_GB/1166 539581430/ [accessed: 25 September 2008].

PART II
The Challenges and Opportunities of Small European States

Chapter 5
Small States and Innovation

Rainer Kattel, Tarmo Kalvet and Tiina Randma-Liiv[1]

Introduction

The concepts of small states and innovation are both subject to a relatively wide range of definitions and usage. While we can agree with Wittgenstein's argument that the meaning of the word is its usage, the problem with these two concepts is that in using them, to stay with Wittgenstein, there are too many different and even contradictory 'language games'. Thus, before describing the aim of the chapter, we will briefly discuss how both small states and innovation can be defined and how they are used in the current contribution.

Definitions

The most widespread definition of innovation originates from Schumpeter and with slight modification is used by international organisations like the Organisation for Economic Co-operation and Development (OECD), the European Union (EU) and others. Perhaps the best-known formulation of this definition is as follows:

> An innovation is the implementation of a new or significantly improved product (good or service), or process, a new marketing method, or a new organisational method in business practices, workplace organisation or external relations (OECD and Eurostat 2005: 46).

Innovation, in other words, has relatively little to do with science or even with research and development (R&D). Innovation is the means by which entrepreneurs seek to overcome competition to earn profits. Indeed, as Schumpeter already noted, entrepreneurs innovate *because* they seek to obtain monopoly or near monopoly situations. However, innovations are usually based on some type or form of skills and knowledge (not necessarily in a codified form; for instance, experience, networks, etc., often involve uncodified knowledge) to gain a competitive advantage. Thus, innovations are often associated with a steep learning curve and

---

[1] We would like to thank the Estonian Ministry of Education and Research (targeted financing grant no. SF0140094s08), the Estonian Science Foundation (grants nos. 7577 and 7441) and the Estonian Ministry of Economic Affairs and Communications' I-PUP program for research grants allowing us to write this chapter.

fast growth in productivity that, in turn, often lead to strong and sustained economic growth. Such an understanding of economic development based on innovation and productivity growth reaches back to theoretical works from at least the seventeenth century (Reinert 2007). Innovation-based productivity explosions create enormous competitive advantages through agglomeration, clustering, positive externalities, and economies of scale and scope that, as cumulative dynamics, engender virtuous circles of growth and rapidly raising living standards. At the root of such complex interactions is highly embedded policy-making of increasing coordination, dialogue, and cooperation managed by a highly capable public administration (Evans and Rauch 1999; Wade 2004).

The small states concept, on the other hand, is much more contested. In this chapter we use the relational understanding of small states provided by the editors of this volume in the introduction:

> Being a small state is tied to a specific spatio-temporal context, not a general characteristic of the state. A small state is not defined by indicators such as its absolute population size or size of GDP relative to other states. Instead, a small state is defined by being the weak part in an asymmetric relationship.

Smallness or size is a dynamic characteristic of a country, its impact changes in time, and it is best understood as a relatively important determinant in welfare of that particular country. The next section will elaborate on this concept.

As a note of caution, the specific characteristics of small states can be easily confused with the problems of development. For example, Benedict (1966: 32) claims that the less-developed countries, even the large ones, are socially characterised by personal role relationships – a finding that has been claimed to be a specific feature of small states. Montgomery (1986) argues that a paradox of administration in developing countries is the great reluctance to make decisions and to take action. This finding is similar to what others have claimed about small states, including Lowenthal (1987: 35) and Sutton (1987: 19). Consequently, issues of development should not be underestimated when studying small states (also Montgomery 1986; Warrington 1997).

The Aim of this Chapter

Innovation, and economic development for that matter, was born in small and by today's standards even in microstates like Renaissance city-states. Cities like Venice, Florence, Delft and others were extraordinarily successful at innovation – using knowledge to create economic gains – and out competing nations much larger in geographic, demographic, or almost any other measure of size (Hall 1999; Landes 1999: 45–59; Reinert 2007). In these cities, it can be argued that smallness was one of the key factors that contributed to an institutionally highly embedded and yet diversified economy – both then already seen as pivotal ingredients of sustained growth. Indeed, early key political economists such as Giovanni

Botero (1590) and Antonio Serra (1613) juxtaposed small city-states with great economic and often military power to natural resource-rich large areas that were economically backward. Today's wisdom seems, instead, to regard smallness as a source of multiple constraints on innovation and economic development in general (e.g., Armstrong and Reid 2003; contrast with Easterly and Kraay 2000). These constraints can be summarised as follows:[2]

1. Almost by definition, small states (particularly the less-developed ones) have small home markets that limit the possibilities for economies of scale and geographical agglomerations;
2. Small home markets and dependence on exports threaten small states with overspecialisation, lock in, and low diversification of the economic structure;
3. Small states do not have the financial capabilities or human resources to invest into cutting-edge science, research, and development, which makes prioritisation, selectivity and adaptability key in policy design;
4. The latter presupposes high administrative capacity that, again, many small states with a lower level of development seem to lack almost by definition;
5. Dangers of rent-seeking and vested interests make the use of Weberian civil service and policy design processes for creation of high administrative capacity, often seen as key for sustained economic development, difficult if not impossible for small states.

However, the last significant attempt to deal with small states and innovation is already 20 years old. *Small Countries Facing the Technological Revolution*, edited by Freeman and Lundvall, appeared in 1988. Still, despite the title, the authors do not in reality deal so much with the issue of smallness as with the issue of innovation systems in general as this concept was in its infancy at that time and was mainly developed by the same authors. Edquist and Hommen (2008), while entitled *Small Country Innovation Systems*, suffers from the exact same problems: it actually only deals with innovation systems issues relevant for highly developed countries from Finland to South Korea. The book does not in fact discuss almost any size-specific issues as far as innovation and innovation policy are concerned. In essence, innovation literature is seemingly aware of the issue of size, while in reality it tends to gloss over size and the small states literature tends to assume that size is a constraint on economic development and innovation.

We argue that a number of new challenges and risks in the international economy have emerged during recent decades that re-emphasise the issue of size. Prevailing theoretical solutions to these challenges, both in innovation and administrative sciences (innovation systems approach and [neo-]Weberian state

---

[2] Classic summary of the first three arguments are Walsh 1988 and Freeman and Lundvall 1988; also earlier, Robinson 1963.

respectively), have clear flaws when applied to small states, i.e., these concepts actually do not help overcome constraints created by the new challenges.

Unlike much of the twentieth century, state size is now again one of the key determinants of how and why companies innovate (state size impacts company-level innovation, although the impact changes somewhat with the level of development). Successful small economies learned to overcome issues arising from size. New challenges in the international economy transform size into one of the key tempo-spatial dynamic characteristics of a polity.

New Challenges and Risks

While innovations and technological change are often seen as key drivers of economic growth and development, it is seldom recognised that many innovations can bring significant adverse side effects as well. There are two key reasons for such effects:

1. Innovations and technological change often work through a process that Schumpeter described as creative destruction, where new products, activities, jobs, and industries are created and old ones evaporate (Schumpeter 1912, 1942);
2. Many innovations create dynamics, such as economies of scale, that become, as Arthur and others have shown, powerful enforcers of learning mechanisms and of various feedback linkages among value-chain actors that all lead up to strong path dependencies and barriers of entry for competitors (companies, regions, countries) (Nelson and Winter 1982; Arthur 1994).

These aspects of innovation necessitate a public-sector-led process that can be called creative destruction management (following the original Schumpeterian idea), where public policies support creation of new knowledge, companies, and jobs and alleviate the destructive effects (Drechsler et al. 2006; Kregel and Burlamaqui 2006). During much of the twentieth century, successful instances of creative destruction management were greatly helped by the particular nature of the then prevailing techno-economic paradigm (detailed in the next subsection).

Mass-production or the Fordist system of production used huge hierarchical organisations and long-term planning that were both directed at creating stability in production and reaping economies of scale and scope (Chandler 1990). Increasing real wages and living standards that guaranteed stable consumption patterns became effectively part of that production and planning system. While first realised probably by Henry Ford when he more than doubled his workers' salaries, this system was perfected by the small Nordic welfare states during the 1960s and the 1970s (Katzenstein 1985; Mjoset 2000). The rise of the East Asian economies can also be understood as an exemplary case of using the mass production paradigm. The then small economies of Asia developed via strong state-led industrialisation efforts that were based on creating strong government-owned enterprises and networks of enterprises in order to create economies of scale (e.g., Amsden 1989; Wade 2004). Essentially, the Nordic welfare states and the Asian tigers showed that size does not matter as long as one was able to capture the logic of the paradigm: mass production assumes mass consumption that in turn feeds on mass employment that is not interrupted by sickness, old age, or any other similar circumstance (i.e., welfare-state regulations, other forms of regulation, or customs such as long-term employment that socialises unemployment risks).

The Fordist paradigm was thus 'naturally' prone to agglomeration effects (as integration into large hierarchies was its fundamental principle) that in turn created middle income jobs (significantly helped by the welfare state type regulations), not only in developed countries but also increasingly in the developing world (for instance, Mexico's real wages were continuously increasing precisely until the end of the Fordist paradigm in the mid-1970s; see Palma 2005). The Fordist paradigm also worked similarly for regions as economic agglomerations and the welfare state also carried the fruits of innovation to geographically remote areas.

The breakdown of this system has been mitigated by four developments:

1. Change in the techno-economic paradigm following the new ICT-based technological revolution (ICT: Information and Communication Technologies) coming to its full force during the 1990s;
2. Adoption of the Washington Consensus economic policies;
3. Growing financial instability; and
4. The administrative reforms of the last 30 years.

The question that poses itself for European small states is the fifth development – how membership in the EU is influencing the abovementioned challenges and states' abilities to deal with them. Each development and how it influences innovation in small states will be briefly discussed.

Techno-Economic Paradigm Shift

The term techno-economic paradigm was coined by Carlota Perez (2002, 2006) and goes back to the theory of long waves of economic development originally developed by Nikolai Kondratiev (in particular 1924, 1926). According to Perez, the paradigms last somewhere around a half century and consist of a 'common sense' about how the capitalism of that particular period works and develops. The paradigm also describes how technological change and innovation in a given period are most likely to take place: what organisational forms and finance are conducive to innovations; what technological capabilities, skills and infrastructure are needed; what policy changes potentially enhance innovation; and what kind of best practices of business development emerge and how they thrive. It is important to note that paradigms always form around a set of key innovations and technologies that then encompass and transform the whole economy.

The current ICT-based techno-economic paradigm goes back to key innovations in the 1970s and has engendered fundamental changes in production processes in almost all industries (including many services and agriculture). Perhaps the most profound feature of the ICT-paradigm is the growing use of outsourcing and the breaking up of various production functions that have, in turn, created strong de-agglomeration pressures, both in highly industrialised as well as in developing countries (for discussion, Samuelson 2004; Krugman 2008). Gains from technological change and innovation do not 'travel' within regional or national geographic boundaries so easily anymore. Large production units and mass employment are substituted by highly specialised networks that operate and source production and knowledge, often supra-regionally or even globally – creating a vicious circle of increasing competition, pressure to cut costs and lower wages, luring foreign investors who often bring few fruits to the specific location with extensive concessions (in taxes, etc.). As a result, enclave economies and de-linkaging effects emerge (Gallagher and Zarsky 2007). At the same time, the ICT-led paradigm also enables creation of niche production that has a potential to become supra-regional or even global, for instance hospitals specialising into specific heart surgery (Prahalad 2006).

The ICT-led paradigm increases pressures for de-agglomeration, de-linkaging, and de-diversifying. This has become the key challenge to many smaller or peripheral nations/areas where such pressures are already quite strong. It is not so much the issue of size as such (e.g., scarcity in human capital) that has become important but, rather, a combination of geographic location and economic specialisation patterns. This can be summarised as the position a nation holds in international value chains. For instance, while Finland is both geographically peripheral and demographically relatively small (ca. 5 million inhabitants), its place in the international, mobile electronics-production value chain is distinctly very high. Finland is also seeing a growing outflow of R&D activities into regions with lower costs and larger agglomeration effects such as India.

Finland's position, however, has little if any positive bearing on Finland's neighbouring country Estonia (80 km to the south, ca. 1.4 million inhabitants). In the mass-production paradigm, Estonia could have devised relatively simple strategies to reap the benefits from its proximity to highly developed markets via specialising into lower end products/markets and moving up the value ladder. National policy-making could have created successful catching-up strategies. Instead, Estonia's electronics industry specialises today in simple production and assembly of products with low wages and substantial de-linkaging effects (Kalvet 2004; Högselius 2005). The ICT-led global-production paradigm makes such strategies highly temporary and largely futile as there is growing evidence that upgrading in such sectors does not happen very often (Giuliani et al. 2005).

While the ICT-led paradigm significantly amplifies de-agglomerations, larger nations/regions are somewhat more hedged against risks imminent in the current paradigm. This means that smaller (and especially developing) countries have a growing dependency on international markets and production networks. Second, for smaller nations it can be argued that the policy space needs to be redefined. If local and foreign companies have growing incentives to de-link production, R&D, etc., from a given geographic position, then investing more into education, creating more cultural possibilities and better social programmes only seems to delay the inevitable (also Cimoli et al. 2005). Small state policy-making needs to become supra-regional (for instance, within the European Union). Size in terms of political influence and power – of having the necessary human resources able to negotiate supra-regional policies – is becoming key to the economic success of small states. While it can be argued that this concept is generally known in small state literature (e.g., Ingebritsen et al. 2006 for a collection of useful discussions), the key new understanding here is that this concept also affects innovation. Indeed, when mass-production innovation policy is local (creating local technological capabilities and markets, and then moving to exports), the ICT-paradigm innovation policy of small states has to be supra-regional from the start. In fact, hardly any small country in Europe is capable of or is practicing such policies yet.

It has been argued that such a logic of dispersion of global production networks that create de-agglomeration and de-linkaging effects is not necessarily inevitable to the ICT-paradigm (Perez 2006). Still, the global macroeconomic environment – namely, the Washington Consensus policies – create significant incentives to instate policies that enable the adverse effects of the ICT-paradigm and innovations to be particularly strong. While these policies might seem to be precisely supra-national in nature as demanded by the new techno-economic paradigm, in many areas such policies have enlarged de-agglomeration effects and not the opposite. While for many small countries economic openness has become the key economic policy mantra, we argue that this situation might in fact increase and not lower the challenges these countries face in global competition.

The Washington Consensus

Initially, a list of '10 policy instruments about whose proper deployment Washington can muster a reasonable degree of consensus' (Williamson 1990), the Washington Consensus may have failed in light of the mainly negative experience many developing countries have had with these policies (World Bank 2006; Rodrik 2007). It has given way to 'Washington Confusion' (Rodrik 2007). On the level of actual policy-making, however, the Washington Consensus still seems to be in full force, coming in many new disguises. While the simple battle cry of the 1990s – stabilise, privatise, liberalise – has given way to more intricate phrases and policy advice, they still boil down to the same core ideas.

Two observations are crucial: first, whatever its intellectual roots and its current health, the Washington Consensus essentially became the vehicle delivering the techno-economic paradigm change globally. Second, the main policy vehicles of the consensus, such as financial globalisation and foreign direct investments based growth policies, have failed to deliver growth (Rodrik and Subramanian 2008) and, instead, have magnified the negative effects of the ICT paradigm. In combination, both observations have a huge impact on the way innovation takes place in many companies, especially in developing countries and poorer regions, and the way most countries see and define the policy space available to them. Indeed, one of the most fundamental characteristics of industrial change in developing countries such as Central and Eastern Europe during the 1990s has been that a majority of companies have actually engaged in process innovation (e.g., in the form of acquisition of new machinery) in seeking to become more cost-effective in the new marketplace.

Since the main emphasis of the Washington Consensus policies is on both macroeconomic stability (low inflation, low government deficits, stable exchange and interests rates) and on open markets (low if any trade barriers, common technical standards, etc.), these policies have two main assumptions: 1) increased foreign direct investments (that should thrive in stable economic environments) bring foreign competencies, know-how, linkages, and increased competition for domestic producers, that 2) create more pressures to innovate in form of better and cheaper products and services. If these assumptions are coupled with the real changes taking place in production networks due to the changing paradigm, however, we get highly dynamic forces engendering structural change in more vulnerable areas. Indeed, these changes were largely the reason for the consensus policies in the first place (Kregel 2008a, 2008b). Yet, as economic performance of the 1990s shows, the dynamic changes in (developing) countries following the Washington Consensus policies have been highly surprising, not to say disappointing (World Bank 2006; Amsden 2007; Chang 2007). The policies were highly effective in destroying admittedly outdated industrial capacities in the developing world, yet they were also similarly spectacularly ineffective in creating new capabilities and opportunities.

In sum, the international policy environment created is a highly fertile ground for the negative effects of the techno-economic paradigm change to come into full force without counterbalancing by international policy initiatives. For small states this situation significantly increases the challenges brought on by the ICT-led globalisation of production networks. While there are clear gains from trade, economic specialisation and trade patterns become key determinants in the way a small country integrates into the world economy (e.g., the clear difference in the way Finland's and Estonia's electronics sectors are integrated into world markets). Small developing countries have to keep in mind that waving the flag of rather simple liberalisation and openness might just as easily undermine their own competitiveness in the long run because of de-industrialisation and de-agglomeration. Under these circumstances, smallness becomes a crucial factor in designing innovation policies. How can the combined potentially negative impact of the ICT-paradigm and the global environment, as defined by the Washington Consensus policies, be counteracted? Innovation and industrial policy measures that have been accepted during the last 500 years, such as infant industry protection (also included in Willamson's 1990 article, but not enforced under the Washington Consensus) are not only discredited and politically hardly acceptable (for instance within the EU), but it is also unlikely that such measures (or R&D tax breaks) would work for instance in the case of Estonia's electronics industry. Existing specialisation patterns and global dynamics are simply too strong for such measures to gain any significant traction. Small states in particular, both highly developed and developing, should reconsider their innovation, industrial, fiscal, and monetary policies in order to counterbalance the potential negative dynamics.

Financial Instability

Financial instability as a concept originates from Keynesian economic theory and was further developed by Hyman Minsky (in particular 1982, 2008). While Minsky used the concept only in the nation-state framework, Jan Kregel's work (especially 1998a, 1998b, 2004, 2008a and 2008b) has extended Minsky's analytical tools to the international economy. The basic idea behind the Minsky-Kregel framework is relatively straightforward: a free-market economy is inherently unstable because stability itself leads to relaxed financing criteria (lower margins of safety) that in turn engender a growing number of businesses that have difficulties with meeting their financial commitments, resulting in financial instability or crises.

Three distinct financing positions exist for assets in a free-market system: hedge, speculative, and Ponzi finance (Minsky 2008: 230–38). All positions are defined according to a business unit being able to meet its financial commitments. In the hedge position, cash flow from operating activities is enough to cover all outstanding debts and other financial commitments. In other words, all of them are hedged. In the speculative position, cash flows do not cover all commitments, and thus the business unit needs to sell some of the assets or cut costs, etc., in order to meet commitments. Ponzi finance is a position where it is clear that the business unit is not able to meet all commitments, which are larger than assets owned. In essence, the unit is insolvent because 'financing costs are greater than income' (Minsky 2008: 231).

Clearly, when one adds the Schumpeterian framework of innovation and creative destruction (as Kregel and Burlamaqui 2006 do), we have a theoretical toolbox to understand how innovation coupled with competition (both in the industry and the financial sector) can create all of the financing positions (e.g., speculative or Ponzi positions can result from successful innovations by the competitors or by failed product development). The toolbox also explains how these financing positions can impact a business unit's incentives to innovate in order to create hedged financing position or not as dangers of sliding into speculative or Ponzi position loom.

As Kregel (2004) has shown, the Minsky framework can also be used to analyse country positions in the international economy. Similar to businesses, sovereign countries can also have hedge, speculative, or Ponzi finance positions. Adding Schumpeterian concepts of creative destruction and innovation to this construction allows us to understand how innovation at the company level and sovereign financial stability or instability are not only connected but also have a fundamental impact on each other.

Such linkages become crucial for economic development in small countries as they have relatively small cushions with which to absorb various external and internal financial shocks and fluctuations (e.g., in terms of the central bank's ability to guarantee private banking deposits). We argue a huge difference exists between the mass-production paradigm and the current globalised and open financial markets. To understand the difference, we look at two typical cases: small state type A being a Nordic economy existing within the mass-production paradigm and small state type B being a Baltic economy operating under open financial markets.

Under the Bretton Woods international financial system (that lasted until early 1970s), it was relatively common to have more or less closed capital markets (further discussion in Kregel 2004, 2008b). Most Nordic economies operated under economic policy regimes that included (in one form or other) wage agreements (and wage indexing), closed capital markets, and strong export dependency that resulted in rapid industrialisation and productivity growth. (Mjoset 2000 is an excellent overview of post-war Nordic economic policy regimes.) This, in turn, brought strong growth not only in wages and profits but also in inflation, resulting in periodic loss of export competitiveness through high wages. Such a situation can be described as a highly speculative position, because loss of export competitiveness means a lessened ability to meet financial commitments (by both private and sovereign borrowers). What a typical Nordic country did during the post-war era to return to a hedge position and to increase export competitiveness was to devalue its currency. This action generally returned the country into a hedge position, and the wage/profit growth started all over again. As devaluation hit both profits and wages, such managed boom-bust cycles were also socially accepted. The typical Nordic country avoided prolonged financial instability and thus being in a Ponzi finance position (e.g., runs on its currency, banks, wave of insolvencies). The type A small country used all the aspects of the mass-production paradigm extremely well and managed wage, export, and profit growth in a more or less systematic way. Via mechanisms that absorbed internal and external shocks relatively well, such a policy framework created strong incentives for (high risk) innovations at the company level as it socialised the risk of sliding into a Ponzi finance position. In addition, under continuous wage growth and welfare-state regulations, home markets for highly sophisticated products also expanded rapidly and again socialised risks for prolonged and high-risk product development and innovation.

Under the Washington Consensus policy framework, Baltic economies (type B) followed a distinctly different path, where avoiding instability and boom-bust cycles were two key policy determinants from the very beginning. These economies were seeking to create stability and international trust through a currency peg, an open economy, a balanced public budget, low tax and administrative burdens, and generally weak power by labour to negotiate wages. This allowed for furious restructuring of the economy through direct foreign investments (Tiits et al. 2008). However, particularly during early 2000s, large amounts of foreign investment and private lending financed consumption and real estate booms (e.g., Fitch 2007a, 2007b, 2007c), driving wage growth into double-digit territory. This forced Baltic economies to face precisely the same kind of speculative position where export competitiveness was threatened and endangered their abilities to meet all liabilities (mostly in the private sector and households because public borrowing remains low). This is the situation that the Baltic economies face in 2008.

A key change that made devaluation under these circumstances an almost impossible policy option was brought through open (capital) markets and a currency peg. Large amounts of private borrowing in the Baltic economies are done in euro. In addition, many export industries, being part of international value chains and often involved in outsourcing activities, pay for their inputs in euro as well. This means that devaluation would hit wages, input prices, and consumption, affecting in turn the public budget through lower revenues from taxing turnover. Devaluation would not necessarily lead Baltic economies back to a hedge position; rather, they would remain speculative and need new financing (investments, borrowing) in order to meet current commitments. This means trying to attract new foreign funds through low taxes, lax labour regulations, etc., causing less public funding for investment into productivity-increasing activities.

In order to avoid that the speculative position does not become a Ponzi finance position, Baltic economies need to constrain wage growth. This can happen either through increased unemployment or bankruptcies, or both. Becoming a euro-area country can serve as an exit strategy out of a possible Ponzi position, but the dangers of remaining in a speculative position would not change. Such economies are bound to become or remain highly unequal in terms of income distribution, and home markets remain import-based and strongly segmented – rather hostile to high-risk product development and innovation.

Under condition of financial liberalisation, Washington Consensus policies that stress macroeconomic stability and outsourcing nature of industry under the ICT-led paradigm, type B small developing countries become highly vulnerable to financial instability. This, in turn, is directly related to the way innovation happens at the company level in these economies (innovation as outsourcing, cost-cutting machinery acquisitions that demand less labour, etc.). Financial instability in effect locks type B small economies into specific innovations that target low value-added sectors and activities. Type B countries face constant de-diversification pressures. Product and other high-risk innovations remain very costly to finance as there are almost no public policy options to socialise these risks without creating high rent-seeking incentives (e.g., prolonged dependence on public subsidies, lock in into dead-end technological platforms, etc.). Small home markets cannot serve as test beds for new products/innovations.

As type A countries thrived under the mass-production paradigm that is no longer there and as type B countries face prolonged financial instability, both need to reinvent economic policy regimes to create conditions for sustained growth in the ICT-led techno-economic paradigm.

Administrative Reforms

Administrative capacity is seen as one of the key conditions for creating policies conducive to innovation and sustained economic development. However, the Washington Consensus and its underlying neo-liberal ideology have had great impact on administrative reforms and the way many scholars and policy-makers understand administrative capacity. Since the early 1980s, many countries have been influenced by New Public Management (NPM) ideas and reform trajectories with its "economic rationalism" and managerialism. NPM reform ideas have also had an impact on state-building efforts in a number of new democratic countries where the early years of transition coincided with NPM popularity in the West. NPM ideology sat well with countries that were abolishing their one-sector economies, carrying out large-scale privatisation, and contracting out government services. Additionally, a number of international organisations (e.g., the World Bank, OECD) promoted NPM reforms with no critical or context-related assessment. Although NPM reforms already started to draw severe criticism in the second half of the 1990s, some of its core ideas are still alive in public administration reform practices. As documented by many researchers (for an excellent summary, Pollitt and Bouckaert 2004), neo-liberal administrative reforms have hollowed out the state at a time when the state's capacity to steer the economy is direly needed.

In addition, administrative capacity is something that small states have problems with almost by definition. NPM reforms, although partly originated in small states such as New Zealand, have posed particular challenges to small societies. By creating private monopolies instead of public monopolies, especially in microstates, market-driven reforms (privatisation, contracting out public services) have had questionable outcomes due to the limitations of small markets (e.g., lack of competition). Public-private partnerships have been difficult to develop because of the personalism and interrelatedness within small societies (Lowenthal 1987), which, in turn, may easily give way to problems with control and accountability, corruption, and nepotism. Finally, two important mantras of NPM – decentralisation and deregulation – pose an essential human capital requirement by assuming the presence of a critical mass of professional leaders. This can be questionable even in large countries and is extremely difficult to develop in small states. At a time when small states are increasingly challenged to step up their policy-making efforts on the international level, a wave of administrative reforms or reform tendencies may easily undermine these very efforts.

NPM is not a suitable medicine for small state problems. Moreover, elements of traditional (Weberian) bureaucracies are also not well suited to the small state context. The high personalisation of institutions in small states contributes to the instability of organisations and policies (Randma 2001), whereas stability is seen as a cornerstone of the Weberian administration. Organisations, situations, and decisions tend to be more personalised in societies where 'everyone knows everyone else'. Rationality requires consistency, which may be missing in the structures and decisions in small state public administration that can be largely based on the knowledge and skills of particular individuals (Randma-Liiv 2002). The problems of implementing bureaucratic principles in small states may not stem so much from the design of rational-legal bureaucracy itself as from the inappropriate application and circumvention of its norms and procedures in small administrations.

A fundamental issue in small public administration appears to be modification of a Weberian bureaucratic model in which large size is a critical variable. If small states operate with bureaucratic models inherited from larger states and comprehension of desirable adjustments remain limited, small states may face severe problems in matching bureaucratic rules with their predominantly particularistic societies. Where traditional bureaucratic models of civil service do not suit small states, they can discover their own approaches to public administration. Consequently, both in designing administrative systems as well as in managing public organisations, the key is to find an optimal compromise between classical bureaucratic principles and flexibility. Small states may not merely represent, to paraphrase Richards (1982), a hybrid or halfway house between primitive and modern systems of administration. The form of administration in which the personal factor is so important is well recognised. The question remains whether and how different countries accommodate, exploit, and regulate personal relationships in a way that facilitates 'good government' and whether common patterns can be identified. First, it is important to note, as Katzenstein (1985) argued, that the post-war success of European small states is at least partially due to prolonged political stability and that, second, Asian tigers also tend to have highly stable policy and administrative environments, because of their limited liberal democracies. Small developing countries fall into neither category and, as we have seen above, NPM reforms have hollowed the administrative stability characteristic of small successful European economies during the mass-production paradigm.

The European Union: An Opportunity for Small States?

The European Union has become one of the most important policy factors for small states within the union (Thorallsson and Wivel 2006). The influence of the union on small states and their economic development and innovation differs quite strongly according to their levels of development. For both 'old' and 'new' European small states (most Central and Eastern European economies, except Poland, are seen as small ones), the integration into and membership in the union has turned out to be an ambivalent affair.

First, the impact of accession into the European Union for the Eastern European small economies has been pivotal for their innovation policies in the 2000s. Since joining the EU in 2004, and already during the accession talks, a strong but almost not publicly discussed change towards a much more active state role occurred in innovation policies in many Eastern European countries. The EU's structural funding played a clear and strong role in this change, particularly in negotiations and the planning that comes with it. These changes come with two specific problems: 1) the over-emphasis in emerging Eastern European innovation policies on linear innovation (from lab to market) which is based on the assumption that there is a growing demand from industry for R&D (Radoševic and Reid 2006; also INNO-Policy TrendChart Country Reports 2006–2007), and 2) the increasing use of independent agencies in an already weak administrative capacity environment lacking policy skills for networking and long-term planning. Such Europeanisation of innovation policy in Eastern European small states, while highly positive in directing these countries to reorient economic policies towards more sustainable growth, is in its implementation often only deepening and exasperating the existing problems of networking, clustering, and coordination.

Second, for 'old' small European states, enlargement of the union has brought, on the one hand, clear advantages in terms of significantly larger markets and access to wider pools of human and technological resources. In some cases, foremost for Ireland, European structural funding has also played a crucial role in building up technological capacities and enhancing economic development in general. On the other hand, in particular for those small economies belonging to the common currency area, the euro has also brought unique challenges. Most euro area countries suffer from real exchange-rate appreciation, as they cannot compete with Germany's productivity and export growth. They are faced with growing downward pressures on their wages and difficulties with export competitiveness (Finland and Ireland are exceptions here; see further Pisani-Ferry et al. 2008). Loss of independent monetary policy and restrictions on fiscal policy are clearly quite serious challenges for many European small states.

New global challenges and risks for small states necessitate regional collaboration in policy making for innovation. While to this day we cannot detect any serious initiatives here, it is clear that, because of the policy-making mechanisms in the EU, small states are bound to work more closely together (Thorallsson and Wivel 2006). The EU may involuntarily push small states towards more collaboration in various policy areas, including innovation policy.

Death of Distance, Rebirth of Size?

While numerous fundamental changes in the international economy and in technological development pose new challenges to small states, no clear theoretical understanding explains how to deal with these risks. Perhaps the most developed and influential approach in innovation studies is the one that emerged in the mid-1980s: the concept of national innovation systems (NIS), defined as 'the network of institutions in the public and private sectors whose activities and interactions initiate, import, modify and diffuse new technologies' (Freeman 1987: 1). NIS emerged to meet a growing need at the country level to understand competitiveness better and how to influence it. Existing theories were felt to be partial. Since then, the NIS approach has strongly influenced national governments and international organisations all over the world (Sharif 2006). Indeed, it can be argued that the

NIS approach is the theoretical framework most often used in academic and policy analysis literature.

NIS literature, however, does not deal with issues specific to small states or with the risks described above. Research on (mainly national) innovation systems has focused on activities related to the production and use of codified scientific and technical knowledge: '... when one turns to policy analysis and prescription, as well as to the quantitative survey-based studies that support and justify policy, we would contend there is a bias to consider innovation processes largely as aspects connected to formal scientific and technical knowledge and to formal processes of R&D' (Jensen et al. 2007: 684). For smaller countries and especially for smaller developing countries, other sources of innovation, especially those related to process and organisational innovations, are more relevant. Innovation policy discussions have also been dominated by discussions about 'high-technology elements' (like emphasis on venture capital funds, support on patenting, technology transfer), which often assume existence of relatively large home markets. Although much research is being done on ICT-sector innovation systems, discussion of the current ICT-led paradigm and its increasing pressures for de-agglomeration, de-linkaging, and de-diversifying effects is only emerging (also Edquist and Hommen 2008). Furthermore, systems of innovation literature rarely deals with the effects of macroeconomic policies on innovative activities at a company level (i.e., how liberalisation of markets or exchange rate fluctuations impact company-level innovation; Cimoli 2000 is a rare exception). The same holds for financial instability.

Finally, while the state is generally considered as an important factor influencing how concrete innovation systems develop, discussion of policy-making itself, administrative capacities, and constraints associated with small size is practically missing in innovation and systems of innovation studies.

Consequently, while clear new challenges and risks in the international economy re-emphasise size-specific issues, we argue that there is no coherent theoretical framework that captures all of these issues. Indeed, there is a clear lack of empirical studies detailing how small states cope with the challenges and risks.

The ICT revolution, and the enormous reshaping of industries it enables, has been called the 'death of distance'. We argue that the same revolution, along with the impact of Washington Consensus policies and NPM administrative reforms, has led to a rebirth of size as a key factor for geopolitical units to take into account while devising innovation and economic policies for growth and development.

Indeed, size matters enormously for innovation. While the logic of the previous techno-economic paradigm, that of mass-production, was in itself highly conducive for agglomeration and linkaging effects to emerge – key factors driving innovation and sustained economic growth – then under the ICT paradigm that is amplified through Washington Consensus type of globalisation, these effects are reversed for many countries. The mass-production paradigm thrived under a top-down policy-making framework: welfare state policies and/or state-led industrialisation policies could also carry the positive spillovers of innovation and technological change to the remote areas of distinct geopolitical entities. This transfer seems to be increasingly difficult.

We argue, that country size matters again, as it is one of the key determinants for company-level innovations (what kind of innovations prevail in the private sector).

The implications for innovation policy are that these policies should be built following bottom-up logic: creating local networks and scaling them up into wider networks, which is essentially the opposite of the mass-production paradigm where the creation of national or supra-regional economies of scale was key.

Creation of administrative capacity for such policy development assumes an administrative stability that is difficult in small states per se and has become even more difficult because of NPM reforms during last decades and small administration constraints.

On the basis of these challenges, we foresee that innovation policy in small states needs to deal with three interlinked issues in order to be successful:

1. First, small states must build administrative and coordinating capacity in order to be able to function in and take advantage of both regional and international networks. This seems to be a highly complex task which requires a complicated balancing act between Weberian features such as merit-based recruitment and legality, as well as more open-ended and novel solutions such as independent agencies for managing innovation policy.
2. Second, policies targeting private sector efforts at innovation need to be sector, technology, and value-chain specific while keeping in mind their global natures. Finding the right policy mix (tax breaks, subsidising hiring of engineers, intellectual property rights support, etc.) depends on the particular circumstances in the country.
3. Third, linking macroeconomic policies with innovation policies in order to be able to deal with the financial fragility inherent in free market economies is crucial for long-term sustainable development in small states. Exchange- and interest-rate policies, labour-market flexibility, and so forth need to take into account what and whose risks are being socialised or hedged with such policies.

As is evident, the latter two aspects are heavily dependent on the first one. Getting the administrative and coordinating capacity right is the key to successful small state development.

In the deeply interlinked issues of innovation and administration, size matters and small states face new challenges. These challenges are not satisfactorily answered by the theoretical literature. We call for further theoretical work that focuses on the specific problems of small states that are perhaps most strongly challenged by the new ICT-led paradigm.

References

Amsden, A. 1989. *Asia's Next Giant: South Korea and Late Industrialization*. Oxford: Oxford University Press.
Amsden, A. 2007. *Escape from Empire: The Developing World's Journey through Heaven and Hell*. Cambridge, MA: MIT Press.
Armstrong, H.W. and Read, R. 2003. The Determinants of Economic Growth in Small States. *The Round Table*, 368, 99-124.
Arthur, B.W. 1994. *Increasing Returns and Path Dependence in the Economy*. Ann Arbor: University of Michigan Press.
Benedict, B. 1966. Problems of Smaller Territories, in *The Social Anthropology of Complex Societies*, edited by M. Banton. London: Tavistock Publications, 23-36.
Botero, G. 1590. *Delle cause della grandezza delle città*. Rome.
Chandler, A.D. 1990. *Scale and Scope: The Dynamics of Industrial Capitalism*. Cambridge, MA: Harvard University Press.
Chang, H.-J. 2007. *Bad Samaritans: Rich Nations, Poor Policies, and the Threat to the Developing World*. London: Random House.
Cimoli, M. (ed.) 2000. *Developing Innovation Systems: Mexico in the Global Context*. New York: Continuum-Pinter Publishers.
Cimoli, M., Ferraz, J.C. and Primi, A. 2005. *Science and Technology Policies in Open Economies: The Case of Latin America and the Caribbean*. Santiago: ECLAC. Available at: www.cepal.org [accessed: 16 June 2008].
Drechsler, W., Backhaus, J.G., Burlamaqui, L., Chang, H.-J., Kalvet, T., Kattel, R., Kregal, J. and Reinent, E.S. 2006. Creative Destruction Management in Central and Eastern Europe: Meeting the Challenges of the Techno-Economic Paradigm Shift, in *Creative Destruction Management: Meeting the Challenges of the Techno-Economic Paradigm Shift*, edited by T. Kalvet and R. Kattel. Tallinn: PRAXIS Center for Policy Studies, 15-30.
Easterly W. and Kraay, A. 2000. Small States, Small Problems? Income, Growth and Volatility in Small States. *World Development*, 28(11), 2013-27.
Edquist, C. and Hommen, L. 2008. *Small Country Innovation Systems: Comparing Globalisation, Change, and Policy in Asia and Europe*. Cheltenham: Edward Elgar.
Evans P.B. and Rauch, J. 1999. Bureaucracy and Growth: A Cross-National Analysis of the Effects of Weberian State Structures on Economic Growth. *American Sociological Review*, 64(5), 748-65.
Fitch, 2007a. *Risks Rising in the Baltic States?* Special report, 6 March.
Fitch, 2007b. *Bulgaria, Croatia, Romania – How Sustainable are External Imbalances?* Special report, 20 March.
Fitch, 2007c. *The Baltic States: Risks Rising in the Trailblazers of Emerging Europe?* Special report, 8 June.
Freeman, C. 1987. *National Systems of Innovation: The Case of Japan Technology Policy and Economics Performance: Lessons from Japan*. London: Pinter.

Freeman, C. and Lundvall, B.-Å. (eds) 1988. *Small Countries Facing the Technological Revolution*. London: Pinter.

Gallagher, K.P. and Zarsky, L. 2007. *The Enclave Economy: Foreign Investment and Sustainable Development in Mexico's Silicon Valley*. Cambridge, MA: MIT Press.

Giuliani, E., Pietrobelli, C. and Rabellotti, R. 2005. Upgrading in Global Value Chains: Lessons from Latin American Clusters. *World Development*, 33(4 April), 549-73.

Hall, P. 1999. *Cities in Civilisation: Culture, Innovation, and Urban Order*. London: Phoenix.

Högselius, P. 2005. *The Dynamics of Innovation in Eastern Europe: Lessons from Estonia*. Cheltenham: Edward Elgar.

Ingebritsen, C., Neumann, I.B., Gstöhl, S. and Beyer, J. (eds) 2006. *Small States in International Relations*. Seattle and Reykjavik: University of Washington Press, University of Iceland Press.

INNO-Policy TrendChart, 2006-2007. Annual Country Reports for Czech Republic, Estonia, Hungary, Latvia, Lithuania, Poland, Slovakia, Slovenia, Bulgaria and Romania. Available at: http://www.proinno-europe.eu/trendchart [accessed: 16 July 2009]

Jensen, M. B., Johnson, B., Lorenz, E. and Lundvall, B.-Å. 2007. Forms of Knowledge and Modes of Innovation. *Research Policy*, 36, 680-93.

Kalvet, T. 2004. *The Estonian ICT Manufacturing and Software Industry: Current State and Future Outlook*. Seville: Institute for Prospective Technological Studies, Directorate General Joint Research Centre, European Commission.

Katzenstein, P.J. 1985. *Small States in World Markets: Industrial Policy in Europe*. Ithaca and London: Cornell University Press.

Kondratiev, N. 1998a. The Concept of Economic Statics, Dynamics and Conjuncture (1924), in *The Works of Nikolai D. Kondratiev*, edited by N. Makasheva, W.J. Samuels and V. Barnett. London: Pickering and Chatto, 1-23.

Kondratiev, N. 1998b. Long Cycles of Economic Conjuncture (1926), in *The Works of Nikolai D. Kondratiev*, edited by N. Makasheva, W.J. Samuels and V. Barnett. London: Pickering and Chatto, 25-63.

Kregel, J. 1998a. East Asia Is Not Mexico: The Difference between Balance of Payment Crises and Debt Deflations. *The Levy Economics Institute of Bard College Working Paper*, 235. Available at: http://www.levy.org/pubs/wp235.pdf [accessed: 16 June 2008].

Kregel, J. 1998b. Yes, 'It' Did Happen Again. A Minsky Crisis Happened in Asia. *The Levy Economics Institute of Bard College Working Paper*, 234. Available at: http://www.levy.org/pubs/wp234.pdf [accessed: 16 June 2008].

Kregel, J. 2004. External Financing for Development and International Financial Instability. *G-24 Discussion Paper Series*, 32, United Nations. Available at: http://www.unctad.org/en/docs/gdsmdpbg2420048_en.pdf [accessed: 16 July 2009].

Kregel, J. 2008a. The Discrete Charm of the Washington Consensus. *The Levy Economics Institute of Bard College Working Paper*, 533. Available at: http://www.levy.org/pubs/wp_533.pdf [accessed: 16 June 2008].

Kregel, J. 2008b. Financial Flows and International Imbalances – The Role of Catching Up by Late-industrializing Developing Countries. *The Levy Economics Institute of Bard College Working Paper*, 528. Available at: http://www.levy.org/ pubs/wp_528.pdf [accessed: 16 June 2008].

Kregel J. and Burlamaqui, L. 2006. Finance, Competition, Instability, and Development Microfoundations and Financial Scaffolding of the Economy. *The Other Canon Foundation and Tallinn University of Technology Working Papers in Technology Governance and Economic Dynamics*, 4.

Krugman, P. 2008. *Trade and Wage, Reconsidered*. Princeton University. Available at: http://www.princeton.edu/~pkrugman/pk-bpea-draft.pdf [accessed: 16 June 2008].

Landes, D.S. 1999. *The Wealth and Poverty of Nations: Why Some Are So Rich and Some So Poor*. New York: Norton.

Lowenthal, D. 1987. Social Features, in *Politics, Security and Development in Small States*, edited by C. Clarke and T. Payne. London: Allen & Unwin, 26-49.

Minsky, H.P. 1982. *Can 'It' Happen Again? Essays on Instability and Finance*. New York: Sharpe.

Minsky, H.P. 2008. *Stabilizing an Unstable Economy*. New York: McGraw-Hill.

Mjoset, L. 2000. The Nordic Economies 1945-1980. *ARENA Working Paper Series*, 6. Available at: http://www.arena.uio.no/publications/wp00_6.htm [accessed: 16 June 2008].

Montgomery, J.D. 1986. Bureaucratic politics in South Africa. *Public Administration Review*, 46(September/October), 407-13.

Nelson, R. and Winter, S. 1982. *An Evolutionary Theory of Economic Change*. Cambridge, MA: Harvard University Press.

OECD and Eurostat, 2005. *Guidelines for Collecting and Interpreting Innovation Data, Oslo Manual*. Third Edition. Paris: OECD Publishing.

Palma, H. G. 2005. The Seven Main 'Stylized Facts' of the Mexican Economy Since Trade Liberalization and NAFTA. *Industrial and Corporate Change*, 14(6), 941-91.

Perez, C. 2002. *Technological Revolutions and Financial Capital: The Dynamics of Bubbles and Golden Ages*. Cheltenham: Edward Elgar.

Perez, C. 2006. Respecialisation and the Deployment of the ICT Paradigm: An Essay on the Present Challenges of Globalization, in *The Future of the Information Society in Europe: Contributions to the Debate*, edited by R. Compañó, C. Pascu, A. Bianchi, J-C. Burgelman, S. Barrios, M. Ulbrich and I. Maghiros. Seville: European Commission, Directorate General Joint Research Centre, 27-56.

Pisani-Ferry, J., Aghion, P., Belka, M., Hagen, J. von, Heikensten, L. and Sapir, A. 2008. Coming of Age: Report on the Euro Area. *Bruegel Blueprint Series*,

15 January. Available at: http://www.bruegel.org/uploads/tx_btbbreugel/ BP2008bruegel_comingofage.pdf [accessed: 16 July 2009].
Pollitt, C. and Bouckaert, G. 2004. *Public Management Reform: A Comparative Analysis*. Second Edition. Oxford: Oxford University Press.
Prahalad, C.K. 2006. The Innovation Sandbox. *strategy+business*, Autumn. Available at: http://www.strategy-business.com/press/freearticle/06306 [accessed: 16 June 2008].
Radoševic, S. and Reid, A. 2006. Innovation Policy for a Knowledge-Based Economy in Central and Eastern Europe: Driver of Growth or New Layer of Bureaucracy? in *Knowledge-Based Economy in Central and East European Countries: Countries and Industries in a Process of Change*, edited by K. Piech and S. Radoševic. Basingstoke: Palgrave Macmillan, 295-311.
Randma, T. 2001. A Small Civil Service in Transition: The Case of Estonia. *Public Administration and Development*, 21, 41-51.
Randma-Liiv, T. 2002. Small States and Bureaucracy: Challenges for Public Administration. *Trames*, 6(4), 374-89.
Reinert, E. S. 2007. *How Rich Countries Got Rich and Why Poor Countries Stay Poor*. London: Constable & Robinson.
Richards, J. 1982. Politics in Small Independent Communities: Conflict or Consensus? *Journal of Commonwealth and Comparative Politics*, 20(2), 155-71.
Robinson, E.A.G. (ed.) 1963. *Economic Consequences of the Size of Nations*. London: Macmillan.
Rodrik, D. 2007. *One Economics, Many Recipes: Globalization, Institutions, and Economic Growth*. Princeton: Princeton University Press.
Rodrik, D. and Subramanian, A. 2008. *Why Did Financial Globalization Disappoint?* Harvard University. Available at: http://ksghome.harvard.edu/~drodrik/Why_Did_FG_Disappoint_March_24_2008.pdf [accessed: 16 June 2008].
Samuelson, P. A. 2004. Where Ricardo and Mill Rebut and Confirm Arguments of Mainstream Economists Supporting Globalization. *Journal of Economic Perspectives*, 18(3), 135-46.
Serra, A. 1613. *Breve trattato delle cause che possono far abbondare l'oro e l'argento dove non sono miniere*. Naples: Lazzaro Scorriggio.
Schumpeter, J.A. 1912. *Theorie der wirtschaftlichen Entwicklung*. München und Leipzig: Duncker & Humblot.
Schumpeter, J.A. 1942. *Capitalism, Socialism, and Democracy*. New York: Harper.
Sharif, N. 2006. Emergence and Development of the National Innovation Systems Approach. *Research Policy*, 35(5), 745-66.
Sutton, P. 1987. Political Aspects, in *Politics, Security, and Development in Small States*, edited by C. Clarke and T. Payne. London: Allen & Unwin, 3-25.

Thorallsson, B. and Wivel, A. 2006. Small States in the European Union: What Do We Know and What Would We Like to Know? *Cambridge Review of International Affairs*, 19(4), 651-68.

Tiits, M., Kattel, R., Kalvet, T. and Tamm, D. 2008. Catching Up, Pressing Forward or Falling Behind? Central and Eastern European Development in 1990–2005. *The European Journal of Social Science Research*, 21(1), 65-85.

Wade, R. 2004. *Governing the Market: Economic Theory and the Role of Government in East Asian Industrialization*. Second Edition. Princeton: Princeton University Press.

Walsh, V. 1988. Technology and Competitiveness of Small Countries: A Review, in *Small Countries Facing Technological Revolution*, edited by C. Freeman and B.-Å. Lundvall. London: Pinter, 37-66.

Warrington, E. 1997. Introduction. *Public Administration and Development*, 17, 3-12.

Williamson, J. 1990. *What Washington Means by Policy Reform*. Peterson Institute for International Economics. Available at: http://www.iie.com/publications/papers/paper.cfm?ResearchID=486. [accessed: 16 July 2009].

World Bank. 2006. *Economic Growth in the 1990s: Learning from a Decade of Reform*. Washington, DC: World Bank.

Chapter 6

Small States, Power, International Change and the Impact of Uncertainty

Toms Rostoks

Introduction

If there is something about small states that makes them particularly interesting for researchers, it is their limited power compared to larger and presumably more powerful states. Smallness is contextual, and it is manifested most clearly when actors find themselves in a position where smallness makes it more difficult for them to get what they want in comparison to other actors whose properties allow them to achieve their goals easier. It has been frequently noted that 'small states are defined by what they are not' (Ingebritsen et al. 2006: 6). Relational power or, to be more precise, relational weakness is the main characteristic of small states (see Chapter 1). Thus, smallness is neither necessarily related to more virtuous or benign behaviour *vis-à-vis* other states, nor is it related to stronger support for international norms, although it is assumed that the survival of small states depends on a prevailing degree of support for basic rules of the game on the part of larger states. Small states are not more stable, more democratic or more efficiently governed than larger countries. Therefore it would be correct to argue that smallness is intimately related to power and insecurity (or security dependency).

This chapter aims to put the survival, the existence and the development of small states in the context of power and international change. It may be a paradox, but small states are at the same time both vulnerable to influences of larger and more powerful states, sometimes to the extent of threatening their security and their very existence, but also, at this particular point in history, resilient to influences of larger countries, as very few would argue that small states' existence is questioned. This paradox has provided impetus for earlier generations of small state studies (e.g. Keohane 1969). In order to explain this paradox of security and anxiety, the concept of uncertainty will be introduced as an important factor that leads to restraint on the part of great powers *vis-à-vis* small states. It is argued that, on the one hand, small states benefit from uncertainty with regard to state capabilities understood in terms of power, and on the other, from uncertainty which is a built-in characteristic of the international system. It will be shown how important aspects of power are difficult to pinpoint and analyse correctly. The aim of this chapter is to assess the implications of uncertainty in the international system and examine whether these implications provide for new insights into the conditions under which small states are looking for security and prosperity in world politics.

Changing Power

Power is one of the most important concepts in international politics, and it is often referred to as the currency of international relations. Hans Morgenthau even made an explicit attempt to separate international politics, as the domain of power, from international relations where power, according to him, was not involved (Morgenthau 1985). From the outset, power has been described as an ability of the strong to get what they want. No one has ever stated this in a stronger form than Thucydides: 'The strong do what they have the power to do, and the weak accept what they have to accept' (Thucydides 2006). If that was true, life of small states would be fraught by fear and insecurity, since these actors would be seen as an easy prey in the struggle for power between great powers. Luckily enough, from the viewpoint of small states, exercise of power is more complicated than the mere ability of the strong to get what they want, because more power may also lead to greater insecurity rather than greater opportunities for the state that has embarked on the road of power acquisition.

When discussing state behaviour under anarchy on the one hand and balancing and bandwagoning behaviour on the other, Kenneth Waltz has argued that power drives weaker states to pursue balancing strategies, and 'states prefer to join the weaker of two coalitions' (Waltz 1979: 126). One can say that developing a coalition of the strong against the weak is highly unlikely, and that the strong are influenced by a security dilemma, which means that any action is bound to create a counter-action and that an increase in power is likely to produce a balancing behaviour. Robert Jervis has noted that the security dilemma exists when 'many of the means by which a state tries to increase its security decrease the security of others' (Jervis 1978: 169). Thus, aggressive behaviour against small states may increase mistrust and turn out to be counter-productive for great powers. Moreover, rash and reckless exercise of power can weaken great power's capabilities and undermine its standing among other countries. Recently this has led a number of scholars to advise restraint in their governments' foreign policies (see Walt 2005), and it is possible that states would go as far as hiding their strength in order to avoid being feared and, as a consequence, being balanced against.

The survival of small states is ensured by the influence of the international system, which pushes states to flock to the weaker side in order to balance against the strongest state. Although a holistic understanding of power is tempting, the concept of power is much more complicated than that. Usually states are depicted as actors who are aware of how much power they actually yield. States are thought to be good at detecting their relative strength against others. This may turn out to be untrue if power becomes more multifaceted and complex. Robert Gilpin argues that, for the purpose of analytical clarity, power should be viewed as a sum of various capabilities of states: 'The concept of power is one of the most troublesome in the field of international relations and, more generally, political science. Many weighty books have analyzed and elaborated the concept. In this book, power simply refers to the military, economic, and technological capabilities of states' (Gilpin 1981: 13). Waltz describes power in a similar way: 'I offer the old and simple notion that an agent is powerful to the extent that he affects others more than they affect him' (Waltz 1979: 192). As Waltz emphasises that power is to be understood as distribution of capabilities, it becomes clear that for Waltz small states are policy-takers rather than policy-makers, and it isn't even critical whether weaker actors are influenced intentionally or unintentionally. A slightly different understanding of power is offered by Edward Hallett Carr. He argues that alongside military and economic power there exists another source of power which he labels 'power over opinion' (Carr 2001: 132). Essentially, it is the power to mobilise people for a common cause. Thus, the difference between ideational and material power is delineated, but at the same time there is a constant interplay between the various sources of power.

Although Gilpin distinguishes between several sources of power (military, technological, economic), there is little indication which sources are considered to be of foremost importance. All sources are considered to be important, but their hierarchy has not been explained. It may be the case that the three sources of power are mutually self-reinforcing (highly developed technologies transform into economic and military power and vice versa), and an effective measurement of power is prevented by the uncertainty about the proportion of importance that is allocated to each of the three sources. Besides, technologies tend to be quite diverse, and advanced technological sectors can sometimes be easier translated into economic rather than military power. Also, due to various reasons, states sometimes fail to develop fruitful linkages between power sources. For example, North Korea is believed to yield considerable military power (having managed to build nuclear weapons), but its totalitarian regime has prevented its economy from developing. Consequently, the North Korean government has failed to provide for the basic needs of its population and does not exert any economic power.

The idea that some states possess more of one kind of power and that other states possess more of another kind of power is of great importance because it leads to the idea that there is more than one power structure within the international system. There may be one power structure when it comes to military power, but the power structure may be different when it comes to technological, economic or some less tangible sources of power. As Keohane and Nye have argued, there is a lack of hierarchy among issues (Keohane and Nye 1977: 26-7). Hierarchy of power in one area may be very different from the hierarchy of power in another area.

Numerous attempts have been made to enhance our understanding of those power resources that are crucial for countries. Joseph Nye has developed a classification of power, and he argues that there has been significant variation in the sources of power over time. Power sources that were highly valued a few centuries ago are regarded as less important today (Nye 2002: 13). He goes on to argue that the power structure of today's post-Cold War period resembles a 'three-dimensional chess game' with military at the top, economic in the middle (more dispersed), and transnational relations, such as information flows, at the bottom level where power is most dispersed (Nye 2002: 39). This, however, does not imply that military power is more important than economic and transnational relations. In fact, both Keohane and Nye have argued in favour of the diminishing importance of military power, and Nye has later developed a set of arguments about the increasing importance of soft power in world politics. By soft power he understands attractiveness of culture, political values and foreign policy (Nye 2004).

Some of the problems related to the concept of power have already been outlined, thus showing that, due to a variety of power sources, it is extremely difficult to measure power and to show how its various sources relate to each other. As a consequence, smallness expressed in terms of power becomes very problematic. There is no agreement on which power sources should be seen as being dominant in a particular era, and it is quite unclear how one kind of power spills over into and transforms other kinds of power. A broad understanding of the sources of power such as economic or military is also problematic, because the simple possession of power does not automatically imply that a particular country would be very successful in exercising its power. Besides, a category such as a military power is very vague, and aggregate military power may be useful for achieving only a certain range of tasks while it may not be very useful for achieving other military goals. There is a wide range of military capacities, and a country's military can be good for certain purposes, while at the same time not capable of achieving other goals. An obvious consequence of this observation is that it is far from certain how much power a certain country possesses at a given point. Therefore a simple definition of power 'as the ability of an actor to get others to do something they otherwise would not do (and at an acceptable cost)' (Keohane and Nye 1977: 11) creates more questions than answers.

To complicate matters even more, the concept of power has been transformed further in recent decades. Although the international relations research still favours a particular understanding of power which is rooted in neo-realist and neo-liberalist schools of thought, alternative views of power are emerging. The understanding that there may be subtler ways of producing desired outcomes has been growing. However, it has also made the concept of power even more difficult to pin down. The realist understanding of power leaves small states at the mercy of more powerful players, while alternative views of power may provide small states with a more positive perspective which would be more consistent with current international settings. These important changes have implications for small states.

Michael Barnett and Raymond Duvall have conceptualised power alongside two analytical dimensions. They argue that power is, first, explained by its *kind*, 'either an attribute of particular actors and their interactions, or a social process of constituting what actors are as social beings[...].' (Barnett and Duvall 2005: 9). Second, they argue that power can be categorised by its *specificity* – whether 'the social relations through which power works are direct and socially specific or indirect and socially diffuse' (Barnett and Duvall *ibid.*). Alongside these two dimensions of power they have conceptualised a fourfold taxonomy of power: compulsory power, structural power, institutional power and productive power (Barnett and Duvall 2005: 11-22).

Compulsory power is the most common form of power. It is quite easy to establish that such a power relationship exists between two actors. The most common definitions of power fall into this category, as power is seen as the ability of A to get B to do something he/she would otherwise not do. Institutional power can be observed on those occasions when interactions between A and B are indirect and manifested in 'the formal and informal institutions that mediate between A and B, as A working through the rules and procedures that define those institutions, guides, steers, and constrains the actions (or non-actions) and conditions of existence of others, sometimes even unknowingly' (Barnett and Duvall 2005: 15).

Structural power, in turn, is the power to define 'what kinds of social beings actors are'. Basically, structural power is about allocating different social privileges to actors who participate in international relations and who are positioned at different structural positions. As Hedley Bull writes, 'great powers are powers recognised by others to have, and conceived by their own leaders and peoples to have, certain special rights and duties' (Bull 2002: 196). Structural power is not only about the actors' capacity to act, it is also about the perception that an actor has certain rights to act which are defined by its position in the structure of power. 'A exists only by virtue of its relation to structural position B' (Barnett and Duvall 2005: 18). Structural power is somewhat similar to hegemony as described by Antonio Gramsci when he argued that hegemonic consciousness 'brings the interests of the leading class into harmony with those of subordinate classes and incorporates these other interests into an ideology expressed in universal terms' (Cox 2001: 12-14). Productive power partly overlaps with structural power, because both are 'attentive to constitutive social processes that are, themselves, not controlled by specific actors, but are effected only through the meaningful practices of actors'. Barnett and Duval also write:

> Specifically, and at the risk of gross simplification, structural power is *structural* constitution, that is, the production and reproduction of internally related positions of super- and subordination, or domination that actors occupy. Productive power, in contrast, is the constitution of all social subjects with various social powers through systems of knowledge and discursive practices of broad and general scope. Conceptually, the move is away from structures, per se, to systems of signification and meaning [...] and to networks of social forces perpetually shaping one another (Barnett and Duvall 2005: 20).

It is evident that productive power, in contrast to structural power, is seen as wider and more encompassing. In fact, structures (ideational, economic, cultural, ideological, political, etc.) are *produced* through meaningful interactions between actors.

There is a common trend in various attempts to conceptualise power, as more diffuse and relational conceptualisations of power are established as an important part of research on power in international relations. Subtle and sometimes difficult aspects of power are granted their righteous place and are recognised as providing important insights into the workings of international relations. Even a country's weakness has been found to have a certain potential for influencing other countries' behaviour (Rumer and Wallander 2004). It doesn't mean that compulsory power is no longer relevant. In fact, it would be a grave mistake to discard instances of direct power relations, but it would be a mistake of equal magnitude to argue that the internal workings of international institutions do not matter, or that identities, roles, knowledge and perceptions of actors participating in international relations are irrelevant. Neo-realist and neo-liberal views on power are still relevant, but they are complemented with more interpretive and constructivist analyses. The recognition of a variety of forms of power, to a large extent, has an impact on our understanding of opportunities of exercising and resisting power. The fact that there is a variety of views on power has implications for research on small states that will be discussed later in this chapter. We will then also examine some of the examples from recent writings on small states with regard to power and capacity of small states to act in international politics, but first it is necessary to look at the process of change in international relations.

International Political Change

Why is international political change important when considering opportunities for small states? In the previous section, various conceptions of power were outlined, but international political change describes conditions under which actors are ready and willing to exercise their power in order to facilitate favourable change in the international system. This section draws heavily upon Gilpin's *War and Change in World Politics*, as Robert Gilpin made one of the most important contributions to analysing change in world politics. In his opinion, the international system has the same characteristics as any other social system. There are actors, and they interact with each other. The system is shaped not only by actors' capabilities, but also by the rules that actors establish with the aim of advancing and securing their interests. Actors attempt to establish rules that further advance their interests, but the rules of the system depend to a large extent upon actors' relative power capabilities. The system is perceived to be in equilibrium when the rules reflect the distribution of the actors' capabilities, that is, 'the behaviours rewarded and punished by the system will coincide, at least initially, with the interests of the most powerful members of the social system' (Gilpin 1981: 9). In short, states form a social system, and the strongest and most powerful states establish rules for their own and other states' behaviour.

One can expect that those actors who determine which behaviour will be rewarded or punished would benefit themselves most from these rules, but Gilpin shows that there are good reasons to believe that a great power would face several problems. First, he argues that states would face the problem of diminishing returns from the empire. Gilpin writes about the rise and decline of dominant states and argues that 'For the empire to survive, the economic surplus had to increase faster than the cost of war' (Gilpin 1981: 115). It means that at some point the cost of keeping the empire becomes too high, and the state either fragments or adjusts its financial burden and retreats. Second, Gilpin writes that with time 'military strength tends to erode; economic efficiency gives way to various diseconomies and a slackening in economic growth; the military and economic competitiveness of a society declines' (Gilpin 1981: 159). Third, there is a tendency for the military techniques and economic strengths to diffuse from their point of origin to other countries. As a consequence, the strongest state starts to loose its competitive edge: 'through a process of diffusion to other states, the dominant power looses the advantage on which its political, military, or economic success has been based' (Gilpin 1981: 176). Robert Keohane argues that hegemonic power tends to erode during peacetime, as 'hegemonic powers have historically only emerged after world wars; during peacetime, weaker countries have tended to gain on the hegemon rather than vice versa' (Keohane 1984: 9). The argument for the hegemonic decline is quite strong, and this process is fostered by both internal and systemic factors, thus creating preconditions for decline. At the core of this argument is the idea that the growth of military, economic and technological power is uneven.

Gilpin argues that state power and rules that govern state behaviour have to be in equilibrium. The strongest state sets the rules, but in time the power distribution changes due to differential growth rates. It is highly likely that rising powers would like to change the rules of the game, because that would allow them to extract greater benefits from the system. Gilpin develops a five step model of international change. First, he argues that the system is stable if the power distribution and the rules that govern behaviour are in equilibrium, that is, the system is stable if no state wants to change it. Second, states are perceived as rational and profit-calculating entities. Therefore states will attempt to change the system if they see that they can benefit from the change. Third, revisionist states will proceed with change-facilitating activities until costs and benefits of the change would reach a new equilibrium. When costs start to outweigh the benefits, revisionist states would probably stop. Fourth, once an equilibrium is established, costs of maintaining the status quo tend to rise faster than the economic, military and technological capacity to maintain the status quo. The dominant power faces an imminent perspective of decline. Fifth, it is very likely that if the disequilibrium in the international system is not resolved, '... the system will be changed, and a new equilibrium reflecting the distribution of power will be established' (Gilpin 1981: 10-11). For Gilpin, history is a chain of repeating cycles of power shifts which are reflected in the changes of the established rules for the system. When power shifts, the rules of the system tend to shift accordingly.

There is no doubt that Gilpin has made an important contribution in terms of theory of international relations. His idea that change in international system reflects fundamental power shifts is valid, but it rests on a number of assumptions that have to be fulfilled in order for states to be able to exercise power, facilitate change and adequately assess opportunities for change. First, states must somehow know or measure how much power they have. Second, states have to be able to assess complex relationships between various sources of power, their linkages and applicability. Third, states have to know how to apply their power and be able to mobilise their resources if such a necessity would arise. Fourth, states need to assess correctly not only their own capabilities, but also those of other countries that are likely to be affected by international political change. Fifth, states need to assess correctly the probability of resistance from other countries to international political change.

These qualifications make it difficult for states to exercise their power and facilitate conscious international political change. Orderly international change is possible, though it is highly unlikely, because states are rarely correct at assessing their own power and that of other countries. States have trouble assessing linkages between various aspects of power, and states certainly have difficulties mobilising their power. It is evident from the first section in this chapter that power is a far more complex phenomenon than simply the sum of various state capabilities. Various aspects of power may be disconnected from each other, and state capabilities may vary depending on which elements of power are under consideration. Military power may transform into economic power, but it doesn't have to. Economic power cannot be regarded as a given that can be used by the state to advance its interests. Economics, more often than not, is an autonomous sphere that is beyond direct state control and acts according to its own logic. Private businesses act as profit-seeking actors, and using them as instruments for enhancing state power may create adverse consequences both for the company and the state.

Relations between states and private businesses have changed a lot in the West since the 1980s. States have loosened their grip on economic agents, and this has resulted in the decoupling of economics from state power to a certain extent. The issue of power fungibility has been analysed in great detail by Keohane. He argues that complete fungibility is impossible and that there are several power structures depending on which elements of power are under consideration (Keohane 1986). Military force, although still important, no longer plays the decisive role, but also other power elements each have a separate structure that affects the outcome of world politics. In sum, the difficulties faced by states when assessing their power are real. Also, states face problems projecting their power, because sometimes states lack the skills to apply their power, or smaller powers are more successful at activating their force (Keohane 1986). Besides, power is often successfully resisted by those on the receiving end (Barnett and Duvall 2005). Although states are very concerned about their capabilities, they constantly operate under conditions of uncertainty. The concept of uncertainty will be further developed in the next section where its impact on small states' prospects in world politics will be discussed.

Uncertainty and Small States

Uncertainty is a concept that is well-known in international relations, but usually it has been mentioned in order to describe the environment – the anarchy – in which states operate. For Waltz, anarchy produces uncertainty, and wars are bound to occur, because there is nothing to prevent them (Waltz 2001). Barry Buzan analyses the implications of anarchy for state security. He concludes that there are different anarchies: mature and immature. The latter are characterised by 'continuous struggle for dominance' with the international system being almost in a state of nature (Buzan 1991: 175). Here, the degree of uncertainty is exceptionally high. In mature anarchies, the international system transforms into an international society. Here, the degree of uncertainty is also high, because it is inevitably produced by the lack of hierarchy. Uncertainty is also an important concept for those interested in foreign policy analysis. It is said to be one of the elements that make rational decision-making difficult, if not impossible (Hill 2003: 102). The fact that states simply don't know about the true intentions of other states has been the main driving force behind the perception/misperception literature (e.g. Jervis 1976), which has not only tried to describe the problem of uncertainty, but, at least partly, also to provide prescriptions to policy-makers for dealing with it. However, uncertainty that is derived from the above analysis is somewhat different from theoretical writings mentioned in this section.

How should we understand uncertainty? First, it is understood as a state's inability to assess its own power correctly, which significantly decreases the state's willingness to facilitate international political change. Second, uncertainty is referred to as the inability of states to adequately assess the consequences of their actions. The international system is a social system. Therefore the consequences of the actions usually extend beyond those effects that have been foreseen and intended. For this reason, unintended consequences of the actions and unintended consequences of unintended consequences are likely. If power is exercised against small states, some of the intended and unintended consequences may prove to be harmful to the long-term interests of the great power and may impede its ability to achieve foreign policy objectives. The following paragraphs will elaborate on both understandings of uncertainty in the context of small states.

First, there is an argument which favours benevolent treatment of small states that stems from the problem of uncertainty with regard to assessing the power of small states. Scholars of international relations have adopted a considerably broader understanding of power over the past decades. However, two contradictory trends can be discerned. On the one hand, our understanding of the concept of power has been enriched by the recent writings, but, on the other hand, as our interpretation of power has become more detailed, empirical assessment of how much power each state actually yields has become much more difficult. In sum, we know more about power as such, but we are less and less capable of assessing the power of any given country. Some recent writings on small states confirm this general trend. Baldur Thorhallsson has acknowledged that traditional variables, which have been used to define the size of a country, such as territory, GDP, military capacity and population, have limited applicability and do not provide sufficient insight into size of any given state, not even to mention the possibility of predicting its behaviour. In order to improve the theoretical framework for assessing state size and explain state behaviour, Thorhallsson develops a more detailed framework that consists of six variables: fixed size, sovereignty size, political size (including military and administrative capabilities), economic size, perceptual size and preference size (Thorhallsson 2006). The latter two variables go beyond the traditional view that depicts small states in a negative light, as having a self-perception or being perceived as lacking power and not being capable of pursuing ambitious foreign policy objectives. Christopher Browning has demonstrated with the example of Finland that 'being small' is not an objective in itself, but a matter of negotiation (Browning 2006; 681). Therefore it is possible to tell the story of small states with a much more optimistic perspective. Smallness becomes a virtue and can become a crucial component of small states' identity in a positive way, especially if small states are seen by others as smart states. Although this framework has primarily been developed in order to enrich our understanding of what a small state is and which states can be regarded as small, the framework of six variables also reflects the evolving debate on the concept of power, because small states are small not only because they lack certain capabilities, but also because they either regard themselves as small or are considered to be small by other countries.

The variables that were developed by Thorhallsson certainly point to the fact that the application of different criteria can lead to contradictory results. Large states may seem small, according to some criteria, and small states may overcome their smallness by either consciously or unconsciously developing capabilities that would elevate them to the status of large states if smallness is measured differently. As a result, the dividing line between small and large states becomes more blurred in case of some states that have been generally regarded as small, but this divide deepens for some other small states if it turns out that their smallness extends to an even greater number of capabilities. The international environment is also considered as very important. There is a growing amount of literature on small states in the European Union (EU) that tends to emphasise the fact that opportunities for small states are greater in the pacified regional settings of the EU than in other regions (Thorhallsson and Wivel 2006). This leads to the conclusion that detecting smallness is far from simple, and, arguably, states are aware of that. When the detecting of smallness becomes problematic, great powers are no longer tempted to act against their smaller peers, because it may turn out that this smallness has been an illusion. However, smallness is still a function of power, but the concept of power is now broader and more detailed than the one expressed in older realist writings. Therefore assessing power (even that of small states) in practice is an arduous task.

Small states have a historic record of being able to resist great power intervention. There are numerous examples of such occasions, both in terms of geography and history (Anderson 2005). Finland successfully resisted Russia's invasion, Vietnam was quite successful in resisting US hard power, and the Soviet Union stumbled in Afghanistan (although this happened with notable assistance from the US and the Middle East countries). The weak may quite successfully resist against the strong, and this is equally true in both domestic and international politics. History shows that great powers cannot take for granted emerging victorious from conflicts with small states. Great powers have committed errors before, and this knowledge acts as safeguards against embarking on ambitious foreign ventures. It is much safer to treat small states favourably and as equals than facing the unpleasant consequences of an inaccurate assessment of one's own and adversary's power.

Second, there is the argument that encourages favourable treatment of small states because of the uncertainty that an action might bring about unintended consequences in the social systems. Uncertainty works in favour of small states and increases their security. Actions have unexpected consequences, and unexpected consequences have unexpected consequences of their own. This restricts freedom of action for all states. It is especially relevant in the case of great powers, because they are more inclined to act as agents of change and have more resources to do so. The implications would be first felt by small states, but the exercise of power may have unintended consequences that may effectively turn against the country that initiated change. Small states act as a litmus test for the conduct of great powers. It is good news for small states that great powers have to pursue prudent policies, because even acting against small states may have harmful and unforeseen consequences for them. The fact that states usually flock to the weaker side when encountering threatening behaviour by larger states should also be taken into consideration (Walt 1987).

Great powers are aware that their success with regard to facilitating change in the international system depends to a large extent upon the way they are perceived by other actors. For example, US leadership in the post-Cold War era has been possible not only due to its obvious military and economic capabilities, but also because of its status as a 'benevolent hegemon'. The discussion on the possibility to extend the unipolar moment has been raging in the US already for almost two decades with one camp of scholars arguing that it is impossible to extend unipolarity because states tend to react to the overwhelming power of the hegemon (for example, see Layne 1993 and Layne 2006), while scholars, in the opposite camp, have been arguing that unipolarity is extendable because states react to threats rather than to power (for example, see Walt 2005). The point, however, is that one of the main arguments in favour of the extended US leadership in the present international system is the fact that America has been perceived as the 'benevolent hegemon'. Its leadership rests on the assumption that the US continues to remain kindly disposed towards other countries. This would change if the US started treating other states in a manner that is incompatible with its status of 'benevolent hegemon' whose leadership also benefits other actors. In other words, the US benefits from its current status, but it is also trapped by it. Uncertainty works against the US and favours small states, because a more forceful foreign policy *vis-à-vis* small states may harm the status of the US and, in the end, produce undesired balking and balancing behaviour against it.

The same principle applies also to other great powers, because their ability to achieve foreign policy objectives, at least partly, rests on their image of responsible stakeholders. If this image is broken or damaged their ability to collect benefits, which depend on favourable perceptions on the part of other countries, is impeded. For example, Russia's role as a reliable energy exporter is valid only until it actually is a reliable partner in this respect. If this image is marred, Russia is likely to see more balancing against it (in terms of energy diversification, common EU energy policy, more decisive shift towards renewable and alternative energy, etc.). In sum, there is a problem of power exercising for great powers. On the one hand, they are categorised as great powers, because they are powerful, but, on the other hand, their freedom of action is heavily restricted in the post-Cold War international system. Therefore, in general, uncertainty (here understood in terms of the impossibility to foresee unintended consequences of state actions) favours small countries.

It has to be admitted though that sometimes uncertainty can work against smaller states. US relations with pre-2003 Iraq, Iran and North Korea are examples of cases when uncertainty tends to work against smaller states. Yet circumstances have been quite exceptional in these cases. Weapons of mass destruction (WMD) may be seen as an instrument for overcoming smallness, but it is likely to provoke reaction from great powers. In such cases smallness becomes threatening and provocative, and uncertainty with regard to the intentions of small states in possession of WMDs may turn against smaller actors, even if their intention has been to increase their security. Also, small states can suffer from being left out of alliances, as in the case of relations between Georgia and NATO. In general, however, uncertainty works in favour of smaller and less powerful actors, because usually they are on the defensive side, and larger countries have to be careful in evaluating their aspirations for control and influence. Larger countries have a record of endowing their adversaries with capabilities which are far beyond their real powers, sometimes even to the point of fearing small states.

Uncertainty prevents great powers from forcefully seeking international political change and effectively inhibits attempts to change the international system. Uncertainty about the consequences of exercising power compels great powers to rely on soft power, because less resistance is expected there. Raw power is met with caution and resistance, but states are expected to be less concerned when softer versions of power are exercised, because they represent a less direct threat to the territorial integrity. The use of soft power may change small states' behaviour, but the shift towards softer versions of power is good news for small states, because smallness is linked with greater exposure to other states' policies. Smallness is also related to constant concerns over international political change.

Having considered various implications of uncertainty on behaviour of large states and great powers, it can be concluded that uncertainty reduces freedom of action of great powers and increases security of small states in a number of ways. However, uncertainty mainly works through the reduced willingness on the part of great powers to act as agents of change, because it is difficult to assess power correctly and apply power *vis-à-vis* small states without creating unintended repercussions.

Conclusions

It was shown in the course of this chapter that more sophisticated understandings of power produce greater uncertainty, but this is good news for small states. Simplistic perceptions of power tend to produce unequal interstate relations, while more nuanced accounts on power favour more balanced relations. Traditional sources of power are still important as general guidelines that can be used for assessing few basic capabilities of states, but a more detailed analysis is needed in order to comprehend states' internal and external capacity to act. Incorporation of less tangible power criteria in addition to those that have been traditionally used for assessing capabilities of countries is a step forward in the field of small states studies. Moreover, it is also useful for practical reasons because the uncertainty which is fostered by such exuberance of power indicators provides more opportunities for small state action in world politics. Theoretically, power is an elusive and multifaceted concept, but it has positive effects in practice, because less clarity about one's own and others' power is likely to force decision-makers to pursue prudent policies that give preference to restraint rather than exercise of raw power.

International change as such is not slowed down by uncertainty, but it is likely that change would take place through unequal growth rates and soft power. Necessity to preserve the status of either 'benevolent hegemon' or 'responsible stakeholder' prevents great powers from manoeuvring against small states' interests, because such actions would alert other states and thus would actively create obstacles for achieving foreign policy objectives. There is enough evidence that threatening behaviour forces other states to act against the source of threats. And, after all, it is much safer to ensure that international change takes place gradually, rather than through the application of raw power. Uncertainty forces all states to look for security, rather than act as power maximisers. If this is indeed the case, today's international environment is more conducive to the existence of small states than ever. Although states are still perceived as rational actors operating in a self-help system, uncertainty increases incentives to pursue status quo policies and decreases the possibility of revisionism. Small states are certainly going to benefit from that.

However, much depends not only on the international, but also on the regional environment. Jeanne A.K. Hey points out that the category of small states can be subdivided at least in three parts: microstates, small states in the developed world, and small states in the developing world (Hey 2003: 2). This means that the context is important, and the regional environment in Western Europe is different from that in Sub-Saharan Africa. Uncertainty in stable regional settings with satisfied great powers is much more favourable to small states than uncertainty in unstable and conflict-ridden regional settings. This is a word of caution against excessive optimism with regard to small states in the modern international system.

References

Anderson, R.D. 2005. Lessons from History on the Limits of Imperialism: Successful Small State Resistance to Great Power Aggression. *Journal of Third World Studies*, 22(1), 21-40.

Barnett, M. and Duvall, R. (eds) 2005. *Power in Global Governance*. Cambridge: Cambridge University Press.

Browning, C. 2006. Small, Smart and Salient? Rethinking Identity in the Small States Literature. *Cambridge Review of International Affairs*, 19(4), 669-84.

Bull, H. 2002. *The Anarchical Society: A Study of Order in World Politics*. Third Edition. New York: Columbia University Press.

Buzan, B. 1991. *People, States and Fear: An Agenda for International Security Studies in the Post-Cold War Era*. Second Edition. Boulder: Lynne Rienner Publishers.

Carr, E.H. 2001. *The Twenty Years' Crisis. 1919–1939: An Introduction to the Study of International Relations*. Basingstoke and New York: Palgrave Macmillan.

Cox, R.W. 2001. Gramsci, Hegemony and International Relations: An Essay in Method, in *International Relations: Critical Concepts in Political Science. Vol. 3*, edited by A. Linklater. London: Routledge, 1207-22.

Gilpin, R. 1981. *War and Change in World Politics*. Cambridge: Cambridge University Press.

Hey, J.A.K. (ed.) 2003. *Small States in World Politics: Explaining Foreign Policy Behavior*. Boulder: Lynne Rienner Publishers.

Hill, C. 2003. *The Changing Politics of Foreign Policy*. Basingstoke and New York: Palgrave Macmillan.

Ingebritsen, C., Neumann, I.B., Gstöhl, S. and Beyer, J. (eds) 2006. *Small States in International Relations*. Seattle and Reykjavik: University of Washington Press, University of Iceland Press.

Jervis, R. 1976. *Perception and Misperception in International Politics*. Princeton: Princeton University Press.

Jervis, R. 1978. Cooperation Under the Security Dilemma. *World Politics*, 30(2), 167-214.

Keohane, R.O. 1969. Lilliputians' Dilemmas: Small States in International Politics. *International Organization*, 23(2), 291-310.

Keohane, R.O. 1984. *After Hegemony: Cooperation and Discord in the World Political Economy*. Princeton: Princeton University Press.

Keohane, R.O. 1986. Theory of World Politics: Structural Realism and Beyond, in *Neorealism and its Critics*, edited by R.O. Keohane. New York: Columbia University Press, 158-203.

Keohane, R.O. and Nye, J.S. 1977. *Power and Interdependence: World Politics in Transition*. Boston: Little, Brown and Company.

Layne, C. 1993. The Unipolar Illusion: Why New Great Powers Will Rise. *International Security*, 17(4), 5-51.

Layne, C. 2006. The Unipolar Illusion Revisited: The Coming End of the United States' Unipolar Moment. *International Security*, 31(2), 7-41.

Morgenthau, H. 1985. *Politics Among Nations: The Struggle for Power and Peace*. Sixth Edition. Columbus: McGraw-Hill.

Nye, J.S. Jr. 2002. *The Paradox of American Power: Why the World's Only Superpower Can't Go it Alone*. New York: Oxford University Press.

Nye, J.S. Jr. 2004. *Soft Power: The Means to Success in World Politics*. New York: Public Affairs.

Rumer, E.B. and Wallander, C.A. 2004. Russia: Power in Weakness? *The Washington Quarterly*, 27(1), 57-73.

Thorhallsson, B. 2006. The Size of States in the European Union: Theoretical and Conceptual Perspectives. *Journal of European Integration*, 28(1), 7-31.

Thorhallsson, B. and Wivel, A. 2006. Small States in the European Union: What Do We Know and What Would We Like to Know? *Cambridge Review of International Affairs*, 19(4), 651-68.

Thucydides 2006. *The History of the Peloponnesian War*. New York: Barnes & Noble Classics.

Walt, S.M. 1987. *The Origins of Alliances*. Ithaca and London: Cornell University Press.

Walt, S.M. 2005. *Taming American Power: The Global Response to US Primacy*. New York: W.W. Norton.

Waltz, K.N. 1979. *Theory of International Politics*. Boston: McGraw-Hill.

Waltz, K.N. 2001. *Man, the State and War: A Theoretical Analysis*. Third Edition. New York: Columbia University Press.

Chapter 7

The Fluid Nature of Smallness: Regulation of the International System and the Challenges and Opportunities of Small States

Plamen Pantev

Introduction

The study and the concept of 'small states' have an almost one century long record (Jones 1939; Van Roon 1989; Rothstein 1968; Baker Fox 1959; Vital 1967, 1971; Keohane 1969; Höll 1983; Bauwens et al. 1996; Reiter and Gärtner 2001). Despite the recognition by international law of the sovereign equality of states, the variety of transformations that the international system underwent in this period and the continuing lack of consensus on how to define a small state, the theoretical endeavours of small state studies have continued (cf. Neumann and Gstöhl 2006). This holds true also for the post-Cold War period of intellectual efforts, aimed at finding the special meaning of a state's 'smallness' for security studies, security environment and security policy as well as for the evolving integration process in the European Union (EU).

Traditionally, studies and discussions on small states derive arguments mostly from power relationships in the international system. However, in this volume we define small states as the weak part in an asymmetric relationship (Chapter 1 in this volume; cf. Mouritzen and Wivel 2005). According to this definition, a state may be weak in one relation, but simultaneously powerful in another. The aim of this chapter is to discuss the fluid nature of this concept of small states and to assess how regulative factors change the nature and importance of the challenges and opportunities faced by small states.

The Fluid Nature of the Concept of Smallness of States

The concept of smallness does not provide an encompassing descriptive, explanatory and predictive power, but bears the potential to add to the theory of international politics in conjunction with the broader field of studies in that area. The theoretical value of the concept of 'small countries' stems not from its definition or potential as an analytical instrument, but from its ability to organise and focus the researchers' attention. Olav Knudsen points to the convenient description of the problem through this concept as well as to its ability to guide the research to the fundamental issue of the political and physical survival of the small state (Knudsen 1996: 4-5).

This assessment still preserves its validity and becomes even more actual and intriguing in the light of the evolving global international relations. In the context of globalisation the destiny of a small state becomes more dependent not so much on the power disproportion and asymmetry with the direct neighbouring 'great power' or other big powers, but on the contents of the global security agenda and on the configuration of the great power relationships, constituting the most significant part of the structure of the international relations system.

The theoretical focus on 'small states' preserves its attractiveness also due to the developing international political and economic integration processes and its impact on the security of the individual countries and the respective regions. 'Functional integration' in international relations, the interaction of its different 'sectors' and the consequences of the 'spill-over effect' give birth to new paradigms of security in the international system.

Whatever the research focus on small states' security has been by now, it has had the positive effect of helping the description of the range of issues and specific influential factors, outlining the general picture of stability of the respective country. Every research focus could practically be added to the rest of similar efforts and approaches, thereby facilitating the drawing of the general picture.

The conceptual literature on the foreign and security policy of the small state (e.g. Mathisen 1971; Handel 1981; Inbar and Sheffer 1997; Hey 2003; cf. Chapter 1 in this volume) has been useful for two other reasons. First, small states are responsible for their survival and progress. Smart, adequate and wise policy of a small state, supported by a good quality diplomacy and security sector, largely determines its successes and failures in international relations. Second, factors that are beyond the magnitude and the capacity of the small countries have a defining impact on their security and, generally, their destiny. Thus, challenges and opportunities are most often determined by factors external to the small states, but the small states themselves are responsible for facing the challenges and taking advantage of the possibilities.

Both theoretical focuses bear an essential practical potential in favour of democratic governments and institutions: they get involved in the treatment and solution of significant issues of the global international, including security, agenda. On the other hand, geopolitical issues, globalisation, integration, the transforming system of security threats and their impact on the policy of the small states, cannot and must never be ignored as they usually have a defining effect on small countries' policies.

Any of these theoretical conclusions should not be overstated. The dangers lie in the possibility that an individual small country could move beyond the limit of rational national mobilisation and enter thinking and behaviour of a destructive nationalistic type. The other risk is in following a subservient attitude on the international arena, leaving too much freedom of action to the powerful actors (Pantev 2006: 244-6).

The changing meaning of the geopolitical position of the state and its strategic role for the neighbouring and other great powers is an important example of the fluidity of the concept of 'smallness of states'. In the conditions of globalisation the strategic value of a small state should not be considered only from the perspective of eventual adversarial intentions of the more powerful player(s). Furthermore, not just the neighbouring great country and its eventual tensions with other big actors concerning the policy of the small state matter today, but the transformation of the whole configuration of the global centres of power. The small country needs to follow closely the status of the power cycles in the international system and use its historical experience in its relations with each of the 'centres of power'. The rising role of powerful international institutions or of such institutions that have lost the credibility of its power potential also matters strongly for small states' analyses, assessments and foreign policy and security decisions.

The developments of the international system have led to a new framework of analysis for the foreign policy of small states, which includes their existential interests, their drive for prosperity, as well as the tendency to democratisation on a national and international level. In addition to this, the global environment of international relations provides small states with new chances of participation in the shaping of its own national destiny by influencing the configuration of relations among the power centres. For example, through joining one political tendency or another, or by aligning with, or differentiating from some of the great countries. The difference a small country would make from previous historical periods is the direct projection of such a behaviour on the global processes and tendencies. The responsibility of a small state can be measured by either its contribution or damage to the global security system, and not just on the country's national interest.

The fluid character of the concept of 'smallness', its shrinking and expansion according to the waves of change in international power relationships, as well as the rising impact of globalisation on the international system, should not preclude the theoretical endeavours of defining workable recipes of the small countries' behaviour on the international arena.

Small States and the Regulative Factor of the System of International Relations: Some Relevant Aspects

The discussion on the regulative factor of the international relations system is an effort to add to this developing theoretical potential of the concept of 'smallness' and diminishing its fluid nature, while showing how it develops its explanatory and predictive potential with time.

The regulation of the international system means contributing to its proper functioning, on the one hand, and influencing its change and development in a chosen direction by the state and other international actors, on the other. The fundamental argument of this thesis is based on the invariant character of 'management'/'regulation' of the organised, technically developing, biological and *social* systems. Undoubtedly, every small state contributes to the regulation of the system of international relations – a social system of great magnitude – in one way or another.

At least three aspects of the regulative capacity of the small states need to be considered: the regulation of 'factual relationships', the increased effectiveness of international law and the soft power potential of small EU states.

The Regulation Role of 'Factual Relationships'

We first discuss the participation of small states in the regulation of the international system through factual relationships. The sovereign equality of states as a major international legal principle with imperative legal power according to the United Nations Charter and other fundamental sources of modern international law does not compensate for other regulative factors of non-legal nature, especially those based on economic, technological and military power – a topic extensively conceptualised by the school of the 'political realists' and 'neo-realists' (Morgenthau 1967; Claude 1962; Cline 1975). This has definitely been an area of domination by the great powers throughout the history of international relations and their responsibility, for the future of humankind has not diminished as the accumulation of resources of various types would be hard to compare to those of the bigger number of small state actors on the international arena.

The various ways of influencing the regulation of the international relations system through traditional 'hard power'-means by a small country depend on the correct interpretation of the factual configuration of the 'power poles' in the world today and in the future, as well as on the details of the multitude of relations, established or developing, among the centres of gravity in global politics. Though insignificant in absolute terms, the economic, financial, technological or military power of a small country may play a major role as a contribution to the pooled resources of a coalition or an alliance of states. The participation of small countries in the UN-mandated and NATO-led operation of stabilising Afghanistan is indicative in this respect. Small states rarely add significant 'hard' power capabilities to an alliance, but they often add legitimacy.

The effectiveness of the state, its capacity for good governance, its capacity to contribute to tackling the global and regional agendas of the present world, including through financial and military means, these are factors that define different assessments and profiles of small states today. A small state operates already within a single global economic, strategic, ecological, information and humanitarian space. This is a source of various limitations, but also of opportunities for a small state on the global arena.

These factors have specific outlines in a world which is characterised by varying polarity in the military-political, economic and diplomatic fields. For instance, the participation of different small states in UN, EU or NATO peace support operations practically matter despite the involvement of limited resources. The Bulgarian and Georgian, and even the Albanian and Bosnian records in joining such coalitions in the last decade substantially compensate for other deficiencies of these small countries in terms of good governance and institutional efficiency of their states. Belgian, Dutch or Austrian police cooperation has often had a substantive effect in the EU efforts of coping with criminality in post-conflict or post-totalitarian societies in the last years, especially in South East Europe.

In other cases the financial or economic contribution by a small country to a broader aid plan for a conflict-stricken state or region might lead to accelerating the general post-war or post-disaster rehabilitation efforts. The participation of Switzerland and Norway as small states in such post-conflict reconstruction activities is of immense importance, despite being 'small countries'. A post-Yugoslav, post-totalitarian and post-conflict small state like Slovenia succeeded to gain a similar positive 'donor experience' with its participation in the Stability Pact for South East Europe, which was succeeded by the Regional Cooperation Council. This last example is of special importance as it shows the way to many other small states with a similar historical record as the one of Slovenia. As a small state, acquiring 'donor' potential has practically become a kind of criterion for separating the meanings of 'smallness' and 'weakness'.

Raising the Effectiveness of International Law

The regulative capacity of the small states is dependent, secondly, on the level of effectiveness of international law.

By definition, according to international law, sovereign states have equal rights in international relations and in its normative and institutional systems. International law is also an indicator that morality in international relations matters. It provides objective standards, facilitating states in finding solutions to contentious issues. Normally these standards have universal character and serve as common denominators to the different conflicting national interests of the states: they display a longer-term engagement of the states willing to implement them; they show a future-oriented attitude; they direct the attention of the states to their interests and not to their declared positions; they are clearly and officially formulated with a high level of stability, being the end result of long and successful negotiations; being a model of behaviour, a kind of algorithm of rights, obligations and responsibilities applicable to similar contingencies, they could serve in the same fashion the interests of third countries; and, lastly, there are good chances for the partner state to respond constructively to such standards. All these possibilities are at the disposal of small countries in their policies.

Furthermore, international law provides also a useful international institutional basis for foreign policy behaviour of small states (Neumann and Gstöhl 2006). Participation in international institutions like the UN, NATO and EU influence positively the formation of group identity, facilitating the adaptation to the other members of the organisations. This definitely is helpful for the decision-making process when small states are confronted with problems. The suitability of the situation is linked to the fact that principles and norms of the fundamental charter of the institution are obligatory to its member states, both big and small. This means the treatment and assessment of the conflicting interests of the participants in the organisation take place within the framework of the institutional bodies and charter rules. The necessity to preserve the bond with the organisation calls for constructive and creative approaches by the member states that have run into conflict of interests in their efforts to cope with them. Thus the membership in the institution diminishes the level of tension for the small state that has arisen because of the conflict with another member of the organisation. While the power disproportions are preserved, the belonging to one and the same institution inevitably softens the differences of the small state and the big power.

Pulling international law from its present state of crisis, making it more effective and putting it in service of the majority of the states of the world – the small ones – is both a decent political objective and a source of assuming a more authoritative 'say' in international affairs.

Strengthening the 'Soft Power' Potential of Small EU States

The small EU states have a special position in driving the regulative system of present international relations: being part of one of the most influential global 'soft powers', they have the potential to induce their own interpretation of what 'soft power governance' means and why it is so needed (cf. Nye 1990; 2002; 2008). In the last few years, the EU clearly realised its global role and its efficiency as a function of the combination of 'soft' and 'hard' power (Ahlin 2006; De Vasconcelos 2007). Leaders of the EU put an accent on the Union's capacity to promote its role, authority and influence on other political actors at the global arena, using the toolbox of 'soft power' – culture, values, standards, legal rules, best practices that turn the EU into an attractive model of realising social progress (Barroso 2007: 40-1). The EU is more a convincing force than a coercive one.

Small states are in a unique position to add to the Union's soft power potential and to multiply their own capacity through the integration momentum. Four areas to which small countries may contribute are of special importance: raising prognostic, intelligence and negotiation capacities and focusing the political energy on the issue of enhancing the international law effectiveness.

While all these four areas are within the capacity and reach of great powers, even in bigger magnitude and better quality of the implementation compared to small powers, this extra potential would still be considered and calculated as an addition to the typical usage of 'the carrots and sticks of payment or coercion' (Nye 2008) by the big and powerful states and represent political instruments rarely applied by smaller countries. Paul Meerts, a long-term explorer of the negotiation behaviour of small states, very vividly portrays this unique capacity of the smaller countries in comparison with the great states: 'the power of innocence ... and the power of the mosquito' (Meerts 2002: 8-10).

Let's also remind ourselves again that the majority of states in the world are smaller ones. This brings an added value to the performance in these four areas by the smaller countries in comparison to the more powerful ones — both along the lines of solidarity and moral influence.

First, organising and improving its scientific and forecasting potential, including in the area of security. Being in possession of an anticipatory strategic assessment of the developing security situation in the world, a given region or sub-region turns a small EU member state into a reliable and intellectually competent partner and member of the Union. This can only be achieved in case there is a specialised knowledge base in the area of foreign policy forecasting, a developed scientific and educational system in the given small state. Higher scientific and educational levels are indispensable factors for an adequate interaction with the other EU member states and for more advantageous competitive positions relative to the other global centres of power.

Timely and farsighted investments, as well as organising the national talent could make small states significant contributors to the intellectual power of the Union. There are no 'great powers' in the area of spirit, intellect, culture and science unless proven by doing. This is a potential 'fast track' for small EU member states to prove their abilities and their capacity to contribute to the Union's 'soft power'. The EU is on the brink of formulating its 'grand' concepts and plans how it would act as a global strategic actor. The contribution of its small member states on the *thinking* in the area of foreign policy, security and defence would be indispensable.

Second, researching and developing adequate and convertible intelligence and information potential on a long-term basis. In parallel to the traditional aims of achieving in an anticipatory way valuable information for the security of the country and of its Union partners, the intelligence services of small EU countries should try to realise an *anticipatory knowledge* of the security environment, of its threats and opportunities for progress. It is the anticipatory knowledge that matters most during the decision-making process by the individual Union members and of the supra-national institutions on issues of the European security and defence policy.

To reach that goal would require a forward-minded, courageous, intellectually-driven and a politically supported reform process of the intelligence services on a national and Union basis. Pooling of intelligence resources would inevitably be one of the difficult issues that would require political will. This is an issue, however, with tremendous consequences for the progress of ESDP of the Union and of the integration process in general. Unless introducing this element in the ESDP, the 'grand' vision and strategy in the security and defence areas would be hardly formulated and practically implemented.

While the practical improvements in this field are directly contingent on the coordinated decisions taken by the big EU member states, small EU member states could influence such a tendency through their active participation. However, the contribution of the latter would matter more if they also could display a potential of providing adequate anticipatory knowledge and intelligence information about the security and defence interests of the Union. This is why organising and mobilising the national capacity of small EU states in these areas would be crucial for stimulating the process of upgrading the single policy of the Union on security and defence.

Third, reaching an adequate international negotiation potential that would be added to the Union's capacity to negotiate, both internally and at the global stage. Generally it is the small countries' problem to overcome the power asymmetries of the various international actors, allies, partners and adversaries. The knowledge and skills for dealing with the limitations imposed by the comprehensive structural power of the small state, the maximum utilisation of the situational power in the concrete negotiations via broadening the alternatives and strengthening the engagements and the capacity to control, as well as acquiring tactical (behavioural) negotiation advantages are the keys to coping with the problems of the power asymmetry (Habeeb 1988; Pantev 2006: 286-324).

Thus, for example, a small country with adequate international negotiation potential may constructively serve as a needed third party of a bilateral negotiation process for different reasons: first, because it is perceived by the negotiating parties as neutral to the ongoing dispute between them; second, because it has given clear indications it would not in any circumstance disregard the fundamental interests of the arguing parties; third, because of the potential to manipulate the negotiation process of the disputing parties – a capacity, stemming from the third (small) country's prestige as a reliable and moral partner.

A small country may contribute intellectually to the phase of the formula drafting of any bilateral or multilateral negotiation process, thanks to its forecasting, information and intelligence capacity. This may become an effective ability during multilateral negotiations while playing the role of a communication centre for the other participants, or as a trusted mediator, contributing to the creation of a positive atmosphere during the complicated process of drafting of a single final document, etc. The 'hidden' intellectual potential of such European small countries as the Netherlands, Sweden, Austria, Bulgaria, and eventually others could be better utilised for Union purposes. The knowledge base on international negotiations in these small EU countries is a 'Union asset' that needs to be utilised to its best.

Finally, fourth, the small countries in the EU could initiate political steps in the direction of raising the effectiveness of international legal regulation of international relations, especially those in the field of security. It is doubtless contemporary international law is in deep crisis. The advantages for the small countries of implementing the norms and principles of international law have been outlined in details in previous paragraphs. The small countries could reinvigorate the moral values in international relations by insisting on the strict implementation of international law and of its progressive development that would reflect the transformations in the international system and in its structure in the last 18-20 years.

There are few 'own sources' of carrying out political initiatives by small countries. The policy of emancipating the international legal effectiveness as a needed factor of regulating the international system is among the rare chances for small states to highlight the power of entertaining the principle of 'sovereign equality'. This policy would inevitably trigger processes of influencing the sense of responsibility by the centres of power in the global world – a decisive prerequisite for the respect of international law, for raising the effectiveness of the international legal regulation of the system of international relations and for highlighting again the unique power of example, possessed by the EU as a provider of legal normative regulation of various social activities.

Conclusions

The fluid character of the concept of small states does not make it irrelevant and useless (cf. Christmas-Møller 1983). The mutations of the concept have been linked to its ability to draft some formula for dealing with the various power asymmetries in the international system and for improving the small countries' relative stance in the foreign political interrelationships. The scepticism as to the theoretical relevance of this concept has always been accompanied by proofs of adequate recipes, based on research findings about the actual small states' relations with bigger powers in the international relations system.

In the post-Cold War period, which historically coincided with the decisive drift of the international system to its global dimensions, the chance of the concept to preserve its relevance and actuality has for sure a clear and definite source: the need of a more efficient and effective regulation of the international relations. The single economic, security, information, environmental and humanitarian space the international relations system presents today due to the processes of globalisation in the last few decades created new problems and opportunities for small states, putting their survival and the preservation of their vitality in jeopardy.

One of the venues small states could embark on and improve their case, politically and conceptually, is the regulation of the international system. The new chances are linked to the 'hard power' and the 'soft power' potential of the small states as well as to their political creativity to stimulate the restoration of the authority and the regulation effectiveness of contemporary international law.

The power centre constituted by the EU in this world bears the potential of big, medium and small countries. Paradoxically, the intellectual know-how of small states' policies might serve in very practical ways to the Union's attitudes as a global actor in its interactions with other centres of power in international relations. Mostly this intellectual potential of the small states is linked to the regulative factor of the international system. One could even conclude the small state's involvement with the regulation of the international system might serve as a model case with potential for application for the great power centres' interactions, in which in certain situations each one of them might be the 'weaker party'.¹

In conclusion, regulative factors change the nature and importance of small state challenges and opportunities in Europe. Most importantly the ever-changing nature of the European Union creates a number of new opportunities for small states, who are likely to play a decisive role in the future development of the EU as a normative power in world politics (cf. Manners 2002).

References

Ahlin, U. 2006. Soft power could put sharper teeth into the EU's neighborhood policy. *Europe's World*, 4, 20-23.
Baker Fox, A. 1959. *The Power of Small States: Diplomacy in World War II*. Chicago: University of Chicago Press.
Barroso, J. M. 2007. *The State of Europe at 50: Looking to the Next 50 Years*. Report of the fourth annual VIP Policy Summit, organized by *Friends of Europe* in partnership with the Belgian Government, CMB, Gallup Europe, Microsoft, Pfizer, Veolia Environment and Vinyl 2010, 4 October. Brussels: Palais d'Egmont.
Bauwens, W., Clesse, A. and Knudsen, O.F. (eds) 1996. *Small States and the Security Challenge in the New Europe*. London, Washington, DC: Brassey's.
Christmas-Møller, W. 1983. Some Thoughts on the Scientific Applicability of the Small State Concept: A Research History and a Discussion, in *Small States in Europe and Dependence*, edited by O. Höll. Vienna: Wilhelm Braumüller, 35-53.
Claude, I. 1962. *Power and International Relations*. New York: Random House.
Cline, R. 1975. *World Power Assessment*. Washington, DC: Georgetown Center for Strategic and International Studies.
De Vasconcelos, A. 2007. After the Lisbon Treaty: Global EU? *Issues*, 24(November), 1-2.
Habeeb, M.W. 1988. *Power and Tactics in International Negotiations: How Weak Nations Bargain with Strong Nations*. Baltimore and London: Johns Hopkins University Press.
Handel, M. 1981. *Weak States in the International System*. London: Frank Cass.
Hey, J.A.K. (ed.) 2003. *Small States in World Politics: Explaining Foreign Policy Behavior*. Boulder: Lynne Rienner Publishers.
Höll, O. (ed.) 1983, *Small States in Europe and Dependence*. Vienna: Wilhelm Braumüller.
Inbar, E. and Sheffer, G. 1997. *The National Security of Small States in a Changing World*. London: Frank Cass.

---

1 For sure the concept of smallness of states and the role of the regulative factor of the international system would have its 'internal-Union' repercussions, too.

Jones, S.S. 1939. *The Scandinavian States and the League of Nations*. Princeton and New York: Princeton University Press.
Keohane, R.O. 1969. Lilliputians' Dilemmas: Small States in International Politics. *International Organization*, 23(2), 291-310.
Knudsen, O.F. 1996. Analyzing Small-State Security: The Role of External Factors, in *Small States and the Security Challenge in the New Europe*, edited by W. Bauwens, A. Clesse and O.F. Knudsen. London, Washington, DC: Brassey's, 3-20.
Manners, I. 2002. Normative Power Europe: A Contradiction in Terms? *Journal of Common Market Studies*, 40(2), 235-58.
Mathisen, T. 1971. *The Functions of Small States in the Strategies of the Great Powers*. Oslo: Universitetsforlaget.
Meerts, P. 2002. The Negotiating Power of Small States in a Globalizing World: Options for Mongolia. *PIN Points Network Newsletter 18*, Laxenburg: International Institute for Applied Systems Analysis, 8-10.
Morgenthau, H.J. 1967. *Politics Among Nations, Fourth Edition*. New York: Alfred Knopf Publishers.
Mouritzen, H. and Wivel, A. 2005. *The Geopolitics of Euro-Atlantic Integration*. London: Routledge.
Neumann, I.B. and Gstöhl, S. 2006. Introduction: Lilliputians in Gulliver's World?, in *Small States in International Relations*, edited by C. Ingebritsen, I.B. Neumann, S. Gstöhl and J. Beyer. Seattle: University of Washington Press, 3-36.
Nye, J.S. Jr. 1990. *Bound to Lead: The Changing Nature of American Power*. New York: Basic Books.
Nye, J.S. Jr. 2002. *The Paradox of American Power: Why the World's Only Superpower Can't Go It Alone*. New York: Oxford University Press.
Nye, J.S. Jr. 2008. *Barack Obama and Soft Power*, June 12. Available at: http://www.huffington.com/joseph-nye/barack-obama-and-soft-pow_b_106717.html [accessed: 8 July 2009].
Pantev, P. 2006. *International Negotiations in the Area of Security*. Sofia: University of Sofia.
Reiter, E. and Gärtner, H. (eds) 2001. *Small States and Alliances*. Heidelberg, New York: Physica Verlag.
Rothstein, R. L. 1968. *Alliances and Small Powers*. New York: Columbia University Press.
Van Roon, G. 1989. *Small States in Years of Depression: The Oslo Alliance 1930–1940*. Assen and Maastricht: Van Gorcum Publishers.
Vital, D. 1967. *The Inequality of States: A Study of the Small Power in International Relations*. Oxford: Clarendon Press.
Vital, D. 1971. *The Survival of Small States: Studies in Small Power/Great Power Conflict*. London and New York: Oxford University Press.

PART III
The Experience of Small States with the European Union

Chapter 8
In a League of its Own? The Netherlands as a Middle-Sized EU Member State

Jan Rood

Introduction

What is the position of the Netherlands in the EU of 27? What capacity does it have to influence decision-making in today's EU? What kind of strategies has the Netherlands adopted to maximise its impact in the EU framework? These questions should be seen primarily against the background of the sensitive relationship the Netherlands has with the big EU member states – France and Germany in particular. It could even be argued that a strategy of binding the big member states has been one of the main reasons for the Netherlands to join the European integration project in the first place, and in particular for the Dutch preference to found this project on a supranational basis. Integration within a framework of strong supranational institutions was seen as offering the best guarantee for maintaining a certain equilibrium among the member states, whether big or small.

Notwithstanding the supranational character of EU integration, there has always been concern in the Netherlands about the big member states dominating the EU at the expense of the smaller ones. For that reason the 'big-small' dimension has traditionally been one of the benchmarks in Dutch EU policy. That was the case in the 1950s and 1960s. But the importance of this notion became once again clear during the negotiations on the constitutional treaty and the Treaty of Lisbon.

The fear of being marginalised already played a role in the Community of six, but that fear is so much stronger in today's Union of 27 member states where the Netherlands not only has to cope with the aspirations and actions of the big ones. In the Union of 27, the Netherlands no longer is one of the founding fathers. It has become one of the many member states, an evolution which implies by definition a relative loss of power and position, and which makes it more difficult to make a difference.

How has the Netherlands responded to this change of position? What options does it have to maintain and perhaps even strengthen its influence in this multi-actor environment, taking into account the constraints of being one of the 'smaller member states'? This issue will be discussed in this contribution against the background of the traditional attitude of the Netherlands towards the EC/EU. To what extent was this attitude the result of its position as a relatively small member state? And has there been a change in attitude and policies towards the integration process as a result of developments at the EU level, *inter alia*, of the enlargement? These questions are so much more relevant in view of the no-vote in the Netherlands referendum of June 2005 on the European constitutional treaty than the actual no-vote itself. This event has been perceived by many observers as a change of attitude of the Netherlands towards the EU, marking in particular a shift from a loyal supporter and founding father of the European integration to a much more critical and reluctant actor.

But before going into these questions, first the Dutch position within the EU in terms of *size* should be discussed. Can the Netherlands be ranked as one of the many small and smaller member states within the EU of 27 or is it a middle-sized country? Next, the Dutch EU policy will be elaborated as to its traditional strategic *basic assumptions*, in particular regarding the relationship with the big member states. What were the basic considerations underlying Dutch membership of the European Community/Union? This part is followed by an analysis of the effects of the enlargement on the Dutch position in the EU and on the strategies to be followed in order to maximise its influence in the Union of 27. This contribution concludes with some more general observations concerning the present Dutch EU policy position and the constraints that the government in The Hague is facing in pursuing its policies.

The Dutch Position in the EU: Small, Middle-sized, or ...?

What is the Dutch position as an EU member state, in terms of size? How is this position perceived by the Netherlands itself? The most simple answer to these questions is the fact that whereas the Netherlands was once one of the six founding fathers, as a result of enlargement it has become one of the many member states, knowing also that the designation 'founding father' is something of a distant past which no longer has any resonance, in particular to member states which joined the EU at a much later date. The impact of, in particular, the enlargement process on the position of the Netherlands (and also of Belgium and Luxembourg) becomes even more visible considering the fact that in the EC of six, the Netherlands was one of the *three* small member states, with Luxembourg being a very small member. Facing them were three big member states, with Germany and France clearly setting the tone in the framework of the Franco-German axis. In the EU of today the number of small and smaller member states has increased to 21. At the same time, the number of big member states has grown to six (i.e., if Spain and Poland are considered as belonging to the group of big member states). As a result of this ongoing enlargement with specifically small countries, the Netherlands has not only become one of the many member states, but even one of the many small and smaller EU countries. One effect of this development on the Dutch position has been that is has become more difficult for the Netherlands to distinguish itself and to wield influence in such a way that it can have an impact on EU decision-making.

But can the Netherlands actually be seen as a small or smaller member state? What is the view of the Dutch themselves? A preliminary observation in this regard is that, as will be elaborated further in the next paragraphs, obviously a country's potential to have influence within the EU is determined by many factors. Size is only one among them and, moreover, is in 'the eye of the beholder' (Hanf and Soetendorp 1998). In other words 'size matters', but less so than is often assumed. In that sense the debate about the purport of the 'big-small' dimension in the EU is to some extent artificial. However, it is also clear that in some instances size *does* matter and that smaller member states are confronted with specific constraints, due to the fact that they are the weak part in an *asymmetric* relationship, and that therefore it does have an impact on the policies and, in particular, the strategies of member states towards the integration process (see, *inter alia*: Panke 2008; Broman 2005).[1] Against this background and taking these observations into account, the question of the position of the Netherlands in terms of weight does play a role in the debate about Dutch EU policy.

In discussing this issue, three arguments could be considered as to underpin the claim that whatever the final conclusion regarding the Dutch position is, the Netherlands certainly should not be ranked among the small or smaller EU member states. The *first* one concerns the rather paradoxical observation that, as a result of enlargement, the *differentiation* within the EU, in terms of groups of member states to be distinguished, has increased substantially. In the EU of today we find big, middle-sized, smaller, small and very small member states, whereas in the EC of the past only big and small member states could be distinguished. As a result of enlargements to be envisaged with in particular small and very small member states from, *inter alia*, the Balkans, this differentiation will only increase. In other words, the 'demographic' factor has become more important (and will become even more important), with the paradoxical effect that, in terms of ranking, the Netherlands has become 'bigger' in relation to the other 'small' member states.

This effect becomes, *secondly*, so much more prominent in view of the fact that with a population of 16 million the Netherlands is substantially larger than the next 'small' member state Belgium, which has a population of only 10 million. From this perspective, the Netherlands could be considered a middle-sized EU country, and when we take into account that the next 'bigger' member state, Romania, has 22 million inhabitants, it rather plays in 'a league of its own'.[2]

This (self-)projection of the Netherlands as a middle-sized country is, *finally*, based on the level of ambition of Dutch foreign policy, by the degree of international

---

1   For the discussion of the concept of small states in general and the relational understanding of small states in particular, see the discussion by Steinmetz and Wivel in Chapter 1 of this book.

2   In a recent publication Panke (Panke 2008) remarks that in the present EU 19 member states have a vote weight that is less than the EU average and can therefore be considered as a small member state. Due to its population size and corresponding vote weight the Netherlands does not belong to this group.

engagement and by the instruments and means at the disposal of the Netherlands in conducting its foreign policy. Since the Second World War the Netherlands has departed from its traditional policy of neutrality, which it adopted after the Napoleonic era during which the Netherlands was occupied by France. Instead, it has become an active and ambitious player on the international scene, specifically regarding issues concerning peace and security, maintaining the international legal order, the combat of poverty and underdevelopment and the build-up and promotion of a stable and open international economic system, in particular for the benefit of international trade. These ambitions are pursued in the framework of the global multilateral system, in NATO and other security arrangements (e.g., the OSCE) and through active involvement in the European Union. They are supported by a relatively large diplomatic apparatus, which disposes of an extensive bilateral and multilateral network of diplomatic establishments, and which has given the Netherlands in particular a traditionally strong position within the UN family of organisations. This position is strengthened by the availability of a comparatively large budget for development cooperation, *per capita* even one of the highest in the world. In addition, the Netherlands has a relatively large defence system, well capable of participating in military operations within the higher spectre of the use of violence (intervention, enforcement and stabilisation by military means). This capability is reflected in the active and extensive involvement in military operations under UN, NATO and EU auspices.

The rather ambitious foreign policy of the Netherlands can to some extent be explained by its past. During its 'golden age' (seventeenth century) the Netherlands was the leading economic (and military/naval) power in Europe. In that period the foundations were being laid for a large colonial empire, which it only lost after the Second World War. In other words, seen from an historical perspective, the Netherlands has for long periods been a 'great power'. The Dutch support for a strong international legal order embedded in an effective system of multilateral institutions is, on the other hand, in accordance with its position as a trading nation with a very open economy. It gave the Netherlands traditionally a clear interest in peace and stability in order to guarantee the safe conduct of its commercial activities. 'Peace, profits and principles' were clearly interrelated for the Netherlands (Voorhoeve 1979). That was the case in the seventeenth century, but also today the Dutch trade dependence to some extent explains the ambitions and orientation underlying Dutch foreign policy.

To summarise, this overview may suggest the image of a country which perhaps is 'punching above its weight', but also of a country that manifests itself in particular within the European Union as a member state which on the basis of its position, its foreign policy ambitions and its means and capabilities distinguishes itself from small or smaller member states and that, moreover, it wants to be recognised as such. This characteristic became perfectly clear, *inter alia*, during the negotiations in 2000 on the Treaty of Nice, when the Netherlands demanded a larger vote weight than Belgium, in order to distinguish itself from the group of smaller member states. Therefore, the self-image as, in any case, 'the biggest of the small ones' or the 'smallest of the big ones' serves to underline the Dutch pretention to be a middle-sized EU member state. At the same time, this self-image as a middle-sized EU member state underlines the Dutch position of asymmetry in relation to the bigger member states. The Netherlands may be 'big' compared to Luxemburg or Malta, but it is 'small', and in general in the position of 'demandeur', in its relation with France or Germany.

The Dutch EU Strategy: Supranationalism as a Means to Bind the Big Ones

In view of this it should not come as a surprise that for the Netherlands its relationship with the big member states has traditionally been a rather sensitive issue. It always feared that the big member states – in particular France – would try to break up the existing balance between 'big' and 'small' within the EC/EU by claiming or creating a special and more prominent position for themselves. This sensitivity has manifested itself on several occasions during the process of European integration. One example is the opposition from both the Netherlands and Belgium in the 1960s against the so-called 'Fouchet proposal', initiated by the French President Charles de Gaulle. The two smaller states saw in this proposal an effort to establish a more intergovernmental European framework, which was dominated by a directorate of the three big member states, and which therefore – in their view – constituted a direct threat to the Community model of integration and to their position. For the same reason of protecting the Community method of integration, the Netherlands from the start has been reluctant to the (again French) initiative to establish the European Council. It feared that within this, by definition, more intergovernmental setting the big member states would dominate at the expense of the smaller ones, and that this new body would overshadow the European Commission, which in the Dutch view was and is the core institution of the Community method of decision-making. In the same vein, the Netherlands has always been suspicious of informal inner-circle meetings of the big member states, for fear of being excluded and confronted with 'faits accomplis'.

This sensitivity may be explained from the fact that in the Dutch perception European integration is an outstanding instrument to bind the big member states and to guarantee a certain balance or equilibrium between big and small member states in the EU (Van Keulen and Rood 2003). Hence for the respective Dutch governments the principle of equality among member states has always been one of the most important rules underlying the integration process. And it explains in particular their sensitivity towards the idea of a directorate of big member states, in which the Netherlands was excluded from decision-making. In the same vein the Netherlands has always reacted rather cautiously towards suggestions for enhanced cooperation or the formation of a core group within the EU. For such schemes could easily be dominated by the larger member states and might have a negative effect on the position of the Netherlands.

This attitude is reflected in the support for a European integration process on a *supranational* or *communitarian* foundation: i.e., a European Union/Community disposing of strong and independent institutions – in particular the European Commission and the Court of Justice – and constituting a legal order in which all member states are without distinction bound by the same rules and in which decisions and agreements can be enforced by judicial means. The reason obviously is that such a supranational arrangement offers the best available guarantee for upholding the principle of equality and the best protection against the big member states taking the law into their own hands. For the latter are bound by the same rules and procedures. In other words, a strategy of *binding* has traditionally been at the centre of Dutch European policy (see: Wallace et al. 1999; Wivel 2009). Such a strategy, i.e. the application of the Community method, was perceived as the best way to protect the interests of small member states (see also: Magnette and Nicolaïdis 2003). This Dutch perception also explains why during negotiations about institutional reform 'maintaining the institutional balance', i.e. the balance between member states and in particular the European Commission, has always been the leading principle for Dutch officials.

The fear for a 'directoire' of big member states also explains to some extent the Dutch reluctance towards European *political* integration. European integration was supported as long as it encompassed the economic domains of trade and market integration. These domains were and still are of the utmost importance for a country like the Netherlands with its very open and trade-oriented economy. On the other hand, European cooperation and integration in the areas of foreign and security policy and concerning military matters were approached with great reluctance and suspicion. In these areas the Netherlands has neither been initiator nor forerunner, but more a fence-sitter or even a laggard trying to prevent or slow down initiatives. This attitude had its roots in the aforementioned sensitivity towards the role and position of the big member states. The Dutch feared that European cooperation on these policies would be dominated by the big member states at the expense of the Netherlands. Moreover, during the period of the Cold War the respective governments in The Hague considered the United States, on account of its world power, a more reliable protector of Dutch security interests, than western European countries like, e.g., France or Germany, which in the Dutch view were not able to fulfil the European security needs. Hence the Netherlands has responded only half-heartedly to initiatives to develop European cooperation in the areas of security and defence. Those efforts were seen as a direct threat to the Atlantic alliance, being the linchpin of Dutch security and to the relationship with the United States. In other words, Dutch preference for European integration was conditioned by a so-called *Atlantic clause*, meaning that the EC/EU was the primary framework for economic integration, whereas security and defence should be secured under the umbrella of NATO.[3]

---

3 For the very reason that the Netherlands has always been lukewarm if not reluctant to the idea of further European political integration, the assumption that the Netherlands

To summarise, the traditional EU policy of the Netherlands was based on a strategy of binding the big member states in a supranational framework of rules and institutions. At the same time the Dutch ambitions towards European integration were limited in scope, focusing primarily on economic integration. And finally, this approach was broadly supported by the political elite and embedded in an attitude of 'permissive consensus' among the population.

The Netherlands and the Constitutional Treaty: Does History Repeat Itself?

So far for the traditional position of the Netherlands in the EC/EU and, in particular, the sensitivity of the relation with the big member states. But in the run-up to the constitutional treaty it became clear that also after half a century of European integration this sensitivity has by no means diminished. Certain proposals for institutional reform initiated by the big member states were met with great apprehension, precisely because the Netherlands feared they would strengthen the position of the larger countries. The Netherlands – together with other small member states – expressed in particular great reservations about a proposal made by the big member states to replace the existing rotating presidency of the European Council by a semi-permanent President from outside the Council. As was already mentioned, the Netherlands has always been rather suspicious of this body, fearing that it would dilute the Community method. The idea that this entity would in future be chaired by a permanent President from outside the group of prime ministers or heads of state was unacceptable to The Hague. It was seen as an effort by the big member states to sideline the small ones and to exclude them from the leadership of what since its creation has become the most important institution within the EU. Especially feared was the emergence of an 'inner circle' of the new President and the big member states, which together would set out the strategic orientation of the EU.

In the Dutch view the introduction of this new figure would also constitute a direct threat to the position of the President of the European Commission, and for that reason to the institutional balance within the European Union. And, finally, the Netherlands was suspicious of proposals to limit the number of European

---

has traditionally been in favour of the creation of a federal Europe must be considered as to be based on a myth. In other words, the Netherlands was in favour of European integration, but only to a certain degree – on a supranational basis, but not with the ambition to advance towards a European federation. At the same time it is obvious that, as a result of the end of the Cold War, of the manifestation of cross-border issues and of ever stronger transnational forces, of the ongoing changes in the international distribution of power and of the processes of globalisation, it has during the past 10 to 15 years become more difficult for the Netherlands to maintain this 'split' between European integration and Atlantic cooperation on the one hand, and its reluctance as to political integration in the EU on the other.

commissioners. Such proposals would be acceptable only if it was guaranteed that big member states, as far as their presence in a smaller European Commission is concerned, would be treated in the same manner as the smaller ones.

Most recently, the sensitivity of the issue manifested itself again during the discussions on the implementation of the Treaty of Lisbon – the successor of the constitutional treaty. In these discussions the Dutch aimed to downgrade the position of the permanent President of the European Council as much as possible: he/she should be the chairperson of the Council and not 'the President of Europe'. In addition, the Council of General Affairs – and by that the regular rotating Presidency – should be responsible for the overall coordination of the various Council formations, and not the newly established permanent President.

The above underlines that the relationship with the big member states still is an important conditioning factor in shaping Dutch EU policies. To a certain extent the Netherlands tends to define its own position relative to the position and behaviour of the larger EU member states, in particular at times when the relations of power and influence in the EU are recalibrated; *i.e.* during negotiations about institutional reform. As was already argued, this reflex can be explained from the Dutch self-image as a middle-sized power and the ambitions underlying Dutch foreign policy. On the other hand, taking into account the way in which day-to-day decision-making takes place in the EU, this emphasis on the 'big-small' dimension seems to be misplaced. One reason is that EU decision-making is based on the principle of consensus, i.e. finding a compromise which is acceptable to all or at least as many member states as possible. This was, is and will remain the leading principle in EU negotiations.

Given this principle, decision-making is not characterised by a structural cleavage between big and small member states.[4] On the contrary, the EU is a pluralistic system of mixed or flexible coalitions, with – depending on the issue – different groups of small and big joining their forces. That is the name of the game within the EU. In other words, in day-to-day politics cross-cutting cleavages determine the outcome of the negotiations and not the distinction between big and small member states. Moreover, to this could be added that, as far as there has been a change in the distribution of power on the 'big-small' scale, this has been to the advantage of the small member states, which saw their number increase to 21, whereas, as was already argued, the number of larger members increased to only six. According to some it is therefore fair to speak of the 'tyranny of the tiny' instead of the domination by the big ones. And, finally, although much will depend on the actual implementation of the Lisbon Treaty, the overall impact of

---

4 Institutional matters are the exception to this rule, as was exemplified by the negotiations on institutional reform.

this treaty on the balance between big and small member states appears to be limited and seems not as dramatic as has been suggested during the negotiations on the European constitution.

The Challenges Facing the Netherlands in its EU Policies

Notwithstanding this final observation, it is clear that, in terms of perception of its position, the relationship *vis-à-vis* the big member states is an important variable in understanding Dutch EU policies. Defined in terms of power, this relationship is asymmetrical, meaning that the Netherlands is the weaker part of the relationship. Accepting the fact that some states 'are more equal than others', i.e. the big member states – France and Germany in particular – have more weight in decision-making than others, it is obvious that from the Dutch point of view having access to those countries on the basis of a good relationship is crucial in the game of coalition formation in the EU. A winning coalition without the support of these countries is illusory.

From this perspective, it is a matter of concern to the Netherlands that, partly in response of the enlargement of the EU, the big member states have recently shown a certain inclination to 'gang-up' as a group in the early stages of decision-making. The extent with which this happens and the Netherlands is excluded from the discussions, this is considered as a threat to the Dutch interest. Having access to the big member states and preventing the emergence of a 'directoire' is therefore considered vital.

But the challenges the Netherlands is facing in pursuing its EU policies must be seen in a broader perspective than the mere relationship with the big member states. In addition, there is the effect of enlargement as such on the position of member states, including the Netherlands. The increase of EU membership to 27 member states implies for all member states a relative decline of influence, an effect that probably hits harder in the case of the smaller member states. Enlargement also means that the EU, in terms of the *number* of relations among member states, has become more complicated, a factor which is particularly important given the fact that in more and more EU policy areas decisions are taken by majority voting. Under this regime, a country can only have influence on the final decision-making if it succeeds in finding and mobilising a sufficient number of member states that support its views. This has become a more difficult challenge as a result of the relative decline in position and power of the Netherlands – an inevitable effect of the Union's enlargement – and of the increase in the number of member states with which to maintain a relationship.

What makes this game of coalition formation even more complicated is that, as was argued above, there are no fixed or privileged coalitions in the EU; i.e. countries that on a more or less permanent basis do agree and cooperate on a broad range of issues. Although they have a long history of cooperation, this latter observation even holds true for the Benelux countries.⁵ Coalition formation, in other words, is a game of *flexible* coalitions, in which, from the Dutch point of view, it is crucial to be able to make a difference and to be considered as an attractive and necessary partner by the other member states. In this game it is also important to take into account that, in order to mobilise a winning coalition, one always needs the support of the big member states, specifically France and Germany.

The Dutch EU position and policies have further been complicated by a change in the mode of decision-making in the EU towards a more *intergovernmental* approach. The traditional strategy of relying on the Community method, and in particular the European Commission as a guardian of the interests of the smaller member states, is more difficult in an EU where the support for extending the Community method has decreased and intergovernmentalism is on the rise. This trend can be explained by the more prominent role of the European Council, the larger number of member states and the spill-over of European integration into policy areas, where the application of this method is less obvious and/or less accepted. This development must be seen in conjunction with an even stronger emphasis on EU decision-making during the informal stages of this process.

A final observation concerns the attitude of the Netherlands itself. Traditionally a strong supporter of European integration, defined in particular as an economic project, the Netherlands has recently become more reluctant regarding deepening and extending the integration process. This change was exemplified most dramatically in the referendum of June 2005 concerning the European constitutional treaty. Its result showed that the traditional consensus amongst the political elite concerning the integration process and the benign support of the Dutch population for the EU have been replaced by a more critical, restrained if not sceptical approach towards the EU. The reasons for this change must particularly be sought in the enlargement process and the fear that, as a consequence, the Netherlands would lose its position in an ever larger EU and in the intrusion of EU policies and rules into areas, which are seen as inextricably linked to Dutch identity and society. This latter consideration underlines the fact that the shift of the integration project from an essentially economic endeavour to a much more political effort is clearly causing frictions and strains in Dutch society, limiting the room of manoeuvre of policy-makers. With a divided political elite at home and a more critical population, it has become more difficult for the Netherlands to maintain a balanced approach towards the integration process.

---

5   The cooperation between the three Benelux countries in the broader framework of European integration has had its ups and downs. The heyday of cooperation in the Benelux framework was in the 1950s and 1960s. Since then the picture is rather mixed, varying from periods of disinterest and little activity to efforts to re-energise the cooperation. More recently the Benelux countries have cooperated successfully to some extent in the framework of the IGC's concerning EU treaty reform, by presenting joint memorandums (the so-called Benelux memorandums), in which they put forward a common position.

Options for Maximising Influence in an Ever Larger European Union

In responding to this challenge there are in theory various options open to the Netherlands. One would be to stick to its traditional strategy of binding, i.e. of supporting European integration on a supranational basis as the best method to further its interests, in particular to level differences in power among the member states. However, in view of the more critical domestic scene and the intergovernmental forces in the EU itself, this option does not appear as viable as in the past. A second option could be to have a more minimalistic approach towards the integration process and to adopt an obstructive position in the EU by acting as a veto power in order to maximise its nuisance value. Such a policy would be in accordance with the more critical attitude at the domestic level in the Netherlands. But this option, too, seems unrealistic in terms of providing an effective long-term policy for the Netherlands to promote its interests. These interests are ultimately best served through an active involvement in EU policy-making and they require a working system of institutions at the Union level. From this point of view it would be highly counterproductive to position oneself as a structural laggard or obstructionist, leaving aside the question whether such a policy would be seen as credible by the other member states, and whether it would not lead to isolation of the Netherlands.[6] It moreover might have the unintended effect of stimulating the big member states to create some form of a 'directoire'. For the same reason it would also be counterproductive to position oneself as leader of the group of small member states, trying to counterbalance the big ones by ganging-up. Such a policy would moreover not correspond with the aforementioned reality of EU decision-making, which is characterised by flexible coalitions on the basis of cross-cutting solidarities. This consideration implies that a final strategy – i.e. a strategy of bandwagoning with the big member states – isn't a viable option for the Netherlands either. Strong and close links with these states are crucial, but it would not be in the Dutch interest to identify itself with the big ones. Although important, the big member states should be seen as part of a wider game of coalition formation, in particular in a EU of 27.

Taking these considerations into account, the Netherlands has adopted a more flexible and open approach towards European integration, based on the following elements. It is still considered in the Dutch interest to have a rule- and institutions-governed system of cooperation and integration at the EU level. However, as a result of enlargement and institutional modifications (role of the European Council, co-decision, new forms of cooperation, etc.), this system has become much more complicated. Binding the big member states and not being marginalised are still important goals of Dutch EU policy. In this sense, size *does* matter to the Netherlands. But in day-to-day policies the emphasis clearly is on a process-oriented strategy: aimed at maximising influence on EU decision-making, by making optimal use of both the formal and informal dimensions of this process.

---

6   In other words, the veto can only be used by smaller member states in a restrictive and selective way.

It is, in other words, *a multiple-options and multiple-channels* approach towards the EU, aimed at all stages of the EU decision-making process; i.e. agenda-setting, coalition formation and negotiating.

One aspect of this approach is a reappraisal of the importance of *bilateral* relations on a capital-versus-capital level – not only with the big member states – in the framework of coalition formation.[7] This aspect must be seen in conjunction with the growing importance of an early pro-active involvement, in particular in the informal stages of the decision-making process, in order to shape and set the European agenda. This requires an early input on the basis of expertise and knowledge, both on the level of the member states and of the European institutions, in particular the Commission. Such a strategy of a mix of bilateralism and multilateralism was pursued *inter alia* during the negotiations on the EU's financial perspectives and the Lisbon Treaty. Being a net payer to the EU, the Netherlands had a clear interest in limiting its contribution to the EU and in restricting the EU's expenditures. To realise this, it cooperated very intensively in the framework of the group of net-payers in the EU. In the case of the Lisbon Treaty, the Dutch interest was to have a new treaty text which would be different from the text of the constitutional treaty. This required, in particular, a close relationship with the then EU presidency – Germany – and with France, being the other country that had rejected the constitutional treaty.

Compared to the 'real small member states', the Netherlands has in this respect a number of advantages. First, being a middle-sized country, it is less hampered by a lack of financial and administrative resources. Secondly, due to the fact that it has been a member since the start of the integration process, it has been able to build strong links with both most of the member states and with the European Commission, as well as other European institutions. Moreover, having been involved in EU decision-making for many years implies that it disposes of the experience and knowledge, which are necessary to act in a pro-active way. Finally, due to its position of not being a big member state but a middle-sized one, the Netherlands might prove to be a more attractive partner for some of the smaller member states and act as an honest broker or mediator in the EU. This final quality, of course, depends very much on its reputation within the EU; i.e. whether it is seen as a reliable partner.

Conclusion: Matching Ambitions, Capabilities and Domestic Support

The challenge for the Netherlands in the EU of today is to act strategically in a multi-actor environment (see also: Broman 2005). In this respect the challenge

---

7 Although the big member states have a higher priority on this bilateral policy, this does not mean that the aim is to develop a special partnership with those countries. The same applies to regional cooperation in the framework of the Benelux. In accordance with the principle of flexible coalitions, the bilateral cooperation is 'issue-dependent': 'the issue defines the coalition'.

the Netherlands is facing is not different from the challenge the average small member state has to cope with. However, one difference is that, contrary to 'real small member states', the Netherlands has not been able to adopt a policy of clear prioritisation and has to be more selective in its ambitions. In accordance with its self-image of a middle-sized EU member state and also reflecting its interest in various policy areas (ranging from market integration to environmental policies), the Netherlands always had and still has a very broad European agenda. One of the challenges is whether, in view of the increasing demands of EU decision-making in terms of administrative resources, the Netherlands will be able to maintain this level of ambitions. This question must also be seen in the context of a more critical domestic scene regarding the European Union. As a result of all this, the Netherlands – like many other member states – has become involved in a classical *two-level game*. On the one hand it is faced with the challenge to maximise its influence in an ever expanding EU, while on the other hand it has to convince a critical population at home of the need for and importance of European cooperation. Finding a balance between these two dimensions and dealing with the tensions and dilemmas they cause, is the real challenge for Dutch EU policy in the twenty-first century.

References

Broman, M. 2005. *Small State Influence in the European Union: 'Small State Smart State'?* Paper presented at the annual meeting of the ISA, Hawaii, March 2005.
Hanf, K. and Soetendorp, B. (eds) 1998. *Adapting to European Integration: Small States and the European Union*. London: Longman.
Keulen, M. van and Rood, J. 2003. The Netherlands Presidency of 1997: Between Ambition and Modesty, in *European Union Council Presidencies: A Comparative Perspective*, edited by O. Elgström. London/New York: Routledge, 71-86.
Magnette, P. and Nicolaïdis, K. 2003. Large and Small States in the European Union – Reinventing the Balance. *Research and European Issues*, 25. Paris: Notre Europe.
Panke, D. 2008. *The Influence of Small States in the EU: Structural Disadvantages and Counterstrategies*. University of Dublin: Dublin Institute Working Paper, 3, May.
Voorhoeve, J.J.C. 1979. *Peace, Profits and Principles*. The Hague/Boston/London: Martinus Nijhoff.
Wallace, W., Jacobsson, B., Kux, S., Andersen, S.S., Notermans, T., Sejersted, F. and Hagen, K. 1999. *Between Autonomy and Influence: Small States and the European Union*. Oslo: Arena.
Wivel, A. 2009. From Small State to Smart State: Devising a Strategy for Influence in the European Union. Published in this volume.

Chapter 9
The Foreign Policy of Luxembourg

Jean-Marie Frentz

This chapter discusses the *why*, *who*, *how* and *what* of Luxembourg's foreign policy by focusing on three different levels of analysis: international structure, domestic factors and individuals. Foreign policy is defined as the 'capacity to make and implement policies abroad which promote domestic values, interests and policies' and encompasses the entirety of the international activities of a country. A shorthand definition describes foreign policy as 'the collective coping with the international environment' (Hill 2003: 39). Understanding a country's foreign policy therefore requires a comprehensive assessment and an evaluation of a country's external needs, internal realities and individual influences.

With a population of approximately 500,000 people and a territory of 2,586 km^2, Luxembourg has been an active and often influential player within the European Union (EU) since its inception and has, particularly after the end of the Cold War, become steadily more involved in international politics. It is fair to say that Luxembourg enjoys more international prestige and visibility today than at any other time since independence in 1839.

By what criteria do we judge whether or not Luxembourg is a small state? Most definitions of a small state can be traced back to three core criteria: substantial features, relational characteristics and perceived criteria (Geser 2001: 90). First, Luxembourg is substantially small in terms of the number of inhabitants and the area of its territory, but clearly a sovereign nation-state. Second, Luxembourg is also, according to the relational criterion a small country which poses no threat to its neighbours, but which can be put in a position in which it would be unable to resist external pressure or defend its independence. Third, smallness can also result from a country's internal or external perception which means that size is attributed externally or internally irrespective of a measurable relationship.

For Luxembourg relational smallness is a *raison d'être* of EU membership.[1] The attempt to protect Luxembourg from a possible new quest for hegemony by Germany marked the beginning of the European integration process. In particular, the comparatively small Benelux countries considered binding Germany's coal and steel production into a common structure under supranational control as an essential security guarantee.

---

1 On the relational concept of small states used in this book, see the discussion in Chapter 1.

Until the accession of Malta in 2004, Luxembourg had by far the smallest territory and population of any EU country, albeit contrasted to the country's disproportionately strong economy. For example, in 1950 Luxembourg produced more steel than Italy and the Netherlands in absolute terms (Baillie 1996: 18). Luxembourg's disproportionate economic weight has not changed and today the Luxembourgeois have, on average, the highest per capita GDP amongst the rich industrialised OECD countries (OECD 2007). Within the EU, Luxembourg has shown that it is capable of setting aside its own immediate interests in favour of the common interest. Luxembourg is also a member of the highly selective club of countries that spend more than 0.7 percent of their GNI on development cooperation. If wealth, acting in the common interest, or commitment to international development are used as criteria there is certainly nothing small about Luxembourg. Notwithstanding these examples that show that smallness lies in the eye of the beholder and depends on what criteria are applied, Luxembourg's self-perception is that of a small state.

Foreign Policy Determinants

Geopolitics

As is the case for all small states, Luxembourg's foreign policy is constrained by systemic factors. The defining foreign policy concern has traditionally been potential hostilities between France and Germany. As a then neutral country with powerful neighbours, Luxembourg learnt at a heavy cost during the World Wars, particularly the Second: that the balance of power does not necessarily protect, but can have devastating consequences. The geopolitical environment and history have combined to make Luxembourg highly aware of its vulnerability to the ambitions of external powers, and foreign policy is therefore especially concerned with minimising vulnerability.

Luxembourg has thus been a driving force behind European integration which is, together with the transatlantic alliance, seen as the best guarantee of sovereignty and security. More generally, the need to reduce vulnerability also explains Luxembourg's strong commitment to multilateralism and international law as a form of shelter. Rather than trying to construct a meaningful military force (like, for instance, Switzerland) that would draw on limited resources, Luxembourg embraced collective security by placing itself under the NATO security umbrella at the outset of the Cold War and actively promoted the EU as a peace project. At the same time, Luxembourg has consistently considered that European unity makes sense only in the context of a dynamic transatlantic relationship, and thus has traditionally pursued a pro-NATO, pro-US foreign policy.

Although Luxembourg finds itself today in a post-modern zone of democratic peace without immediate inter-state security threats (Cooper 2003), Luxembourg's basic foreign policy objective remains peaceful relations with its neighbours and, above all, avoidance of another, today most implausible, Franco-German armed conflict.

Economic Factors

Another key foreign policy objective is to maintain and enhance the country's prosperity by trade, promotion of business interests, and maintenance of its status as an actor of globalisation with one of the world's main financial centres for private banking and investment management.

International openness and economic integration into broader groupings can be expected from a small country with a small internal market and a need for external resources. Thus, protectionism was never an option and the country has sought to integrate into bigger markets by joining the German Zollverein (1842–1918), the Belgium-Luxembourg Economic Union (1921), the Benelux Customs Union (1944) followed by the Benelux Economic Union (1958) and the European Economic Community (1957). It comes as no surprise that Luxembourg alone was part of all these economic unions. Today, the country is a model of economic openness with the main economic sectors (banking, steel and telecommunications) operating in global markets and the rest of the industries export-oriented and dependent on foreign supplies. Each working day some 130,000 foreigners cross the borders to work in Luxembourg (OECD 2007). Luxembourg also promotes trade within the EU common market and in EU trade policy.

Political stability, easy access to other European centres, skilled multilingual staff, and a tradition of banking secrecy have contributed to the growth of the financial sector. The Luxembourg financial market provides more than one-third of the Government's tax revenue, although taxation of its activities is modest. Europe's largest investment fund industry, which is second only to the US, and a stock exchange contribute to Luxembourg being one of the largest financial centres in the world.

Luxembourg's decision-makers are well aware that the country's wealth enhances its international voice and can be seen as a major determinant of Luxembourg's foreign policy (Hey 2003: 75-94).

Multilateralism

Luxembourg has consistently based its foreign policy on active participation in multi-level cooperation, on the regional and international levels, and is a founding member of the EU, the Council of Europe, the OECD, the OSCE and the UN. Strongly engaged in the European integration process from the outset, Luxembourg has been described as possibly the most 'European' of EU member states (Asselborn 2006) and remains, by and large, a model of European integration (e.g. Lancelot 2008). Since the creation of the European Coal and Steel Community in 1952, successive governments have been convinced of the necessity and benefits of an integrated Europe in economic terms and regional stability. Hence, the country is today home, *inter alia*, to the judicial and some of the financial institutions of the EU. Luxembourg has a high standing as a member of the EU where its influence and prestige exceed what small size might indicate. The Union projects Luxembourg's voice and makes its international bargaining position much stronger.

While the EU has enhanced Luxembourg's participation in international politics, the EU mitigates many consequences of being a small state so that what appears at first sight like a reduction in sovereignty has in fact become an increase. Small countries have the same rights as large ones and the acquis communautaire provides legal security overseen by the European Court of Justice. Luxembourg, as a founding member of the European project, secured rights and benefits from 1957 that it would probably have difficulty obtaining today. This status might have played a role, when at the Nice Summit, the country successfully managed to hold on to its six seats in the European Parliament, a number disproportionately high compared to Luxembourg's relative population size. Its representation and voting rights actually make Luxembourg an 'over-equal-member-state' (Kirt and Waschkuhn 2001: 38). The country's leadership and bureaucracy benefit from an intimate knowledge of the EU's inner workings that comes from having joined at the outset. This has particularly enabled Luxembourg EU presidencies to leave their mark on the recent history of European integration.

To maintain and enhance its influence within the EU, Luxembourg seeks to keep EU institutions in the country *inter alia* by heavy investments in their infrastructure (e.g. Hansen 2008). Luxembourg governments have always sought to maintain the existing equilibrium within the European institutions and between big and small states within the EU, e.g. the Benelux countries collectively have the same number of votes in the European Council as any of the big four (Germany, France, the UK and Italy). Luxembourg governments have consistently advocated enlargement in the interest of consolidating peace and stability in Europe and promoting investment and trade.

Internationalism

Internationalism, the liberal idea that foreign policy must ultimately be formulated with moral ends and, if possible, means, has become a stronger determinant of the foreign policy of Luxembourg since the end of the Cold War. In a conducive environment of political and economic stability, the country has committed itself to and met such goals as the UN's target for official development assistance (ODA), contributions to European and NATO peace-keeping, crisis prevention and peace-building, humanitarian assistance, promotion of human rights and global environmental protection. Luxembourg intends to support these efforts by aspiring to a seat as a non-permanent member of the UN Security Council in 2013–2014 (e.g. Asselborn 2006).

Development cooperation programmes cement international solidarity and have become a marked component of Luxembourg's foreign policy. They help place the country on the international map (OECD 2008). Luxembourg is one of the very few rich countries that devote more than 0.7 percent of GNI to ODA. Having reached 0.92 percent in 2007, the country aims at an ODA level of 1 percent of GNI in the years to come. It urges its partners in the EU to increase their development commitments to ensure that the EU countries will honour their ambitious ODA targets set in 2005 under the Luxembourg presidency in response to the urgent need to step up efforts to achieve the Millennium Development Goals (Schiltz and Michel 2008). Luxembourg's internationalism is also marked by an increasing presence in the UN system and the adoption of the most ambitious greenhouse gas reduction target of any industrialised country under the Kyoto Protocol. The contributions to the Funds and Programmes of the UN have steadily increased and usually rank the country amongst the top 20 donors in absolute terms and amongst the leading ones in per capita terms. In 2009, Luxembourg holds the presidency of the Economic and Social Council of which it has been a member three times, and is member of the Executive Boards of UNESCO and UNHCR. At informal UN level, Luxembourg is amongst the 'Friends of the Alliance of Civilisations', the 'Friends of the Special Representative for Children and Armed Conflict', the 'Friends of the International Criminal Court' and the 'Friends of Climate Change'.

Since the end of the Cold War, Luxembourg has regularly taken part in peace-keeping operations, notably in former Yugoslavia (UNPROFOR, IFOR, SFOR and KFOR), in Lebanon (UNIFIL) and in Afghanistan (ISAF). In the framework of the EU's Security and Defense policy, Luxembourg has assumed its share of responsibility by participating in missions in former Yugoslavia, in the Democratic Republic of Congo, in Chad and in the Occupied Palestinian Territory.

Foreign Policy-Making

Who makes foreign policy and *how*? Sutton explains (1987: 7) that a small population and national territory does not necessarily coincide with a 'small-scale political system'. Luxembourg is a case in point: it has a parliamentary democracy, a developed bureaucratic structure, stable institutions and economy, together with the Luxembourg model of tripartite social partnership (Lorig and Hirsch 2008). A discussion of foreign policy-making can, however, not be limited to domestic factors such as the role of bureaucracy, institutions, public opinion and individuals in shaping it, but also needs to take the European context into account. Furthermore, the country's wealth is also influencing foreign policy-making: indeed, hardly anybody would disagree that Luxembourg's foreign policy in fostering economic development through EU integration, foreign investment opportunities and trade has been successful.

Population, Public Opinion, Pressure Groups and Domestic Politics

The Luxembourgeois share a rather strong social cohesion, national identity and sense of vulnerability. This leads to cross-party consensus on foreign policy goals and relatively widespread agreement on international matters. Major controversies as a result of foreign policy remain unusual, but can occur as the debates in the run-up to the US-led war in Iraq showed (e.g. Wort 2003). Politicians and the wider population are largely aware that any bitter division on foreign policy could further weaken the already small voice of Luxembourg in international politics.

Business groups influence foreign policy-making through their close contact with government which would avoid taking an international decision going against strong business interests. Similarly, trade unions, traditionally linked to political parties, also understand that their interests are tied to the success of private international business and generally support government foreign policy decisions on that basis. Most NGOs which are often dependent on government funding also seek consensus or at least avoidance of confrontation with government policy.

Hey (2003: 87) notes that 'despite a strong democratic structure, the influence of public opinion in Luxembourg is notably weak'. Although it is fair to say that the culture of debate on foreign policy issues has traditionally been rather weak, public opinion exists on certain issues and can at times express itself forcefully, a case in point being the strong mobilisation of the public against the war in Iraq. A remarkable drifting apart between public opinion and decision-makers has surfaced at the occasion of the referendum on the European constitution in 2005. Although some 43 percent of the voters were against the adoption of the document, 55 out of 60 members of the parliament voted in favour of it. While public opinion remains one of the most pro-European, polls in recent years show increasing indifference and loss of interest in the EU. It appears that the verifiable advantages of Luxembourg's membership in the EU have, for one reason or another, not convinced all citizens of the benefit of further European integration and/or enlargement.

For Luxembourg, as for most small states in Europe, national political peculiarities seemingly tend to enhance the country's influence at the EU level. Katzenstein (1985) argues that the close economic ties and resulting economic openness that small countries have with their neighbours have promoted the formation of corporatist decision-making structures. Competition does not form the core of societal discourse but the permanent search for political consensus does. Therefore, readiness and willingness to compromise and to negotiate decisions are more pronounced in small Luxembourg than, for instance, in big France or Britain. It would appear then that the ability to reach national political consensus benefits Luxembourg within the decision-making mechanisms of EU institutions which by definition rely upon the balancing of interests and the actors' willingness to compromise.

Foreign Policy-Making in the EU

Luxembourg maintains a high diplomatic presence in the EU, especially within the European Council, where member states have the same representation. The country's foreign policy is tightly linked to EU policies, particularly the Common

Foreign and Security Policy (CFSP) with its main goal of spreading peace, security and prosperity beyond the EU's borders. The EU's common positions in external relations form the basis of Luxembourg's policy towards other regions, international players and thematic challenges. As a member of the Council of the EU, the country contributes to the definition of common policies and thus enhances its influence. Luxembourg officials participate in some 250 working groups in Brussels which prepare Council decisions.

Not least because of its disproportionately strong economy, Luxembourg's political influence within the European decision-making structures by far exceeds the numerical weight of its votes and seats in various bodies (Baillie 1998). How can this influence be explained? Empirical studies reveal that smallness can be an ideal condition for assertiveness in EU decision-making procedures. Luxembourg's economic weight is only one of a number of possible factors influencing negotiations on a level playing field with the large states; national cultural particularities and the special working mechanisms of EU institutions are other explanatory factors. Moreover, many politicians from Luxembourg and other small countries have mastered remarkable skills and abilities to search for compromise (von Steinsdorff 2005).

Given the pluralistic, supranational decision-making structures of the EU, there is room for astute political initiatives. Research suggests that small states benefit from the model of supranational integration in decision-making precisely because of their relative or perceived inferiority compared to the large states. Joenniemi (1998: 62) even argues that small country size is an essential prerequisite for successfully influencing European politics so that 'small could indeed become a synonym for smart in the post-Cold War era'.

Small Foreign Policy Administration

Luxembourg's foreign policy executive suffers from chronic overstretch, and even more so during an EU presidency. A foreign ministry with slightly more than 200 staff members can hardly have the same overview and cumulated expertise as for instance the Quai d'Orsay with around 9,400 employees (Hocking and Spence 2005). This translates into a more modest geographical outreach of Luxembourg's diplomatic network (Wurth 2006: 221). Luxembourg's foreign policy priorities have been set at the European level, for vital economic interests, particularly in the areas of finance and tax. The modest foreign representation, that functions without having an in-house analysis and planning unit at its disposal, suggests reserve, prudence and low profile in foreign relations, which make 'go it alone' initiatives rather unlikely. It further suggests that Luxembourg takes part in many decision-making processes as low-key participant.

Small size also gives the non-politicised administration a number of advantages. Internal communication links between departments are short with few administrative layers to confound communication and support relationships with relative ease (Baillie 1998: 196). Politicians and officials tend to know each other personally, resulting in trust and considerable autonomy in decision-making. In order to be influential, representatives from smaller national administrations also need to build closer than usual friendships and working arrangements with their counterparts from larger countries (Hearl 2006: 52).

Luxembourg's foreign policy can rely on existing EU structures to do much of the diplomacy it would otherwise have to do itself. Together with the career-official structure of the public administration, it is the longevity of political leaders that brings continuity to the decision-making process and facilitates the development of relations of confidence which are so crucial in diplomacy. The executive also enjoys a relatively supportive parliament which rarely raises impasses. Hey (2003: 92) has argued that the state's small administration makes foreign policy close to that of a rational actor, one that makes rational decisions based on preference ranking and value maximisation.

Individuals

Individuals have influenced Luxembourg's foreign and, in particular, European policy-making (Trausch 2006). Moreover, ministers often serve their country for a long time. The last five prime ministers' average period of office was over 23 years with over ten years as head of government (Trausch 2006). Similarly, ministers of foreign affairs tend to exercise for more than one five-year mandate. The personal imprint on foreign policy by an individual can be strong. Gaston Thorn was arguably the first individual who as foreign (1969–1980) and prime minister (1974–1979) was able to raise the profile of Luxembourg's diplomacy and to enable it to play a more active role in international politics (Hirsch 2008: 334). The credibility of politicians from Luxembourg at the European stage has allowed two amongst them to become presidents of the European Commission: Gaston Thorn (1981–1985) and Jacques Santer (1995–1999). Today, as prime minister, Jean-Claude Juncker's foreign policy skills make him a leading European diplomat and, as the EU's longest-serving head of government, he has the reputation of a reliable interlocutor, combining linguistic and negotiating skills with dogged Europeanism. These characteristics made him a crucial mediator in negotiations that led to the European Stability and Growth Pact in 1997 and to its revision in 2005 under Luxembourg presidency. The prime minister and other ministers involved in international affairs have become masters of public diplomacy and of what Putnam (1988) called the two-level game, i.e. the ability of decision-makers to simultaneously play on the international and the domestic chessboards. Luxembourg's small foreign policy administration permits a political leader with initiative and expertise to assume a great deal of influence over the foreign policy-making process and particularly the EU gives leading politicians levels of attention and recognition on the international stage that they would scarcely get otherwise.

Foreign Policy Behaviour

What long-term strategies, patterns of conduct, and changes can be perceived?

Luxembourg's foreign policy makers enjoy clarity and consensus in prioritising and pursuing the main foreign policy goals (Hey 2003: 77). As stated, choosing priorities, maintaining excellent relations with neighbours, strengthening and relying on the EU, promoting economic openness and being committed to multilateralism and internationalism are the main tenets of Luxembourg's foreign policy behaviour.

Luxembourg is not different from other countries in the sense that it wants to maintain peace, security and prosperity, even though the means it is able to apply to achieve these basic objectives are necessarily different from larger nations. Luxembourg can be at once influential and non-threatening, able to exert influence without power (Hirsch 1976). As a Benelux country, and co-founder of the European Communities, as a source of politicians, diplomats and mediators, its influence is undeniable (Campbell 2000: 8). Without coercive military power, Luxembourg uses the power of attraction or soft power (Nye 2004), i.e. leading by example (strong economy, internationalism, commitment to European integration) and diplomatic skills. However, it has to wisely choose the issues on which it attempts to exert influence. This behaviour is reflected by a case-by-case pragmatism.

The common thread running through Luxembourg's foreign policy behaviour is that the country wants to make the most of what it has. Wealth certainly helps in this endeavour and allows Luxembourg to provide foreign aid, to work on international issues within the EU and the UN, to contribute to regional diplomacy and to act as an international cultural centre.

Promotion of a Rules-Based Multilateralism and Internationalism

For Luxembourg, security and prosperity depend on an effective multilateral system. Luxembourg considers its foreign policy activities as contributing to a stronger international society, well-functioning international institutions and a rules-based international order.

Remain an 'Over-Equal Member State' of the EU

Successes achieved during Luxembourg's EU presidencies owed much to the close working relationship with the European Commission and to commitment of the presidency team to conciliation and compromise. Luxembourg wants to remain a fully fledged member of the Union and will not allow its membership to be downgraded by others (Schmit 2004: 17).

Luxembourg therefore finds itself obliged to constantly prove the reliability and worth of its contribution. The rotating presidencies illustrate its skill of diplomacy. Luxembourg discharged its responsibilities well in 1985, 1991 and 1997 with the adoption of the Single European Act, the intergovernmental conference that was later to be concluded at Maastricht, and the implementation of an employment and enlargement policy (Hirsch 2004: 3). During its 11th and most recent presidency in 2005, Luxembourg, *inter alia*, reached agreement on revision of the Stability and Growth Pact, prepared the basis for the financial perspectives 2007–2013, secured signature of the accession treaties of Bulgaria and Romania, and brokered the EU 15 commitment to spend 0.7 percent of GNI for ODA by 2015.

In principle, Luxembourg will support strengthening of the Commission's supranational responsibilities even at the expense of national sovereignty. Luxembourg trusts that the Commission as the 'guardian of the treaties' and with its 'right of initiative' will facilitate a fair balance of interests between large and small members. Support of EU interests can serve national interests better than attempting to pursue issues individually, which would, in any case, have little chance of success and be much riskier.

Luxembourg conforms to the general direction of European politics, which is usually in line with its own choices. Only in one area, it had to fight hard to preserve one of the foundations of its economic success: banking secrecy. In 1989, the country used its power of veto for the first and so far last time, to prevent (together with the UK) the introduction, at European level, of taxation on savings. Although a withholding tax is now gradually being introduced, the country has shown 'resilience' and may prevent the automatic exchange of information between tax authorities which would mean the end of banking secrecy. Luxembourg accepts the European solutions only on condition that Switzerland and other competing European banking markets submit strictly subjected to the same laws, but has conceded at the June 2000 ECOFIN Council that its position might evolve 'in light with international developments'. Above all, Luxembourg, together with others, has preserved the principle of unanimity in fiscal matters (FAZ 2004). In parallel, Luxembourg has been consistently involved in favour of a balanced development between economic and social integration. It regularly pleads for a strengthening of European social policy in the interest of greater social cohesion (Feyder 2007).

Acting with Selectivity as a Skilful Negotiator and Broker

It has been explained that the country's small size creates a perception of weakness that translates into a strategic opportunity for successfully conducting negotiations (Baillie 1998). Moreover, other states are more likely to grant requests and be sympathetic to proposals from Luxembourg which are never the result of pressure or threats. There is also generally less political bargaining involved in issues put forward by Luxembourg than in those put forward by a bigger country (Hey 2003: 84). Luxembourg's 'natural' role as a broker between the member states, facilitated by its privileged geographical position between France and Germany, remains a permanent and strong feature of its foreign policy behaviour. This role does not at all contradict the teachings of Joseph Bech, a former prime minister (1926–1937 and 1953–1958) who advised: 'When you have a good idea, find a bigger state to sponsor it and then keep quiet' (*The Times* 2007).

To negotiate successfully, absolute size or power is less important than the perception of the negotiation options by all parties involved: a paradox from which Luxembourg benefits. Precisely because they are considered weak, Luxembourg diplomats sometimes gain negotiation power which cannot be explained simply on the basis of objective factors (Baillie 1998: 202). Luxembourg has asserted its position in a few cases where its national interests were not in harmony with those of the rest. Characteristically, small states take action selectively – then, however, with a high level commitment and success (Thorhallsson 2000: 53). Luxembourg's willingness to compromise on numerous other issues increases the acceptance by the larger states, engaged in all issues, of the few but skilfully defended requests. On numerous occasions, this behaviour has put the country forward as a mediator, and created a conducive atmosphere of negotiation (Hirsch 2008: 333).

Being Open to Alliances

Belgium has traditionally been Luxembourg's closest ally and the Belgium-Luxembourg Economic Union was strengthened in 2002 to also cover political questions. The two governments meet twice a year and the scope of the areas covered by Benelux has been widened by the signature of a follow-up treaty in June 2008. Benelux heads of government meet before every European Council meeting to determine common positions, particularly when it comes to negotiating a new treaty. Luxembourg also enters into different alliances which are issue-specific or in case it has to take sides. For instance, on matters relating to the liberalisation of transport, Luxembourg votes with France and Belgium, reflecting a cautious approach to the privatisation of public services, whereas when it comes to financial markets, Luxembourg has a more liberal view and usually votes with the UK against a potentially protectionist approach (Schmit 2004: 16).

Yet, since the 1990s, and particularly under the premiership of Jean-Claude Juncker from 1995, foreign and European policy has become more pro-active and more clearly aligned with France, Germany, and to a lesser extent Belgium, while at times opposing positions taken by the Netherlands. This became clear before the Iraq war when Luxembourg joined opponents to military intervention; a reversal of Luxembourg's foreign policy, traditionally in line with the US on strategic and military matters. At the height of the American-led coalition's war against Iraq in April 2003, Luxembourg also agreed to take part in a meeting discussing European security policy together with the leaders of Germany, Belgium and France, which was ridiculed by some as the 'Pralinengipfel' and considered as an affront by the US administration. Jean-Claude Juncker considered this initiative essential to give Europe a credible security and defence policy, for diplomatic action would be effective only if it could rely on civil and military capacity. Moreover, when a ground-breaking European initiative, like calling for the creation of a 'European Security and Defence Union' is taken, Luxembourg must be on board (Juncker 2003). Equally, in 2003, the position taken by Luxembourg was essential to avoid a deficit hearing being held against Germany and France, because of their infringement of the Stability and Growth Pact, whereas other small countries like the Netherlands or Austria were in favour of such a hearing.

Some Challenges

While Luxembourg has pursued European integration to advance its own goals and influence, EU enlargement can jeopardise its protected status and limit room for special arrangements that suit the country. At least some of the 20 other small EU member states may well want to imitate Luxembourg's model. However, Luxembourg seeks to ensure that it will not be forced to give up privileges that others would continue to enjoy (Campbell 2000: 8) and, therefore, a creative niche policy should remain possible. Furthermore, it is in Luxembourg's interest that a strong European Commission maintains its position in the equilibrium of institutions to promote the general interest of the Union and to take the necessary initiatives to pursue this goal. It cannot be excluded that the creation of the position of a President of the European Council, as foreseen by the Lisbon Treaty, could potentially undermine the position of the President of the Commission, and lead to larger member states gaining power at the expense of smaller ones.

According to the national Economic and Social Council, a consultative body, Luxembourg needs a medium-term, pro-active European strategy to identify and address questions of national interest at an early stage of the EU decision-making process (Conseil Économique et Social 2004: 6). More generally, the international system demands a perpetual awareness of the outside world and therefore an active diplomacy (Hill 2003). This means responsiveness to international challenges, the ability to create new alliances, also with other small states, the launching of initiatives and the assumption of responsibility to improve international cooperation.

Given that the country's economy is heavily dependent on a few globalised economic sectors, it remains exposed to global economic shocks which could, in turn, have an impact on foreign policy behaviour. While the space to manoeuvre on national economic policy is becoming narrower as a result of globalisation and economic liberalisation (Hilgert 2008), it appears that Luxembourg's economy is not immune to global downturn and as a consequence faces domestic challenges of economic recession and ensuing unemployment. Therefore, in order to reduce economic vulnerability, a diversification policy has to be resolutely implemented.

Conclusion

In spite of Luxembourg's small size, limited resources and military weakness, the country has managed to establish a respectable position in European and international politics.

Many factors contribute to explaining the *why*, *who*, *how* and *what* of the foreign policy of Luxembourg. At the system level, geopolitical position and small status set the foundation which explains Luxembourg's support for European integration and multilateralism. The strongest determinants are found at the system level, and much of Luxembourg's foreign policy efforts focus on that level, although this level can only be influenced to a limited extent.

At the state level, the strong Luxembourg economy explains Luxembourg's efforts to maintain its status as a global financial centre and successful actor of globalisation. The country's wealth and stability also make it easier to achieve national consensus in the policy-making process.

At the individual level, the role played by leading politicians has certainly contributed to a more assertive diplomacy, while circumstances such as the end of the Cold War, European integration together with stable economy and democracy have created a conducive environment for politicians from Luxembourg to stand out.

It is largely because of the EU, as the most successful regional organisation in the world, that Luxembourg could enhance its international voice. Being a small state does not hinder Luxembourg from pursuing its own foreign policy objectives by using the means it has at its disposal. Because of its survival as a sovereign state with a specific history and geography, the pooling of sovereignty in the EU, economic resources and rational decision-making, the small state is able to conduct a confident foreign policy at European and international levels.

References

Asselborn, J. 2006. Beitrag zu konsequentem Multilateralismus. Ein Gespräch mit Jean Asselborn über Luxemburgs Außenpolitik. *Luxemburger Wort*, 21 November. Available at: http://www.mae.lu/mae.taf?IdNav=2717 [accessed: 29 July 2008].

Baillie, S. 1996. The Seat of the European Institutions: An Example of Small State Influence in European Decision-Making. *EUIAS Working Paper RSC*, 96(28). Florence: European University Institute.

Baillie, S. 1998. The Position of Small States in the EU, in *Small States Inside and Outside the European Union: Interests and Policies*, edited by L. Goetschel. Dordrecht: Kluwer Academic Publishers, 193-205.

Campbell, J. 2000. Luxembourg: A Small Country in a Large Organisation – A Comparision of the Role of Luxembourg in the Benelux Union and European Union, in *Essays on Politics, Language and Society in Luxembourg*, edited by G. Newton. New York: Mellen Press, 1-8.

Conseil Économique et Social, 2004. *Avis sur L'Évolution Économique, Sociale et Financière du Pays*. Luxembourg.

Cooper, R. 2003. *The Breaking of Nations: Order and Chaos in the Twenty-First Century*. London: Atlantic Books.

FAZ, 2004. Die Mitgliedstaaten bleiben die Herren der Steuerpolitik. *Frankfurter Allgemeine Zeitung*, 7 September.

Feyder, J. 2007. Le rôle du Luxembourg en Europe et dans le monde. *En Question – Revue du Centre AVEC*, 81(June), 25-8.
Geser H. 2001. Was ist eigentlich ein Kleinstaat?, in *Kleinstaaten-Kontinent Europa: Probleme und Perspektiven*, edited by R. Kirt and A. Waschkuhn. Baden-Baden: Nomos, 89-124.
Hansen, J. 2008. Machine de guerre. *D'Lëtzebuerger Land*, 18 July, 8-9.
Hearl, D. 2006. The Luxembourg Presidency: Size isn't Everything. *Journal of Common Market Studies*, 44(Annual Review), 51-5.
Hey, J.A.K. 2003. Luxembourg: Where Small Works (and Wealthy Doesn't Hurt), in *Small States in World Politics*, edited by J.A.K. Hey. Boulder: Lynne Rienner, ch. 5, 75-94.
Hilgert, R. 2008. It's NO, Mr. Mittal! *D'Lëtzebuerger Land*, 8 August, 11.
Hill, C. 2003. What is to be Done? Foreign Policy as a Site for Political Action. *International Affairs*, 79(2), 233-55.
Hirsch, M. 1976. Influence without Power: Small States in European Politics. *The World Today*, 32, 116-17.
Hirsch, M. 2004. Luxembourg at the Helm: Experience, Determination and Self-denial. *Notre Europe: Studies and Research*, 37. Available at: http://www.notre-europe.eu/uploads/tx_publication/Etud37-en.pdf [accessed: 29 July 2008].
Hirsch, M. 2008. Luxemburg und die europäische Integration, in *Das politische System Luxemburgs,* edited by W.H. Lorig and M. Hirsch. Wiesbaden: VS Verlag für Sozialwissenschaften, 330-43.
Hocking, B. and Spence D. 2005. Towards a European Diplomatic System? *Netherlands Institute of International Relations: Clingendael Discussion Papers in Diplomacy*, 98. Available at http://www.clingendael.nl/publications /2005/20050600_cli_paper_dip_issue98.pdf [accessed: 29 July 2008].
Joenniemi, P. 1998. From Small to Smart: Reflections on the Concept of Small States. *Irish Studies in International Affairs*, 9, 61-2.
Juncker, J.C. 2003. Interview avec le Premier ministre Jean-Claude Juncker au sujet de la défense européenne. *RTL Top Thema*, 29 April, Available at: http://www.gouvernement.lu/salle_presse/interviews/2003/04/20030429juncker_rtl/index.html [accessed: 29 July 2008].
Katzenstein, P.J. 1985. *Small States in World Markets: Industrial Policy in Europe*. Ithaca and London: Cornell University Press.
Kirt R. and Waschkuhn A. (eds) 2001. *Kleinstaaten-Kontinent Europa: Probleme und Perspektiven*. Baden-Baden: Nomos.
Lancelot, A. 2008. Passé, présent et avenir de la construction de l'Europe: le point de vue de l'opinion publique européenne, in *L'Etat de l'Union: Rapport Schuman sur l'Europe*. Paris: Lignes de Repères, 21-33.
Lorig, W.H. and Hirsch, M. (eds) 2008. *Das politische System Luxemburgs*. Wiesbaden: VS Verlag für Sozialwissenschaften.
Nye, J.S. Jnr. 2004. *Soft Power: The Means of Success in World Politics*. Cambridge, MA: Public Affairs.
OECD, 2007. *Examens territoriaux de l'OCDE: Luxembourg*. Paris: OECD.

OECD, 2008. *Luxembourg DAC Peer Review: Main Findings and Recommendations*. Paris: OECD. Available at: www.oecd.org/dac/ peerreviews/Luxembourg [accessed: 29 July 2008].
Putnam, R.D. 1988. Diplomacy and Domestic Politics: The Logic of Two-Level Games. *International Organization*, 42, Summer, 427-60.
Schiltz, J.L. and Michel, L. 2008. En 2007, l'aide publique au développement a baissé. *Le Figaro*, 4 April.
Schmit, N. 2004. Die Präsidentschaft präsidiert: Nicolas Schmit zum Programm der Präsidentschaft. *Forum*, 242, December, 14-18.
Steinsdorff, von, S. 2005. EU-Kleinstaaten: Motoren der Integration? *Aus Politik und Zeitgeschichte*, 46, 23-30.
Sutton, P. 1987. Political Aspects, in *Politics, Security and Development in Small States*, edited by C. Clarke and T. Payne. London: Allen and Unwin, 3-25.
Thorhallsson, B. 2000. *The Role of Small States in the European Union*. Aldershot: Ashgate.
The Times, 2007. Gaston Thorn: Luxembourg's Honest Broker President of the European Commission, 28 August.
Trausch, G. 2006. *Von Bech zu Juncker: Luxemburg's Beitrag zur Union*. 9 May. Available at: www.gouvernement.lu/dossiers/viepol/karlspreis/discours_ trausch/ index.html [accessed: 29 July 2008].
Wort, 2003. Irak-Krise: Glasklare Linie oder Schlingerkurs? *Luxemburger Wort*, 26 February. Available at: www.gouvernement.lu/salle_presse/Interviews/ 20030225juncker/ [accessed: 29 July 2008].
Wurth, H. 2006. La Politique étrangère du Luxembourg. *La Revue Internationale et Stratégique*, 61, 217-27.

Chapter 10
Slovakia and the Czech Republic in the European Integration Process: Birds of a Feather Flying Apart?

Mats Braun

Introduction

In this chapter I look at the Czech Republic and Slovakia, two countries that despite their common Czechoslovak origin have adapted widely different strategies when it comes to questions related to the future of the European Union and institutional matters. The difference in the countries' approaches to the EU can be illustrated by how further steps in the integration process have been approached after accession. Slovakia was positive to the Constitutional Treaty, quick to ratify the Lisbon Treaty, with only insignificant internal opposition and made the early introduction of the euro a priority. The opinion of the political elite in the Czech Republic, on the contrary, has been split on the proposed treaty revisions and failed to make the euro a priority.

Based on the relational understanding of smallness (Mouritzen and Wivel 2005; Thorhallsson and Wivel 2006; Chapter 1 in this volume), I argue that the Slovakian political elite has accepted more fully that it is the weaker part in an asymmetric relationship with the other EU member states than the Czech one has. This has little to do with the fact that Slovakia has approximately 5.4 million inhabitants compared to the 10.4 million of its western neighbour. Rather this is caused primarily by the Slovak experiences in the 1990s of a bumpy road to EU membership and the country's newly-gained independence. This acceptance of being small has in turn manifested itself in a strong interest in maintaining a pro-European image of Slovakia, both internationally as well as domestically.

The Czech's more divided and reserved approach can be understood as a consequence of the transition period of the 1990s, which made the Czech political elite more self-confident of being an equal partner *vis-à-vis* the existing EU member states, and the country's history provided an argument for the country's rightful place in the club of more prosperous European countries. The EU-reluctant part of the Czech political elite wants to see the EU develop towards a more intergovernmental Union. This seems to contradict the conventional wisdom of the literature in the field that suggests that small states favour an institutionalisation of interstate relations in regional politics (Thorhallsson and Wivel 2006: 655).

In the first part I will briefly outline the two countries' road to EU accession and how they have positioned themselves regarding three questions on further steps of integration; i.e. the two proposed treaty revisions and membership of the third stage of the EMU. In the second part I shall explain these different approaches by focusing on the political elites in the two countries.

Slovakia and the Czech Republic: Two Different Approaches to the European Union

After the break-up of Czechoslovakia in 1993, Slovakia and the Czech Republic entered the road to EU membership as independent countries. During the membership negotiations we can see these countries as being the weaker parts in an asymmetric relationship with the then EU member states, especially the small states, in two ways. First, like all candidate countries they were the ones wanting something from the EU and thus not equal partners, but rather the weaker partners in an asymmetric relationship (cf. Vachudova 2005). Second, in contrast to the only clearly 'big' candidate country, in terms of population size, Poland, there was a plausible scenario of the EU enlarging without these two countries (Szczerbiak 2001). This was in particular true for Slovakia that was excluded from the first group of candidate countries at the Luxembourg summit in 1997. This was an experience that actually made Slovakia an even 'smaller' country than it already was in relation to the EU-15 and also compared to the Czech position.

The Slovakian experience of 1997 was especially painful because both the governing regime and the majority of the voters remained firmly committed to EU membership (Rupnik 2003: 28). The Slovakian failure, thus, was not caused by any public Euroscepticism. The government actually did little to challenge the EU in its rhetoric and remained committed to membership as did the majority of Slovak voters. Yet it failed to take the actions necessary to get a green light for continuing membership negotiations (Vachudova 2005: 159).

In fact, despite Slovakia's more complicated road to EU membership, the political elite did even less to challenge essential parts of the EU project than did their Czech counterparts. In both countries, prior to EU accession, all relevant political forces remained committed to EU membership, with the exception of the Czech communists and the extreme nationalists in Slovakia. A major difference between the countries was that in the Czech Republic, one of the two major parties in the country, the Civic Democratic Party (ODS), did coin the term 'Eurorealism', to underline its critical stand towards European integration. They did, however, not challenge Czech EU membership.[1] In Slovakia as consequence of the Luxembourg Council decision, there was an increase in Euroscepticism but only for a very

---

1   In the vocabulary of Aleks Szczerbiak and Paul Taggart the ODS approach could be described as a case of 'soft-Euroscepticism' (for a definition see, Szczerbiak and Taggart 2008: 8; see also Hanley 2008: 258).

limited period. The Slovak Euroscepticism has in general been restricted to two smaller political parties: primarily the Slovak National Party (SNS) (outspokenly only after the 1998 election) and the Slovak Workers Association (ZRS) (which however lost political relevance in the late 1990s). No major political party in Slovakia took on a similar critical position similar to the one taken by the Czech ODS.

The more critical stand of the ODS as a major party has been reflected in the Czech approach to further steps of integration. As a consequence, the Czech political elite was divided and more reluctant in their attitude at the Convention on the Future of Europe, as well as later in their position on the ratification of the Constitutional Treaty, the Lisbon Treaty and on the introduction of the euro.

At the Convention on the Future of Europe, even if on some issues both countries took a typical small state position, e.g. they were reluctant towards any limitations of the rotating presidency and wanted to protect the principle of one country one commissioner (Bilcik 2003: 96; cf. Thorhallsson and Wivel 2006: 662), there were clear differences between the two countries. Slovakia in general supported further integration with the major exception in the field of tax harmonisation and social policy where state sovereignty was considered crucial (Malová et. al. 2005: 18). The Czech delegates, on the other hand, held diverting views on most essential questions regarding the future treaty, such as the inclusion of the Charter of Fundamental Rights, the use of the term constitution, etc. (cf. Kratochvíl and Königová 2005).

Slovakia was therefore also quick in having a positive vote on the Constitutional Treaty in the parliament in 2005; only a few MPs voted against it. The President did not, however, put his signature on the treaty to complete the ratification process. This has to be seen only as a consequence of the negative outcome of the referenda in France and in the Netherlands (EU-25 Watch 2006: 94). In the Czech Republic, the Constitutional Treaty, on the contrary, was the topic of an intense political debate. The ODS profiled itself as being strongly against the treaty, as did the country's president Václav Klaus[2] (e.g. ODS 2004). Despite general consensus, the treaty was never submitted to a referendum.

Regarding the Lisbon Treaty, the situation repeated itself. Slovakia ratified this treaty rather smoothly (except for the small Christian Democratic Party who rejected it). On the other hand, in the Czech Republic, even if the government now including the EU-critical ODS[3] came out in favour of the treaty, there was a strong opposition in both chambers of the parliament from ODS MPs. The treaty was first of all delayed and sent to the Constitutional Court following a request from ODS senators, and thereafter both chambers of the parliament postponed their vote

---

2   In office since 2003.
3   A coalition government including the ODS and two smaller pro-European parties; the Christian Democrats and the Greens.

several times. Finally, in Spring 2009, both chambers of the parliament ratified the treaty, yet it remains[4] uncertain when and if the president will ratify the treaty.

Another illustration of the two countries' different approaches to further integration after membership can be seen in their different attitude towards the introduction of the euro. Whereas Slovakia has been keen to adapt to the euro as soon as possible and introduced the currency in January 2009, the Czech Republic has adopted a more hesitant approach with key politicians (such as the prime minister and the president) questioning the importance of this project for the Czech Republic (e.g. *Právo* 22 September 2007; *Aktuálně.cz* 20 January 2008).

After having shown that further steps of integration after accession have been more challenged in the Czech Republic than in Slovakia the question is now how to explain these different approaches in the two former parts of Czechoslovakia. A possible hypothesis would suggest that the Slovak approach would correspond to a more pro-European public opinion, and the Czech approach, following the same logic, is a response to a more EU-reluctant opinion. After all, in several EU member states there is a conflict between the pro-European political elite and more EU-critical electorates (e.g. Falkner and Laffan 2005: 225-6). However, as I will argue, the differences in public opinion towards the EU in the two studied countries cannot really explain their different approaches.

Although the more pro-European approach of Slovakia is reflected in a more positive public opinion, the difference compared to the Czech Republic is not dramatic. If we look at the figures in the Eurobarometer after accession concerning the question whether EU membership is considered a 'good thing' in Slovakia, the support for EU membership has been slightly above EU average, whereas the opposite is true for the Czech Republic. Neither of the countries belongs to the five most pro-European or reluctant countries according to these figures.[5]

The pro-European electorate in Slovakia was clearly crucial in 1998 for punishing the Mečiar regime once the disparity between its rhetoric and its actual policy became obvious (cf. Vachudova 2005: 250). This might also be one reason why the bigger parties have avoided Euroscepticism as a strategy in Slovakia (Leška 2006: 255).Yet the differences in public opinion does little to explain why the Czech Republic has shown a more mixed attitude towards further steps of integration. Despite the fact that it is the big rightwing party in Czech politics that is EU-reluctant, the vast majority of rightwing voters is pro-European, which suggests that the party is not reacting to any public demand. For instance 64 percent of the rightwing voters consider EU membership a good thing whereas the same figure for leftwing voters is 39 percent (Eurobarometr 69, National Report

---

4 This still was the case when this paper was written in June 2009.

5 According to the Eurobarometer 69, 57 percent of the Slovaks consider EU membership a good thing compared to 48 percent of the Czechs. This pattern was reflected in opinion polls also prior to accession (Eurobarometer 69 2008: 24). In 2003 58 percent in Slovakia to 44 percent in the Czech Republic considered EU membership a good thing (Eurobarometer 2003. 4: 82 and 86).

2008). According to opinion polls, the support for the Lisbon Treaty was also bigger among the ODS voter than in the electorate at large (STEM 2008). It seems therefore that voters at best tolerate the ODS Eurorealism and that the coherent Euroscepticism of parts of the elite rather has influenced the public opinion than the other way around (see Hanley 2008: 248). Thus the differences in public opinion cannot explain the Czech's more reluctant approach. For this reason, the main focus in the following discussion is on differences in the political elites of the two countries.

Understanding the Differences

How can we then understand the more pro-European approach of the Slovak political elite and the more reluctant of the Czech? In the small state literature a rather substantial part of the work has been devoted to the Nordic countries (e.g. Arter 2000; Tiilikainen 2006). Some scholars have, as a consequence, compared the Slovak integration strategy to the Finnish small state approach, considered to be a good European approach (see Malová et al. 2005).[6]

If Slovakia could be compared to Finland then a parallel between the Czech Republic and Sweden might not be too farfetched. Sweden, a country only slightly smaller than the Czech Republic, has allegedly found it harder to adapt to a small state identity (Tiilikainen 2006: 70) and the country has been described as a 'reluctant late-comer to Europe' (Trädgårdh 2002: 130). Yet there is nothing to indicate that it is the actual size (i.e. around 10 million inhabitants) that makes these two countries reluctant to a small state identity. Still, there might be one similarity between Sweden and the Czech Republic. Lars Trädgårdh argues that Swedish EU reluctance can to a large degree be explained by a self-perception based on 'being better' than Europe (2002: 131). The Czech self-perception is not based on 'being better' than Europe, but there is a similarity in perceiving the own state as relatively strong (in the Czech case, only as strong compared to the other new post-communist member states and understood in a relational sense *vis-à-vis* the old member states) (see Braun 2008a).

In the Czech case, which I will explain more in detail below, two explanations for the perceived stronger Czech position compared to the Slovak one seem in particular valid. First of all, the initial success of transition made the political elite self-confident regarding early Czech accession. Secondly, the time of the first Republic of Czechoslovakia in the interwar period is perceived as positive; it is seen as the time when the country allegedly belonged to the group of more prosperous European countries. However, we will first, analyse the Slovak case in more detail.

---

6 For a clarifying discussion on the Finnish approach see Tiilikainen (2006).

Slovakia: Increased Awareness of Being the Weaker Part of an Asymmetric Relationship

So far we have established that Slovakia has adopted after the enlargement a more positive approach on several crucial questions regarding continued integration than the Czech Republic. Despite the many commonalities shared by the two countries regarding their motives for joining the EU: i.e. economic, security and idealistic reasons (e.g. Vachudova 2005), two differences are particularly notable. First of all, the fact that it was Slovakia that broke away from the common federation. Secondly, Slovakia had a bumpier road to EU accession.

Starting with the first of these differences, Slovakian politicians used EU membership as an argument to making the breaking-up of Czechoslovakia seem a less dramatic event and to assure the legitimacy of the new state. Some even argued that the separation was a precondition for a smoother integration of the two nations into the EU. The last Czechoslovak foreign minister, the Slovak Jozef Moravčík, explained it in the following way:

> We do not carry out the transformation of Slovakia into an independent state with the intention of isolating it. On the contrary, we do it in order to contribute to the process of international co-operation as a sovereign unit (quote cited by Kopecky and Učen 2003: 165).

The Slovakian political elite needed to advocate the creation of the Slovak state in this way, since it was not obvious that they had popular support for independence among their own electorate. As it happened, the people did not get the opportunity to have a say in the matter with a referendum, nor did any of the bigger parties propagate the complete dissolution of Czechoslovakia during the parliamentary elections in 1992 (Wolchik 1995: 240). Thus, at the time of separation, the Slovakian political elite needed to assure its population that the end of Czechoslovakia would not be the beginning of an isolated Slovakia. Some even took the argument one step further and suggested that in particular in the period of EU accession, it would be better to have an independent state, and, thus, have the possibility to participate as an equal partner at the European table than to be merely a region within a country (Čarnogurský 2008: 19).[7]

However, Slovakia started off in a much weaker geopolitical and economic position than its newly-created Western neighbour. Its geopolitical position was less favourable since at the time of independence the country did not border any EU member state,[8] and the eastern border with the Ukraine led to concerns regarding

---

7 This argument was also sometimes presented as a Czechoslovak argument. The natural alliance between Czechs and Slovaks would give them bigger influence in Europe as two countries than as one by increasing their number of votes in the Council and the Parliament (Čarnogurský 2008: 19).

8 The EU moved to the Slovak borders only after Austria's accession in 1995.

possible spreading of political instability (Leška 2006: 18). The Slovak economy was also in the early 1990s in a more difficult situation since most of the heavy industry during communist times was located in Slovakia and these industries faced serious problems during the economic transition (Senior-Nello 2003:123).

Therefore, there was a broad consensus among the political elite that the newly independent Slovakia had to head for EU membership as opposed to isolation. EU membership was, thus, a condition already at the time of the state's independence for its legitimacy. The future EU membership remained important to all successive governments of the country until accession. This became obvious when Vladimír Mečiar's regime (1994–1998) failed to meet the criteria for rapid EU membership. The government remained in its rhetoric firmly committed to EU membership and managed for a long period to ignore the repeated criticism of Slovakia in the EU demarches from 1995, 1996 and 1997. The EU criticism mainly targeted the authoritarian tendencies of Mečiar's regime, in particular the regime's lack of respect for the rule of law (Schimmelfennig et al. 2005: 35).

After the Luxembourg Council in 1997 and as a consequence of the exclusion from the group of forerunners for EU membership the Mečiar government, however, only briefly started to outspokenly criticise the EU (Vachudova 2005: 157-59). Prior to this event, only one of the two junior parties in the coalition, the Slovak Workers Association (ZRS), was a EU rejectionist, but this was never reflected in the statements of the government. The second junior partner of the coalition, the Slovak National Party (SNS), turned to Euroscepticism only after having been ousted from power.

Mečiar tried to brand Slovakia's exclusion as an act of Western unfairness, but this explanation was only accepted by his core voters. Mečiar's party, the Movement for a Democratic Slovakia (HZDS), in fact lost the support of the swing voters and failed to attract new voters. Among the core electorate, however, the voters increasingly turned to Euroscepticism (Vachudova 2005: 174-75). Once in opposition, after the election in 1998, Mečiar's party HZDS revised its European policies again and became more pro-European since Euroscepticism had turned out to be more of an obstacle than an asset for the party. This strategy seems to have been rather successful since the HZDS remained the largest party in the chamber of deputies until 2006 (Leška 2006: 255).

The Slovak political elite had to draw two lessons from the events of 1997–1998. Firstly, the country was seen as small and negligible in the eyes of the EU and, subsequently, an exclusion from the first wave of EU enlargement was a real possibility. The Mečiar regime tried to emphasise Slovakia's importance for the EU 15 by emphasising its special relationship with Russia, however without any great success (Kopecky and Učen 2003: 170-71). Secondly, it became obvious that EU's confirmation of domestic policies was important to the domestic legitimacy of governance. Opinion polls of that time showed that concerns for the future Slovak EU membership was one reason why a pro-European coalition could win the elections in 1998 (Schimmelfennig et al. 2005: 40).

The events of 1997–1998 illustrated that Slovakia was in a more vulnerable position compared to the Czech Republic. Slovakia also had other reasons for fearing isolation. The country was excluded from the first wave of NATO enlargement and became member only in 2004, whereas the Czech Republic entered NATO in 1999. Therefore Slovakia's membership in the OECD in 2000 was celebrated as a significant enhancement of international prestige of the country (Drulák 2005: 236). The OECD membership was also important for the centre-right government coalition of Mikuláš Dzurinda that came into power in 1998. His coalition won the elections, among others, by promising that Slovakia should enter again the road to EU membership and OECD membership was an important step towards this goal as well as a confirmation of the government's successful economic reforms (Leška 2006: 175).

However, EU membership was not only important in the sense that it would bring actual economic benefits to the population but also that it would confirm the successful end of the transformation process which in its initial stage was problematic. The new Slovak coalition government that took up office in 2006 and replaced the pro European Dzurinda coalition did not appear to be, at a first glance, a very pro-European government. In fact, the coalition between the Social Democratic SMER and the nationalist parties, SNS and the HZDS, sent a shockwave through Europe.[9] Especially, the fact that Mečiar's HZDS and the nationalist SNS were again involved in a government, even if this time as junior partners, led, among others, to the suspending of SMER's membership in the Party of European Socialists (PES).

Yet despite the doubts concerning the commitment of these parties to further integration, the government has remained committed to the rapid introduction of the euro and also to the ratification of the Lisbon Treaty. Commentators have pointed out that the EU treaty revisions have received surprisingly little public attention in Slovakia (Kořan 2007: 25-7). It is, of course, possible that a country fully engaged in catching up with other countries in the region would be little interested in discussing the nature of this union (Haugton and Malová: 2007: 73). However, even if this claim might be valid, this does not answer why the treaty revisions did not become a topic in Slovakia when the same was being addressed in the Czech Republic. Another hypothesis regarding the attitude of new EU member states is that once inside the club, when conditionality had lost its power, they would become more reluctant to further integration. This did not happen in Slovakia. One reason might be that left/nationalist parties of the since 2006 governing coalition had to have a strong interest in maintaining a pro European image due to its initial lack of credibility.

The Fico-led government also realised the introduction of the euro in Slovakia on the first of January 2009. There was some uncertainty regarding the euro since the SMER had earlier signalised that the date for the introduction of the euro could

---

9 As a matter of fact all three parties were considered Eurosceptic at one point in time (Malová et. al. 2005: 106-7).

be postponed to the time after the implementation of the necessary social reforms. The quick introduction of the euro could be seen as a confirmation for the strength of the business lobby, as argued by Tim Haughton and Darina Malová (2007: 73). Yet it could also be seen as a proof for the importance the current government attributed to international recognition. Even, if public opinion has been hesitant in accepting the euro (EU-27 Watch 2008: 244), the cabinet can use the introduction of the euro as recognition of a well performing Slovak economy. Moreover, this is a confirmation that Slovakia is not any more facing the risk of being excluded from the West, rather it has overtaken the Czech Republic in the competition of being more Western. The former Slovak Prime Minister Ján Čarnogurský (April 1991–June 1992) described it in the following way: 'If Slovakia is able to introduce the euro before the Czech Republic it means that Slovakia, for the first time in history, is more anchored in the West than the Czech Republic. Slovakia succeeded and reached this stage only 16 years after gaining independence (Čarnogurský 2008: 20).[10]

The Czech Republic: The Importance of Equality Between States

In the Czech case two explanations for the more diversified approach to further integration seem particularly valid: first, the initial success of transition which made the political elite self-confident regarding early Czech accession, and second, the heritage from the first Republic of Czechoslovakia in the interwar period, when the country allegedly belonged to the group of more prosperous European countries.

Therefore, leading politicians, such as Prime Minister Václav Klaus, in 1992 believed that the country could become EU member already by 1997–1998 (e.g. *Hospodářské noviny*, 6 November 2006). The Czech elite believed that the political and economic transition would be more successful in their country than in the neighbouring states. This explains also the negative Czech approach to the Visegrád cooperation with Poland, Hungary and Slovakia at the time. Václav Klaus famously denounced this organisation as a 'poor man's club' (Klaus 1994: 136).

Initially, the economic transition was also successful. Until 1997 most figures pointed in the right direction and the per capita income was second only to Slovenia among the transition countries. Even if in 1997 the country suffered from a banking crisis which was followed by a two-year economic recession (Senior-Nello 2003: 116), by then membership negotiations were already well underway, there was never any real fear among the Czech political elite that the country could be excluded from the first big enlargement.

Given the initial success of Czech transition and the fact that membership negotiation had been launched already, the Civic Democrats, who from 1997–2006 were in opposition, could afford a EU-reluctant approach. They criticised

---

10 Own translation.

the Social Democrat led governments for being too weak towards Brussels. The EU was criticised as being too socialist and as being an artificial political unit interfering with the natural political unit, i.e. the nation state. Despite this, the party ODS remained committed to EU membership, they described it as a marriage of convenience and not a marriage of love (for a discussion see Braun 2008b).

As a result of ODS' attitude toward the EU, the Czech political elite has been split regarding the future of the EU, and the Czech Republic was not able to speak with one voice at the Convention on the Future of Europe. The delegate from the Chamber of Deputies, Jan Zahradil, representing ODS, rejected the idea of framing the new treaty as a European Constitution and argued instead in favour of a more intergovernmental EU, which he described as a 'Europe of Democracies', whereas the other two delegates from the Czech Republic, representing the government and the Senate had a more pro-integration view (Kratochvíl 2003: 29; Kratochvíl and Königová 2005: 35).

After the Convention, the ODS persisted in its critique of the Constitutional Treaty. The Lisbon Treaty was also negatively viewed by a large part of the party. The party leadership, however, took on a more pragmatic position as firstly, a rejection of the treaty could endanger the coalition government between the ODS and two smaller parties, and secondly, because of the upcoming Czech presidency in 2009. The party leadership, however, had difficulty convincing their representatives in the two chambers of the parliament to support the treaty.

Since it is the Civic Democrats that make the Czech Republic stand out as a rather reluctant European, it is of interest here to look a bit closer at the party's EU discourse. The party started in the late 1990s to describe its approach as being Eurorealist. The term 'realist' was used as being the opposite of the 'naïve visionarism' of the more pro-EU spectrum of the Czech elite. The party describes the EU as a tilt-yard of interests dominated by the big member states (e.g. Zahradil et al. 2001). Therefore, the European institutions are, according to them, particularly vulnerable to the influence of the big powers (in particular Germany). Therefore, a small or medium sized country should protect its means of influence, i.e. the power of veto. Since the EU institutions are viewed as being easily manipulated by the bigger states, they are not viewed as being the 'natural allies' of the small state (cf. Tiilikainen 2006: 78), rather as the contrary. For this reason the party takes a reluctant position regarding the development of European institutions in a more community-centred direction (i.e. the strengthening of the Commission, European Parliament and Court of Justice). The following quotation is illustrative for the party's position:

> Possible dictates from the big powers can be rejected by the very use of the broadest possible intergovernmental approach. That is equality between single member states, without taking into account size, giving each of them

the possibility of blocking changes in crucial fields by using the national veto (Zahradil et al. 2001: 14).[11]

As the quotation also shows, the party emphasises that all states in the EU should be equal, independent of size and wealth. In this respect, the strategy chosen by the party is one of making sure that small states count as much as big powers. However, other arguments of the party also show that some countries should be treated more equally than others. The party, referring to the glorious days of the first Republic of Czechoslovakia, argues that the country has a certain right to '... an honourable and equal position, proportional to our geographical and geopolitical position' (ODS 2004: 1).

Even if the Czech political elite viewed the country's position as stronger *vis-à-vis* the EU and the old member states than did their Slovak counterparts, only the communists and a few prominent ODS members did actually reject EU membership in the referendum of 2003. The mainstream position in the ODS was that the EU membership was unavoidable, primarily for economic reasons. It was however, not only hard macro-economic data that showed that EU membership was necessary. The EU membership was seen as a confirmation that the transition period had come to a successful end. The description of EU membership as being the final goal of the transformation process was so common in the political discourse that Václav Klaus saw the need to denounce this association between EU membership and 'state success' (Klaus 2003).

The position of the ODS is in opposition to the idea that small states would benefit more from the institutionalisation of interstate relations in regional politics. In particular, the ODS contests the idea that the Czech Republic without the European institutions would have been in a weaker position with regard to other European countries, including Germany, than it is now as a member of the EU. They don't suggest that in intergovernmental relations all countries actually are equal, but that the game is the same within the European Union.

Finally, what can be learned from the fact that the euro has yet to be introduced in the Czech Republic? In the Czech Republic, as well as in Slovakia, the business interests and their lobby organisation are in favour of the euro. The public opinion, although hesitant, is slightly positive. Therefore, clearly the introduction of euro is not a priority in the Czech Republic for *political* reasons (see EU-27 Watch 2008: 217). The lack of political will can be explained by the costs of necessary political reforms to meet the Maastricht criteria as well as a general negative view regarding the euro project among parts of the Civic Democratic Party. There is little discussion in the Czech Republic that this reluctance to adopting the euro could have negative consequences on its reputation in the EU. It is viewed as a decision completely in the hands of the Czechs, which also fits with the argument that the political elite has a self-image of the country as being more in control and, thus, perceived as strong rather than weak or as big rather than small.

---

11 Own translation.

Conclusion

In this chapter I have stressed that the different approaches towards the EU between the Czech Republic and Slovakia can be understood primarily by differences in the countries' transition and accession periods and by differences in the view of the state, either as continuance of Czechoslovak statehood or as a newly independent state. These two factors seem to have been crucial in explaining the Slovakian acceptance of being small, i.e. the weaker part in an asymmetric relationship with the EU, compared to the Czech more diversified approach. There, however, is nothing to suggest that the underlying material factors, i.e. a stronger economy and a more favourable geographic location for a candidate state, as in the Czech case, automatically would lead to a more reluctant approach. Rather it is suggested that these material conditions provided a necessary prerequisite for the possibility of a certain discursive articulation, which then established itself as dominant among a part of the political elite. Similarly, the bumpier road of Slovakia to EU membership was a condition which increased the importance of external recognition for domestic political legitimacy and limited the range of alternatives for the political elite.

References

Arter, D. 2000. Small State Influence Within the EU: The Case of Finland's Northern Dimension Initiative. *Journal of Common Market Studies*, 38(5), 677-97.

Bilcik, V. 2003. National Report Slovakia, in *Positions of 10 Central and Eastern European Countries on EU Institutional Reforms: Analytical Survey in the Framework of the CEEC-Debate Project*, edited by C. Franck and D. Pyszna-Nigge. Louvain-la-Neuve: Université Catholique de Louvain, 93-7.

Braun, M. 2008a. Talking Europe: the Dilemma of Sovereignty and Modernization. *Cooperation and Conflict*, 43(4), 397–420.

Braun, M. 2008b. *Modernisation Unchallenged: The Czech Discourse on European Unity*. Prague: Institute of International Relations.

Čarnogurský, J. 2008. Osamostanenie Slovenska prispelo k jeho dospievaniu. *Mezinárodní politika*, 1/2008, 18-20.

Drulák, P. 2005. Probably a Regime, Perhaps a Union: European Integration in the Czech and Slovak Political Discourse, in *Enlargement in Perspective*, edited by H. Sjursen, Oslo: ARENA, Centre for European Studies, University of Oslo, Report No 2, 209-46.

EU-25 Watch. 2006. *Issue 2*. Available at: http://www.eu-consent.net/library/EU25 Watch/EU-25_Watch-No2.pdf [accessed: 20 July 2009].

EU-27 Watch. 2008. *Issue 7*. Available at: http://www.eu-consent.net/library/ eu25watch /EU-27_Watch_No7.pdf [accessed: 7 July 2009].

Eurobarometer 2003/4. *Public Opinion in the Candidate Countries*. Available at: http://ec.europa.eu/public_opinion/archives/cceb/2003/cceb2003.4_full_report.pdf [accessed: 17 July 2009].
Eurobarometer 69. 2008. *Public Opinion in the European Union*. Available at: http://ec.europa.eu/public_opinion/archives/eb/eb69/eb_69_first_en.pdf [accessed: 17 July 2009].
Eurobarometr 69. 2008. *Národní Zpráva Česká Republika*. Available at: http://ec.europa.eu/public_opinion/archives/eb/eb69/eb69_cz_nat.pdf [accessed: 17 July 2009].
Falkner, G. and Laffan, B. 2005. The Europeanization of Austria and Ireland: Small can be Difficult? in *The Member States of the European Union*, edited by S. Bulmer and C. Lequesne. Oxford: Oxford University Press, 209-28.
Hanley, S. 2008. Embracing Europe, Opposing EU-rope? Party-Based Euroscepticism in the Czech Republic, in *Case Studies and Country Surveys: Opposing Europe? The Comparative Party Politics of Euroscepticism*, edited by A. Szczerbiak and P. Taggart. Oxford: Oxford University Press, 243-62.
Haughton, T. and Malová, D. 2007. Emerging Patterns of EU Membership: Drawing Lessons from Slovakia's First Two Years as a Member State. *Politics*, 27(2), 69-75.
Klaus, V. 1994. *Česká cesta*. Praha: Profile.
Klaus, V. 2003. Měli jsme si více užít naší samostatnosti, ale nejde to. *Lidové noviny*, 11 June.
Kopecky, P. and Učeň, P. 2003. Return to Europe? Patterns of Euroscepticism among the Czech and Slovak Political Parties, in *The Road to the European Union, Volume 1 - The Czech and Slovak Republics*, edited by J. Rupnik and J. Zielonka. Manchester: Manchester University Press, 164-79.
Kořan, M. 2007. Slovensko rok po volbách: úspěšná vláda nebo úspěšná země. *Mezinárodní politika*, 9/2007, 25-7.
Kratochvíl, P. 2003. National Report on the Czech Republic, in *Positions of 10 Central and Eastern European Countries on EU Institutional Reforms: Analytical Survey in the Framework of the CEEC-Debate Project*, edited by C. Franck and D. Pyszna-Nigge. Louvain-la-Neuve: Université Catholique de Louvain, 27-38.
Kratochvíl, P. and Königová, L. 2005. Jak utváret Evropu: konvencne nebo konventne? Konvent jako alternativní metoda prípravy základních smluv evropské integrace. *Mezinárodní vztahy*, 2/2005, 24-41.
Leška, V. 2006. *Slovensko 1993-2004: léta obav a nadějí*. Praha: Ústav mezinárodních vztahů.
Malová, D., Láštic, E. and Rybář, M. 2005. *Slovensko ako nový členský štát Európskej únie: Výzva z periférie*. Bratislava: Friedrich Ebert Stiftung.
Mouritzen, H. and Wivel, A. 2005. *The Geopolitics of Euro-Atlantic Integration*. London: Routledge.

ODS, 2004. *Stejné šance pro všechny. Program pro volby do Evropského parlamentu.* Available at: http://www.ods.cz/volby/programy/2004e.php [accessed: 7 July 2009].

Rupnik, J. 2003. Joining Europe Together or Separately? The Implications of the Czecho-Slovak Divorce for EU Enlargement, in *The Road to the European Union. Volume 1 – The Czech and Slovak Republics*, edited by J. Rupnik and J. Zielonka. Manchester: Manchester University Press, 16-50.

Schimmelfennig, F., Engert, S. and Knobel, H. 2005. The Impact of EU Political Conditionality, in *The Europeanization of Central and Eastern Europe*, edited by F. Schimmelfennig and U. Sedelmeier. London: Cornell University Press, 29-50.

Senior-Nello, S. 2003. The Economic Criteria for EU Accession: Lessons from the Czech and Slovak Republics, *The Road to the European Union. Volume 1 – The Czech and Slovak Republics*, edited by J. Rupnik and J. Zielonka. Manchester: Manchester University Press, 113-37.

STEM 2008. *Informace z výzkumů STEM trendy 10/2008.* Available at: http://www.stem.cz/clanek/1635 [accessed: 17 July 2009].

Szczerbiak, A. 2001. Polish Public Opinion: Explaining Declining Support for EU Membership. *Journal of Common Market Studies*, 39(1), 105-22.

Szczerbiak, A. and Taggart, P. 2008. *Case Studies and Country Surveys: Opposing Europe? The Comparative Party Politics of Euroscepticism.* Oxford: Oxford University Press.

Thorhallsson, B. and Wivel, B. 2006. Small States in the European Union: What Do We Know and What Would We Like to Know? *Cambridge Review of International Affairs*, 19(4), 651-68.

Tiilikainen, T. 2006. Finland – An EU Member with a Small State Identity. *European Integration*, 28 (1), 73-87.

Trägårdh, L. 2002. Sweden and the EU: Welfare State Nationalism and the Spectre of 'Europe', in *European Integration and National Identity: The Challenge of the Nordic States*, edited by L. Hansen and O. Wæver. London: Routledge, 130-81.

Vachudova, M.A. 2005. *Europe Undivided – Democracy, Leverage, and Integration After Communism.* Oxford: Oxford University Press.

Wolchik, S.L. 1995. The Politics of Transition and the Break-Up of Czechoslovakia, in *The End of Czechoslovakia*, edited by J. Musil. Budapest: Central European University Press, 225-44.

Zahradil, J., Plecitý, P., Adrián, P. and Bednář, M. 2001. *Manifest českého eurorealismu, dokument k ideové konferenci ODS.* Available at: http://www.ods.cz/docs/dokumenty/zahradil-manifest.pdf [accessed: 7 July 2009].

Chapter 11
Cyprus, Small-Powerhood and the EU's Principles and Values

Costas Melakopides

Introduction

Arguably, most current bibliographic and journalistic references to 'Cyprus' are dominated by questions regarding its idiosyncratic EU status, its protracted 'reunification' efforts and its inclusion among the 'main obstacles' to Turkey's own EU accession. However, for those untutored in the intricacies of Cyprus-EU-Turkey-Greece relations and of the Cyprus-UN-Turkey conundrums, the corresponding legal and political landscapes are wrapped in mysteries inside enigmas. It may be well-known that the Republic of Cyprus is a full EU member state since 1 May 2004, that the *acquis communautaire* does not yet apply to 37 percent of its territory and that the international community – primarily through the UN – is constantly attempting to mediate for the 'reunification' of the Island. And yet, absent is a strong familiarity with 'the Cyprus problem', and the precise nature of these issues and their implications escape *full understanding*.

Therefore, in order to place the Republic of Cyprus squarely in the framework of this book, it is necessary first to sketch the historical background and the essential dimensions of 'the problem' that preceded and accompanied EU accession, to be followed by a laconic description of Cyprus's post-accession dramatic events in order to be then able to discuss the Republic's present challenges and future opportunities inside the EU.

To anticipate, it will transpire that Cyprus is a *sui generis* small state for at least eight reasons: first, in addition to a population around one million and a territory of less than 9,300 km², Cyprus is geostrategically privileged and hence attractive to powerful and/or amoral states in a partly 'Hobbesean' world. In other words, Cyprus' limited own power has resulted in it being invaded and colonised throughout history, up to even the 1970s. Second, the aforementioned characteristics of its power *in tandem* with the geopolitical properties of the eastern Mediterranean have involved the country not merely in the superpowers' Cold War antagonism, but also in current *asymmetric relations vis-à-vis*, at least, Turkey, the UK and the USA. Third, as a result of Turkey's invasion in 1974, 37 percent of the Republic's territory is under *occupation*. This means that the human rights and fundamental freedoms of all legitimate Cypriots have, until this day, been grossly violated for 35 years. Fourth, the international legal condemnation of both invasion and occupation has had substantial political implications for Turkey, yet not sufficient to force it to settle the problem fairly, functionally and according to international and European legal and ethical norms. Fifth, Cyprus' EU accession on 1 May 2004 was preceded by unconscionable pressures, through the so-called 'Annan Plan', which was overwhelmingly rejected by the Greek Cypriots as essentially unfair, illicit and unworkable. Sixth, EU integration has given the citizens of the Republic primarily a strong psychological boost, a number of tangible benefits and the anticipation of ultimate security. In turn, the Republic, as the EU's most south-eastern voice, promotes EU interests, principles and values in an ever-expanding region. Seventh, given that the Union's self-identification is primarily expressed in normative terms or via Joseph Nye's notion of 'soft power', it can be argued that (*even*) small states that adopt and celebrate these EU features can increase their international respectability and prestige. To capture such an effect, I will introduce the concept of *small-powerhood*. And eighth, the EU has supported Cyprus' case in various ways albeit, to this date, not decisively enough to reach a fair and functional settlement.

Historical Sketch

The Republic of Cyprus was born on 16 August 1960. Since 1925, it was a British Crown Colony. In earlier centuries, after 1570, Cyprus was under Ottoman rule. Following the Russo-Turkish War (1877–1878), the administration of the island was ceded to the British. The United Kingdom annexed it after the First World War, since the Ottomans participated on the side of the Central powers. Under the Treaty of Lausanne (1923), Turkey relinquished any claim to Cyprus. In 1950, when the population ratio was about 80 percent Greek Cypriots (GCs) and 18 percent Turkish Cypriots (TCs), a referendum organised by the Cypriot Orthodox Church and boycotted by the TCs, yielded a 90 percent in favour of *enosis* (union with Greece). The British rejection of this desire, despite the 'winds of change' blowing in the rest of the colonial world, led to a Cypriot campaign to gain independence with the help of Greece at the UN. But the UN campaign failed due to the combined opposition of the UK, the USA and some NATO members. As a result, the GCs formed the liberation organisation EOKA, which fought for independence and union with Greece through armed struggle. After the TCs founded their own organisation (TMT) aiming at *taksim* (partition of the island), the British resorted to a series of 'divide-and-rule' measures which, among other things, made the emergence of conflict between Greek Cypriots and Turkish Cypriots inevitable (Hitchens 1984).

The GCs' anti-colonial struggle was successful. London was forced to grant independence (1960). But the agreements for the creation of the Republic of Cyprus also included the simultaneous involvement of the UK, Greece and Turkey as guarantors, the two British 'Sovereign Base Areas' representing about 5 percent of Cypriot territory and a Constitution which gave the minority TCs asymmetrically large powers.[1] Independent analysts concur that the Constitution was marked by evident weaknesses that made it inherently dysfunctional. Thus, the Cypriot President, Archbishop Makarios III, proposed 13 amendments to improve it in late 1963. Immediately, inter-communal fighting erupted, which the GCs ascribed to 'the Turkish Cypriot rebellion'. In any case, the TCs left the parliament and the government and many of them withdrew into enclaves. For the GCs, all these decisions and actions were seen as strictly conforming to the TCs' vision of partition. In March 1964, the UN Peacekeeping Force in Cyprus (UNFICYP) arrived and has remained on the island ever since.

As suggested earlier, Cyprus's presence in the superpowers' Cold War calculus was inevitable. George Wildman Ball, the former US Under Secretary of State, revealed with disarming honesty the way Washington perceived this geopolitically privileged state. Commenting on the Cypriot inter-communal strife of 1963–1964, he wrote:

> Viewed from Washington, the issues were clear enough. Cyprus was *a strategically important piece of real estate* at issue between two NATO partners: Greece and Turkey. *We needed to keep it under NATO control* (Ball 1982, emphases added).

Needless to say, in view of this perception and Cyprus's post-Second World War history, Moscow was eager to extend numerous gestures of support to Nicosia.

Domestically, while many TCs continued to stick to *taksim* as a nationalist dream, the GCs abandoned their erstwhile vision of *enosis* by the mid-1960s, firstly because the Republic and its President Makarios (a popular figure in the Non-Aligned Movement) were already enjoying international respect. Hence the United Nations never questioned the legitimacy of Makarios' constitutional changes and never endorsed the TCs' and Turkey's protests. Secondly, the Colonels' coup in Greece in April 1967 created a vulgar and humiliating seven-year long dictatorship, hated both in Greece and Cyprus. Therefore, no Greek Cypriot would wish to be associated with *that* Greece. And thirdly, the Greek dictators signalled the blacklisting of Archbishop Makarios from the outset. For a few years, their attempts against his life were numerous and diabolical. However, the coup against him in July 1974 led to a series of catastrophic events.

While Washington was labelling Makarios 'the red priest' and 'the Castro of the Mediterranean', the US was being widely perceived by most Greeks as the instigator of the Greek dictatorship. However, it might be wiser to argue that the Greek junta would not have *survived* without the open and warm support extended to it by the US. Therefore, Washington did not act to prevent the anti-Makarios coup in Cyprus, just as it did not react to Turkey's known preparations for a massive military response (Hitchens 1984; Stern 1984; Melakopides 2006). Be that as it

---

1 The 18 percent minority was given 30 percent participation in the parliament and the administration and permanent veto power.

may, Turkey's military forces struck twice, in July and August 1974. According to a senior Turkish diplomat in Washington, the anti-Makarios coup gave it a 'golden opportunity' to act (Couloumbis 1983).

The military intervention was bloody, ruthless and highly costly in human suffering and material loss. On the Greek side, there were 6,000 dead and about 3,000 missing persons. More than 180,000 Greek Cypriots became refugees in their own country. Turkey occupied 37 percent of Cypriot territory and claimed that it acted in conformity with the Treaty of Guarantee (attached to the Cypriot Constitution), which permitted 'taking action' in order to restore constitutional order. Independent legal opinion, however, and the verdicts of international courts and organisations have treated it as an *invasion*, which means by definition, an *illegal* military intervention. Therefore, given the current efforts, by Turkey and its supporters for EU membership, to rewrite Cypriot history in order to exculpate Turkey, the next section will remind us – albeit schematically – why the international community keeps condemning Turkey's invasion of Cyprus and the implications thereof.

International Condemnation

According to Article 2(4) of the UN Charter, which prohibits even the *threat* to use force in interstate relations, Turkey's action was clearly illegal. Consequently, Ankara had to resort to a 'justification', claiming that the Treaty permitted the use of *armed force* in this case. However, in order to show that this 'justification' is false, I will present here two principal arguments. First, any interpretation of the Treaty in this sense would have been null and void *ab initio* since Article 103 of the UN Charter declares that, in case of conflict between the obligations of UN members under the Charter and obligations under other agreements, 'their obligations under the present Charter shall prevail'. This is the main reason why the distinguished Canadian professor of law, R.St.J. Macdonald, stipulated that Ankara's actions clearly violated international law (Macdonald 1981: 15).[2] Second, the Treaty of Guarantee (1960) stated expressly in article IV that any 'action' taken by the guarantors should occur *'with the sole aim of re-establishing the state of affairs created by the present Treaty'*. However, Turkey's occupation and *de facto* partition has lasted for 35 years. In short, this is the essence of 'the Cyprus problem' that the international community painfully tries to settle ever since.

Equally important to note is that the Turkish Cypriots' secessionist regime (called 'Turkish Republic of Northern Cyprus', or 'TRNC'), which was declared unilaterally in 1983 under the auspices of Turkey, was immediately condemned by

---

2 Professor Macdonald added that this interpretation (i.e. 'that treaty provisions inconsistent with the UN Charter are void ab initio') is also 'preferred by Guggenheim, Lauterpacht, Fitzmaurice, McNair, and Schwarzenberger' (*ibid.*).

the UN Security Council.³ To this day, it remains unrecognised by the international community, except by Turkey. In addition, the European Court of Human Rights has issued numerous condemnatory decisions, most prominently the decision in the *Loizidou v. Turkey* case (Council of Europe 1996 and 1998) and the fourth case of *Cyprus v. Turkey* of May 2001. By the former, Turkey was forced to pay Ms Titina Loizidou about one million euro in November 2003 to compensate for the violation of her *right to enjoy* her occupied property. Then, as recently as April 2009, the European Court of Justice produced its own indictment of the secessionist regime: it confirmed the inviolability of the property rights of Greek Cypriots by reasserting the pan-European jurisdiction of a Nicosia Court, which reaffirmed that the purchase of GCs properties in the occupied territory is clearly illegal.⁴

Such legal sentences have been politically costly for Turkey. Equally costly has been the EU's straightforward condemnation of the unilateral declaration of independence (UDI) of 1983 by the 'TRNC': 'The Ten reiterate their unconditional support for the independence, sovereignty, territorial integrity and unity of the Republic of Cyprus. They continue to regard the Government of President [Spyros] Kyprianou as the sole legitimate Government of the Republic of Cyprus. They call upon all interested parties not to recognise [the UDI], which creates a very serious situation in the area (Bulletin of the European Communities 1984: 68). For these reasons – and in contrast to most small states in Europe today – the Cypriot foreign policy is best described as *existential*. Given its curtailed sovereignty, violated territorial integrity and the indignity of occupation (with the concomitant violation of the human rights and fundamental freedoms of its citizens), the foreign policy of Cyprus is all but consumed by the efforts to restore full *statehood*.

The solid condemnation of Turkey and the 'TRNC' constitutes the major premise of the logic of the Republic's foreign policy. The challenges of Cyprus and the, at times, somewhat lukewarm support from the United States was recognised by three prominent representatives from the United States in the late 1990s: by the then US President Bill Clinton, by Nicholas Burns, then US Ambassador to Athens and by Richard Holbrooke. All three used nearly identical terms in what amounted to an indirect apology. Holbrooke's statement of November 1997 in Nicosia included the following:

> *American history in this area is not entirely clean.* There are some things that previous American administrations did in this area, particularly between the mid-1960s and 1974, which, I think, *were shameful*...There are certain things that

---

3   See Resolution 541 (1983) and Resolution 550 (1984).

4   See Court of Justice of the European Communities, *Meletis Apostolides v David Charles Orams & Linda Elizabeth Orams*, 'A judgment of a court in the Republic of Cyprus must be recognised and enforced by the other member states even if it concerns land situated in the northern part of the island', Press Release No 39/09, 28 April 2009.

happened, that the United States *should not have done* (quote from Theophanous 2004: 169, emphases added).

Enters the 'Annan Plan'

The most recent instance of *Realpolitik's* immorality 'in this area' is the attempt to sell the 'Annan Plan' as a 'UN reunification plan' for Cyprus.[5] It was obvious that the Plan was tailor-made to serve the strategic interests of the US, the UK, Turkey and the Turkish Cypriots, aspiring EU membership. Aiming at *getting rid of* the Cyprus problem, as opposed to resolving it, the Plan intended primarily to *exculpate* Turkey fully for the invasion and the occupation, strengthening thereby the probability of Turkey's EU accession. Simultaneously, the Plan hoped to confirm the legitimacy of the British 'Sovereign Base Areas' in Cyprus, to give George W. Bush a desperately needed 'diplomatic victory' and to secure (once again) the TCs asymmetric power in the envisaged new state. Therefore, the Plan had to circumvent the full restoration of human rights and fundamental freedoms for all Cypriots and to ignore the existential insecurities and anxieties of the Greeks. Given the ongoing efforts by Turkey and its supporters (i.e. supporters of its EU accession) to revive the 'Annan Plan', a brief look at its core features is required.

The Plan was unworkable, and viewed as blatantly unfair to the GCs due to its fundamental structural flaws.[6] In addition, by employing calculated ambiguities, the Plan tried to legitimate most illegal Turkish settlers, disregarding their serious – social, economic, psychological and political – conflicts with the indigenous TCs. This fact was recognised in the Jaakko Laakso Report on Cyprus (Council of Europe, Parliamentary Assembly 2003: 2) as follows:

> The settlers come mainly from the region of Anatolia, one of the less developed regions of Turkey. Their customs and traditions differ in a significant way from those in Cyprus. These differences are the main reason for the tensions and dissatisfaction of the indigenous Turkish Cypriot population who tend to view them as a foreign element.[7]

---

5   Inverted commas in 'Annan Plan' are meant to inform the reader that its real author, as he himself admits, was Lord David Hanney (Hanney 2005). For an illuminating review of Hanney's book, see Miltiades Hatzopoulos (Hatzopoulos 2008).

6   In *Unfair Play* (Melakopides 2006), I have shown how the Annan Plan violated cardinal principles and norms of international ethics and international law, forming a deleterious precedent in the European and global legal and ethical culture.

7   Furthermore, the Plan contained additional legal and ethical sins, such as, first, the surreptitious granting of even continental shelf to the British 'Sovereign Bases' (in Cypriot waters reportedly promising large hydrocarbon deposits) and second, the annulment of the citizens' right to appeal to the ECHR for compensation (for the violation of the right to

Remarkably, no discussion has taken place among Cyprus-watchers who these 'Turkish Cypriots', who voted in favour of the Plan, really were. It goes generally unnoticed that any generalising is very deceptive. For the *indigenous* Turkish Cypriots have long been a *minority in occupied Cyprus*, far outnumbered by the illegal Turkish settlers, methodically brought in to distort the Republic's pre-invasion demography. As the Laakso Report observed:

> Despite the lack of consensus on the exact figures, all parties concerned admit that Turkish nationals have been systematically arriving in the northern part of the island. According to reliable estimates, their number currently amounts to 115,000. [The Turkish Cypriots'] number decreased from 118,000 in 1974 to an estimated 87,600 in 2001. In consequence, the settlers outnumber the indigenous Turkish Cypriot population in the northern part of the island (Council of Europe, Parliamentary Assembly 2003: 2).[8]

Convinced that the Annan Plan and its associated procedures were openly violating any sense of fairness, the GCs rejected it by an overwhelming 76 percent. According to its own terms, the Plan was thereby rendered 'null and void'. And yet, some powers in Europe and beyond embarked immediately on 'punishing' the Republic for the GCs' rational rejection while attempting to 'reward' the TCs for the Plan's endorsement.

Recent EU-Cyprus Relations

London, Washington and Ankara emerge as protagonists of a hard-nosed *Realpolitik* (Melakopides 2006). The United Nations, in turn, appear as a less-than-honest broker. Greece and the European Union are praised for supporting the Cypriots' rights. After all, the EC/EU's *ethical* role has taken various forms, both before accession and since integration. First, the occupation remains among the main obstacles to Turkey's own EU ambitions. Second, as we know, the Community condemned immediately the unilaterally declared independence of the northern part of Cyprus in 1983. Third, it decoupled the Republic's EU accession from the resolution of the Cyprus problem at the Helsinki summit in December 1999. Fourth,

---

enjoy their occupied properties), obliterating thereby the *Titina Loizidou v Turkey* precedent. There also were anomalous procedural novelties, such as asphyxiating timetables and the imposition by the UN Secretary General of 'discretionary power' to fill in any 'gaps' remaining after the negotiations to finalise the Plan.

8   Since the rejection of the Annan Plan, the number of the illegal settlers keeps increasing. Eight years after the Laakso Report, it is reportedly exceeding 200,000, over twice the number of the indigenous Turkish Cypriots. The United Nations, however, allowed tens of thousands of *Turkish nationals* to vote in the *Cypriot referendum* as equals to the indigenous Turkish Cypriots.

at the December 2002 meeting in Copenhagen the European Council decided that the (indivisible) Republic of Cyprus should sign the Treaty of Accession in April 2003 – which it did. Fifth, the Republic acceded officially on 1 May 2004, surviving the protracted dramatic events and the campaign of intimidation associated with the adoption of the Annan Plan (Melakopides 2006).

Then came Turkey's 'declaration' of 29 July 2005, which stated that the Protocol extending its customs union with the EU to the new EU members did not imply recognition of the Republic of Cyprus. After weeks of intra-EU wrangling during the British presidency, the Council issued a decisive 'Counter-declaration' on 21 September, which stated *inter alia*:

> The European Community and its Member States make clear that this declaration by Turkey is unilateral, does not form part of the Protocol and has no legal effect on Turkey's obligations under the Protocol (Paragraph 2).

In paragraph 4 it was declared:

> The European Community and its Member States recall that the Republic of Cyprus became a Member State of the European Union on 1 May 2004. They underline that they recognise only the Republic of Cyprus as a subject of international law.

Finally, after stating its continuing support for the UN Secretary General's efforts to reach a comprehensive settlement of the Cyprus problem, the Counter-declaration demanded that this settlement should also be based on '*the principles on which the EU is founded*' (emphasis added).[9]

In 2006, the Republic of Cyprus received additional political and moral support from many European capitals, the European Parliament – most importantly through the Camiel Eurlings Report – and by some of its prominent members. They have all been strengthening what may be called a pro-Cyprus '*ethical acquis*'. For instance, responding to the November 2006 publication of the *Regular Report on Turkey's Progress towards Accession*, Elmar Brok (EPP) lamented 'a shift of responsibility' by the Commission to the December 2006 summit:

> The Commission evades a final evaluation of Turkey, in particular with respect to the unresolved Cyprus question. This means not only a lack of credibility towards the European public, but also continues to weaken the EU negotiation position *vis-à-vis* Turkey (EurActiv 2006).

---

9 See both Turkey's declaration and the EU's 'counter-declaration' in Costas Melakopides 2007: 203-5.

Similarly, Jan Marinus Wiersma, then Socialist Group Vice-President, stated in the same context: '... [T]he Ankara Protocol is *an important question of law*: it is not up for negotiation and it must be implemented fully' (*ibid.*, emphasis added).

Cypriot Small-powerhood and EU Principles and Values

The 2006 EU Annual Report on Human Rights emphasised: 'Human rights defenders and victims of human rights violations in different parts of the world expect a lot from the EU. Rightly so: the EU *as a value-based community* can be expected to further the cause of human rights and democracy with great ambition' (Council of Ministers/European Commission 2006, emphasis added). Ian Manners already elaborated on the normative character of this 'value-based community' in 2002: 'The broad normative basis of the European Union has been developed over the past 50 years through a series of declarations, treaties, policies, criteria and conditions. It is possible to identify five 'core' norms within this vast body of Union laws and policies which comprise the *acquis communautaire* and *acquis politique*' (Manners 2002: 242). For Manners, these five 'core norms' consist of the centrality of peace, the idea of liberty, democracy, the rule of law and respect of human rights and fundamental freedoms. The EU is, as it were, 'brokering honestly' these norms and values in the world.

If this is the case, then I would suggest that besides the EU institutions, EU member states should embark on the authentic and consistent application of EU principles, values and norms, multiplying a more positive attitude towards the EU. There is an opportunity even for *small states* to be representatives of, or 'positive proxies' for, EU values, both in their vicinity and even beyond. While Brussels increasingly becomes the diplomatic EU capital and the EU as a whole becomes an increasingly better global actor, the foreign policy of member states will inevitably also gain in 'soft power' and, therefore, in authority and prestige if they adopt the aforementioned norms and values. Following this logic, it seems that the *overall power* of any small EU state that consciously adopts these norms and values will be enormously enhanced.

Therefore, I suggest that we need a new concept to connote and denote the above-mentioned prospects. This concept may well be called '*small-powerhood*'. *Small-powerhood* can be defined here as the potential for enhanced international authority, influence and prestige, by even uncontroversially defined small states (such as Luxembourg) or some perhaps more controversially defined small states (such as Denmark and the Netherlands), that were regarded as 'middle-sized powers' during the Cold War. *Small-powerhood* illustrates the instance in which EU membership may entail rich opportunities for small states to become an advanced and prestigious international actor, provided these states integrate and pursue the best forms of the EU's self-declared 'soft power' strategies. In other words, since the EU's programmatic declarations of its essential principles and values – liberty, democracy, human rights, rule of law, solidarity and justice

– amount to a celebration of 'soft power' or 'normative power' (Manners 2002 and 2008), any small EU member state can distinguish itself in terms of international authority, influence and prestige, provided it implements these principles and values. Thus, if endorsed, *small-powerhood* could enjoy a role directly analogous to the humane or ethical connotation of *'middle-powermanship'* used primarily regarding the Canadian foreign policy during the Cold War (Melakopides 1998). *Small-powerhood*, in other words, as applied to small EU states, has a 'family resemblance' with the EU's 'soft power', with the 'EU's normative power' and with the international performance of 'norm entrepreneurs' (Ingebritsen 2002).

Values, principles and norms akin to *small-powerhood*, had already been embraced by Cyprus, even before EU accession. Both by virtue and necessity, the foreign policy of the post-1960 Republic had adopted and was complying with the norms and values of international law and international ethics. Cyprus sought and received UN protection since the early 1960s. It had shown authentic solidarity with the Third World as an active member of the Non-Aligned Movement. Finally, it applied for EC membership primarily for reasons of 'belonging' and for the implications of this 'belonging' in order to settle its problem according to 'cosmopolitan' norms. Following the accession and ongoing integration, the political culture of the country's free territory has endorsed enthusiastically the Union's declared principles and values. This is manifested in the genuine commitment to uphold international law, in Cyprus' refusal to recognise the independence of Kosovo on the basis of the UN-Charter and also in the manner the country adopted in regards to its own reunification. It showed moderation when Nicosia resisted twice – in 2004 and 2005 – to use its veto against Turkey's accession negotiations. It demonstrated unwavering respect for the rule of law through the impressively rapid implementation of the *acquis communautaire* (with only rare phenomena of loss of nerve by the police), steadfast satisfaction of human rights in the Republic's free territory, help for people in need – be it Cuban victims of hurricanes Ike and Gustav or victims of the Asian tsunami, commitment to the causes of liberty and justice and generous assistance to neighbours – most remarkable during and after the 2006 Lebanon war and after the August 1999 earthquake in Turkey.

Now, for fear that the above picture might be interpreted as a 'Cypriot hagiography', I will assure the reader that, despite palpable post-integration achievements, Cyprus still needs to work hard in many fields. First, environmental issues, such as more renewable energy resources, de-salination plants and more rational water consumption, have to be addressed. Second, Cyprus urgently needs a better public healthcare system. Third, the country needs and deserves an even better academic elite. Fourth, and under the pressure of the increasingly outspoken civil society, the political system must be gradually modernised so as to drastically reduce the old-fashioned clientelism. Fifth, Cyprus needs to strengthen and deepen public voluntarism. Finally, measures need be taken to enhance gender equality. Therefore, the earlier positive picture was only meant to suggest that, given its dramatic fortune, it was only natural for Cyprus to embrace what I denote as *small-powerhood*.

Public Opinion Anxieties

Inevitably, while counting on eventual EU assistance to settle their existential problem, the Cypriots live every day under extremely stressful circumstances. Hence, depending on the perceptions of EU support, there is occasional oscillation regarding pro-EU sentiments and views. For instance, in autumn 2007, only 40 percent of Cypriots considered Cyprus' EU membership as a good thing (Standard Eurobarometer 68). Asked whether Cyprus has benefited, or would benefit, from its EU accession, only 37 percent answered positively, far below the EU-27 average of 58 percent (whereas in spring 2007, the Eurobarometer figure stood still at 44 percent).

But this outcome could well be explained by the survey's particular timing. It was the start of a tempestuous presidential election campaign, a dreaded new stalemate regarding inter-communal negotiations, and massive illegal construction of houses and hotels on GCs properties in the occupied north. The Turkish President Gül renewed his assertion of 'two peoples and two states in Cyprus' and illegal immigration via the occupied territory worsened. Such developments, and the looming accession to the euro zone, had disheartened an already anxious public.

But then, the adoption of the euro on 1 January 2008 proved to be surprisingly smooth. The new President, Demetris Christofias, was reassuring that the Cyprus problem *could now* be resolved, and EU officials were enthusiastic about the dawning inter-communal negotiations. With the earlier melancholy dispelled, a sense of revitalisation was reflected in the Eurobarometer of spring 2008. Cypriots now exhibited the highest level of support for the EU, as 71 percent said that they trust the EU. With 61 percent, Cypriots also showed the highest level of support amongst the EU member states for their newly elected national government. Similarly, '[the] majority of citizens residing in areas under the control of the Republic of Cyprus trust the Cypriot legal system, the police and the army. 75 percent trust the National Guard, 62 percent trust the police and 59 percent trust the justice and the Cypriot legal system.' Equally crucial, 52 percent now considered Cyprus' membership in the EU as a good thing, a mere 15 percent thought it bad, and 58 percent of Cypriots said that they have a positive image of the Union. A significant increase of 18 percent was also recorded in the belief that Cyprus has overall benefited from its EU membership, reaching 55 percent (Eurobarometer 69 2008: 6-9).

Cypriots also now appear to be 'pro-European' when it comes to decisions being taken at EU level, with the greatest support recorded for defence, foreign policy and inflation. When asked in spring 2008 to prioritise the most important issues faced by their country, Cypriots ranked, in order of importance: crime, inflation and the economic situation.

Unsurprisingly, opinion polls in the Republic's free territory are immediately affected by developments in the island's convoluted political problem and the conflicting perceptions of its resolution prospects. The EU has long been promoted by the majority of the political elites, influential academics, columnists and political analysts, as sincerely committed to safeguarding human rights and international law. Cyprus' application for accession was directly linked to the small state's aspiration for liberation/reunification. Hence, the signature to the Treaty of Accession in April 2003 and the beginning of the formal EU membership on 1 May 2004 were treated as a cosmogonic turning point.

In this spirit, any suspected foul play on the way to resolving the Cyprus problem in a fair and functional manner is treated as hostile to the principles of justice and the EU's normative culture. This is why the April 2004 rejection of the 'Annan Plan' constitutes a test case for Cypriot normative commitment. It bears repeating that the Plan was perceived as an attempt to dodge the European legal and political principles as well as cosmopolitan ethical values. Therefore, its rejection was viewed by Greek Cypriots as an act of moral courage and an authentic celebration of 'the principles on which the Union is founded'.

Other Benefits From Integration

Five years since accession, the EU membership is deeply appreciated in Cyprus for two main reasons. Firstly, it is treasured as enforcing the island-state's international role and prestige, and second, during the difficult times of the global financial and economic crisis, it has provided the Republic with solid relief. An 'existentially' concerned public, Cypriot decision-makers, opinion-makers, the business community and organised groups, all acknowledge belonging to the European family as a serious asset. In addition, Cypriot businesses, NGOs, other organised groups and even the Church of Cyprus are developing ever closer ties with Brussels. Many of them have been establishing offices there and some are appealing for EU assistance in various projects. During 2008, due to a number of (local, regional and broader) setbacks – such as the second worst drought since 1901, an outbreak of Foot-and-Mouth-Disease and the increase in energy and food prices – the appeal for EU assistance increased.

The EU accession in 2004 and the entry into the euro zone in 2008 have also positively affected economic performance of Cyprus. It is, of course, rather premature, and some would say unwise, to even attempt to assess the full impact of those momentous events at such an early stage. However, we can already identify four areas where there are clear signs that the economy is entering a new stage of development. First, Cyprus is experiencing an invigorated competitive environment that is starting to improve the hitherto low productivity of Cypriot enterprises. Second, the macroeconomic conditions, already very good, are becoming even more so, thus enhancing the overall stability of the economy. Third, improved intra-EU labour mobility is starting to infuse – badly needed – flexibility into the labour market. And fourth, the quality of the overall financial/economic regulatory and supervisory framework is showing clear signs of improvement, with Cypriot consumers being the first to benefit.[10]

---

10 I thank my colleague Professor Andreas Antoniou for refining this paragraph.

Moreover, as the 2008–2009 global financial and economic crisis was deepening dramatically in most EU member states, Cypriots felt sheltered by the euro, which came into force on 1 January 2008.[11] Together with the apparent solidity of the banking sector – which had, among other things, avoided exposure to 'toxic' international products – the euro is considered to be the main reason for the Cypriot vitality of the economy, marked by continuing growth even in the first half of 2009. The Finance Minister, Charilaos Stavrakis, predicted in mid-May 2009 that Cyprus would achieve the highest rate of growth among the EU-27 with one of the lowest rates of inflation and the second lowest unemployment rate.[12]

In addition, conceiving the global economic crisis as also an opportunity, the present government has been actively campaigning for foreign direct investments. Beyond the Russian Federation, a consistent major investor in the country for years, the eyes of the Cypriot government have recently also turned towards other neighbouring countries in the Middle East, such as Egypt, Lebanon, Libya, and Syria, to the Persian Gulf, here primarily Qatar, as well as Iran and even China.[13]

While China occupied the sixth place in terms of Cyprus' imports in 2008 (with euro 389 million), the other countries were all EU member states, except for Israel, which was fifth with euro 591 million. Thus, the list of the ten top countries from which Cyprus imported most goods in 2008 appears as follows (in euro millions): Greece (1,232.4), Italy (772.2), United Kingdom (640.5), Germany (603.1), Israel, China, the Netherlands (294.9), Spain (262.3), Japan (189.3) and United States (128.2).[14]

Cypriot exports went, in 2008, to the following top 12 countries (in euro millions): Greece (218.6), United Kingdom (119.1), Germany (66), Lebanon (31.8), Italy (24.8), Russia (24.5), Spain (21.3), Japan and United Arab Emirates (both at 20.2), Syria (19.5), Egypt (17.6) and the Netherlands (16.5).[15]

---

11 The late President Tassos Papadopoulos should be credited for his unwavering insistence on this date, whereas the (now governing) left-wing party, AKEL, had favoured the date of January 2009.

12 Minister Stavrakis' press conference was reported in *Phileleftheros* (Nicosia daily), 13 May 2009, www.philenews.com/digital/PrintForm.aspx?nid=496709.

13 For instance, in addition to encouraging Iranian interest in purchasing residential homes at the coastal areas, more recent reports suggest that the government of Qatar, following the state visit of President Christofias to the country in early May 2009, is all but ready to invest half a billion euro into the construction of a 'six-star' hotel in central Nicosia.

14 Statistical Service of the Cyprus Government, External Trade, at www.mof.gov.cy/mof/cystat/statistics.nsf/ externaltrade_en/externaltrade_en?OpenDocument, accessed 3 June 2009.

15 *Ibid.*

Additional Dimensions of Cypriot Foreign Policy

If Cyprus represents an emerging paradigm of *small-powerhood*, it can fairly be expected to expand its EU-associated role in the sensitive vicinity of the eastern Mediterranean and far beyond. Already a member of the euro zone, a transportation and telecommunications hub, with a huge merchant marine fleet, an ambitious trade and banking centre, Cyprus is also historically friendly with both the Arabs and Israel. Like a veritable 'unsinkable aircraft carrier' (as neighbouring Crete used to be called during the Cold War), the Republic of Cyprus can utilise its material resources and diplomatic means to expand the EU's interests, collective influence and prestige. Needless to say, this regional role will be enhanced enormously when Cypriot reunification is achieved with the EU's help.

Meanwhile, Cyprus' current foreign policy remains 'existential'. It is primarily occupied with the efforts to inform the EU institutions, fellow EU members and various other influential states about its violated rights and to seek support for the restoration of freedom and justice. After Athens, other capitals that have traditionally provided Cyprus the much-needed support are Moscow and Beijing. Besides excellent bilateral relations (economic, commercial, cultural, etc.) they have consistently defended the Republic's case in the UN Security Council.

In recent years, especially Paris has also emerged as a principled supporter and a close partner of Cyprus both at UN and EU fora. In addition, this bilateral relationship is being progressively strengthened not only commercially and culturally, but even militarily. Noteworthy therefore is the Defence Cooperation Agreement signed in Paris on 28 February 2007, by Foreign Minister Giorgos Lillikas and the French Defence Minister, Madame Alliot-Marie. In addition, President Nicolas Sarkozy's deep knowledge of the region and his repeatedly expressed positive signals to Hellenism are presumed to have immediate positive implications for Cyprus. And yet, it may appear paradoxical that Nicosia and Athens do not concur – *as yet* (see below) – with Sarkozy's often-expressed opposition to Turkey's full EU membership. The Cypriots have long believed that Turkey's 'Europeanisation' is a *sine qua non* for Ankara's radical change of policy towards Cyprus and Greece.

It should also be stressed that Cypriot foreign economic policy is not perceived as an end in itself. Given Cyprus' curtailed present statehood, its foreign economic policy is not detached from its broader diplomatic goals. In fact, Nicosia's foreign relations in the twenty-first century have inherited the rich legacy of warm and healthy relations with all the Arab states, especially since the years of the Non-Aligned Movement and Makarios' aforementioned recognition therein. But Cyprus has managed to balance the traditionally successful relations with the Arab states with simultaneous good relations with Israel. Among other things, trade with Israel is flourishing, to the point that, as already mentioned, total imports from that country in 2008 placed it fifth on the relevant list. Cyprus also cultivates and enjoys strong friendly ties with all the aforementioned neighbouring states: Egypt,

Lebanon, Libya, Qatar and Syria as well as Iran and China. In May 2009, Nicosia announced the opening of embassies in Amman and Abu Dhabi, and more Cypriot embassies later in 2009 are forthcoming: one in Asia, two in Latin America and one in Havana. Given the size of its diplomatic service – it does not exceed 250 people – the above would seem to amount to a Herculean feat.

Current Challenges

In December 2006, the European Council gave Turkey a three-year 'grace period' to fulfil its obligation flowing from the Ankara Protocol, namely to open its ports and airports to Cypriot vessels and planes. Although the December 2009 deadline is fast approaching, Turkey's policy *vis-à-vis* Cyprus not only remains unchanged, but also shows signs of escalating muscle flexing. Besides employing arrogant and provocative rhetoric, Ankara has also harassed Cypriot vessels, which were searching for hydrocarbons in Cyprus' exclusive economic zone. In late May 2009, Turkish military circles were quoted in Turkish newspapers as threatening to use military force even against American vessels employed for the same reason! All this brings back to mind the frequent direct threats against Nicosia emanating from Ankara, as in the case when Cyprus envisaged the installation of Russian S-300 ground-to-air missiles (1997/98), or the threat 'to take extreme measures' in case the EU accepted Cyprus as a full member state.

At the same time, many Cypriot opinion-makers, most centrist political elites and large sectors of the public all seem deeply sceptical about the chances for a fair and functional settlement of the Cyprus issue through the current 'face-to-face negotiations' between the Cypriot President and the leader of the TC community. This has many reasons. First, although the 'Annan Plan' was supposed long ago to be 'null and void', it is still alive and on the negotiating table. Second, Mr Mehmet Ali Talat (leader of the de-facto 'TRNC') manifestly lacks autonomy; hence he follows faithfully Ankara's apparent strategy. He *pretends* to negotiate in all earnest, hoping to use this (appearance) as a ground for pre-empting further measures against Turkey's candidacy in December 2009, and he insists, simultaneously, on a crypto-'Annan Plan' that would ultimately turn Cyprus into a quasi-protectorate of Turkey. Third, although President Christofias has already made remarkable concessions, his interlocutor not only refuses to reciprocate, but he, in fact, backslides, altering continuously the terms of negotiations.[16] Fourth, after months of negotiations, there are widening differences between the two sides on such fundamental issues as governance, 'guarantees', the economy, property issues and the illegal settlers. Finally, there is this new notion, cultivated by some UN and EU circles, that any settlement should be 'by the Cypriots for the Cypriots', which can be described at best as

---

16 Most telling are the concessions to accept 50,000 illegal settlers and a 'rotating presidency' in the envisaged new regime.

disingenuous, since it implies that the problem is 'essentially bi-communal' and, therefore, not an international and European legal and moral problem created by the Turkish invasion and the 35-year long occupation. In other words, there is a rising fear that this new approach aims once again primarily at exculpating Turkey and to facilitate its EU aspirations. Therefore, Greek Cypriots and their friends are founding once again their aspiration for liberation/reunification of the island on the rights and opportunities of EU membership. In sum, Cyprus sees this as a cardinal opportunity opened by EU membership, and the EU sees it as an unavoidable challenge.

Remarkably, although small Cyprus certainly holds a decisive key to Turkey's trajectory to EU membership, the Cyprus Government has to this date shied away from raising the spectre of using it, for fear of causing a serious intra-Community conflict. Thus, *in tandem* with Greece, it pursues the 'European' diplomatic style, based on the Union's (non-conflictual) principles and values, even though this policy, following the aforementioned strategy of Turkey's 'Europeanisation', has so far only yielded negative results. However, I venture to foresee signs of metamorphosis, thanks to persistent pressure from Greek Cypriot (and Greek) public, from numerous influential opinion-makers and some prestigious academics. In other words, precisely because the occupying power and EU candidate refuses to budge and, instead, is employing the entire repertoire of its power (including promoting an enthusiastic support for its EU accession among its friends), the intellectual, analytical and political pressure is mounting on the Christofias Government to stop using exclusively carrots and begin, at long last, to employ Cyprus' valuable diplomatic sticks.

Conclusions

This chapter has tried to bring into sharp relief the labyrinthine nature of the recent and current phase of 'the Cyprus problem', as a prerequisite to understanding that the travails of Cyprus not only predated its independence in 1960, but are, in an obvious sense, even more dramatic since 1974. Of course, the Republic's EU accession on 1 May 2004 and the adoption of the euro on 1 January 2008 constitute its most positive historic moments since independence. The latter, because it has helped its economy during the unprecedented post-war economic crisis to the point that it may emerge unscathed. The integration into the EU satisfied the citizens' need for belonging – politically, psychologically and socio-economically – to the 'European family', affirmed their conviction that their (legal-political-ethical) case would ultimately be respected and raised their optimism that, with the Union's appropriate help, their problem would be handled as it should.

The above analysis entails a series of final conclusions. First, the case of Cyprus has shown that even small EU states are capable of fighting for their rights, as long as they subsume them under the essential (or defining) norms, principles and values of the Union. Second, Cyprus's power is clearly hurt by, on the one hand, the radical asymmetries it is experiencing *vis-à-vis* Turkey and, on the other, the UK and the US which are openly favouring Turkey's nearly unproblematic accession to the EU. This accession is expected to bring the aforementioned benefits for those countries but, on the contrary, enormous cost to the Cypriots' own interests and needs. Third, in pursuing what I have called Cyprus' 'existential foreign policy', the Republic is building methodically a network with friendly and/or like-minded states that are either (a) endorsing Cyprus' claims to liberty and justice or (b) are opposing Turkey's full EU membership or (c) are interested in strengthening Cyprus' role as a commercial/communications/transportations hub in the eastern Mediterranean which they see as reliable gateway to the gigantic EU market. Under (a) we can safely place countries like China, France, Greece, Russia and perhaps Spain; under (b) belong Austria, France and Germany (at the governmental level) and a number of small(er) states whose public opinion consistently opposes Turkey's full membership; under (c) I am referring to a host of primarily neighbouring countries, such as Egypt, the Gulf States, Lebanon, Libya, and Syria as well as India, Iran, Russia and, again, China. Fourth, even if the Republic of Cyprus is following pragmatically the 'rational actor model' in executing its foreign policy this does not mean that it has not fully endorsed the norms, values and principles of the EU's 'worldview'. This, I hope, has been demonstrated in this chapter. Hence the notion of *small-powerhood* was introduced precisely to capture the mutual benefits resulting from the authentic embracing of the Union's 'worldview' for both small EU states and the EU itself.

The above-mentioned asymmetry as well as the fact that, in Cyprus' case, *Realpolitik* is still prevailing over *Moralpolitik*, even at the UN Secretariat and even in some EU fora, may suffice to explain the inherent frustration of the Cypriots and their supporters. Of course, as acknowledged earlier, overall, the EC/EU must be counted among the international actors that have repeatedly protected the Republic in its post-1974 and post-2004 struggles. What is needed, however, is the big, last, decisive step.

The small Republic of Cyprus is showing the 'EU flag' in quite a large and ever expanding region and it promotes ably the Union's interests, principles and norms, paying back for the benefits it received after accession. However, most importantly Cyprus has emerged as test case for the Union's normative consistency, axiological identity and international credibility. Since the EU defines itself in terms of the aforementioned principles and values and since it is prepared to apply severe sanctions to third parties when they violate their citizens' human rights (Smith 2003: 205-208) it should follow that the protection of the fundamental rights of all legitimate citizens of a member state is, *a fortiori*, an EU moral obligation. By assisting in the settlement of the notorious problem of one of its small members, the EU will strengthen its normative respectability and international prestige, will help further improve Greek-Turkish relations and, by final implication, will contribute decisively to creating a trilateral zone of peace and cooperation between Cyprus, Turkey and Greece for the simultaneous benefit of the Union itself.

References

Ball, G.W. 1982. *The Past Has Another Pattern*. New York: W.W. Norton & Company.
Bulletin of the European Communities, 1984. Vol. 16(1). Brussels: General Secretariat, Commission of the European Communities.
Couloumbis, T. 1983. *The United States, Greece and Turkey: The Troubled Triangle*. New York: Praeger.
Council of Europe, 1998. European Court of Human Rights. *Case of Loizidou v. Turkey*. Judgement 40/1193/435/514.
Council of Europe, 2003. Parliamentary Assembly, Committee on Migration, Refugees and Demography. *Colonization by Turkish Settlers of the Occupied Part of Cyprus*, Doc. 9799, Rapporteur Mr Jaakko Laakso (Finland).
Council of Ministers/European Commission, 2006. *EU Annual Report on Human Rights 2006*.
EurActive, 2006. *'Last Opportunity' for Turkey*, 8 November. Available at: http://www.euractiv.com/en/enlargement/opportunity-turkey/article-159527 [accessed: 29 July 2009].
Eurobarometer 69, 2008. *Cyprus (Areas Under the Control of the Government of the Republic of Cyprus)*. National Report, Executive Summary. Available at: http://ec.europa.eu/public_opinion/archives/eb/eb69/eb69_cy_exe.pdf [accessed 25 November 2009].
Hanney, D. 2005. *Cyprus: The Search for a Solution*. London: I.B. Tauris.
Hatzopoulos, M. 2008. 'Pride and Prejudice' in a British View of the Annan Plan Negotiations, in *The Cyprus Yearbook of International Relations 2007*, edited by C. Melakopides, A.C. Emilianides and G. Kentas. Nicosia: Power Publishing, 231-42.
Hitchens, C. 1984. *Cyprus*. London and New York: Quartet Books.
Ingebritsen, C. 2002. Norm Entrepreneurs: Scandinavia's Role in World Politics. *Cooperation and Conflict: Journal of the Nordic International Studies Association*, 37(1), 11-23.
Macdonald, R.St.J. 1981. International Law and the Conflict in Cyprus. *Canadian Yearbook of International Law*, 3-49.
Manners, I. 2002. Normative Power Europe: A Contradiction in Terms? *Journal of Common Market Studies*, 40(2), 235-58.
Manners, I. 2008. The Normative Ethics of the European Union. *International Affairs*, 84(1), 45-60.
Melakopides, C. 1998. *Pragmatic Idealism: Canadian Foreign Policy 1945–1995*. Kingston and Montreal: McGill-Queen's University Press.

Melakopides, C. 2006. *Unfair Play: Cyprus, Turkey, Greece, the UK and the EU.* Kingston, Ontario: Queen's Centre for International Relations.

Melakopides, C. 2007. *The Cyprus Yearbook of International Relations 2006.* Nicosia, Power Publishing.

Smith, K. 2003. *European Union Foreign Policy in a Changing World.* Cambridge: Polity Press.

Stern, L. 1984. *The Wrong Horse: The Politics of Intervention and the Failure of American Diplomacy.* New York: Time Books.

Theophanous, A. 2004. *The Cyprus Question and the EU: The Challenge and the Promise.* Nicosia: Intercollege Press.

Chapter 12

Neutrality Inside and Outside the EU: A Comparison of Austrian and Swiss Security Policies After the Cold War

Jean-Marc Rickli[1]

Neutrality has increasingly become an obsolete conception (Dulles 1956).

Introduction

The harsh criticism of former American Secretary of State John Foster Dulles towards neutrality seems to be borne out by the facts but not quite. Whereas in the past, Belgium, Cyprus, Finland, Ireland, Luxembourg, Malta, the Netherlands, Portugal, Spain and Sweden, adopted neutrality, two countries in Europe, Austria and Switzerland, have legally retained neutrality as the basis of their security policy.[2] Swiss neutrality dates back to the Swiss defeat at Marignano in 1515 that signified the end of Swiss involvement in international affairs. The international legal recognition of neutrality only occurred at the Vienna Congress in 1815, after the Swiss Confederation had been invaded by Napoleon. Since then, the Swiss have conducted a policy of permanent neutrality so as to avoid being involved in European wars. In the aftermath of the Second World War, the sine qua non condition for the withdrawal of all allied troops from Austria's soil was the avoidance of unbalanced relations with any of the occupying powers. Neutrality became the only viable option for Austria to regain its independence. After Austria pledged to the Soviet Union to adopt a form of neutrality similar to the Swiss model in the so-called Moscow Memorandum, Vienna unilaterally declared its permanent neutrality on 26 October 1955 by the adoption of a constitutional law on neutrality.

During the Cold War, the study of neutrality attracted a lot of attention due to the strategic buffer position of the neutral states in the bipolar balance of power (Karsh 1988). After the end of the Cold War, the relevance of neutrality as a small

---

1 The author would like to thank Webster University Geneva for the research grant provided to write this chapter.

2 Ireland, Finland and Sweden will not be considered in this study because their security policy is not legally defined by neutrality.

state's security policy instrument has been increasingly questioned (Bächler 1994; Braillard et al. 1990; Joenniemi 1993; Kruzel 1989; Kux 1994; Thürer 1995). The objective of this chapter is to shed light on the relevance of neutrality in the current strategic environment. To this purpose it asks the following question: what is the security function of neutrality in Europe nowadays?

This chapter demonstrates that the security policy function of neutrality has indeed become marginal after the Cold War. On the other hand, neutrality has become an identity provider which has prevented the neutral states from totally moving away from neutrality. This essay demonstrates this argument by first defining neutrality and its security function. Then it looks at the role of neutrality in Austrian and Swiss security policies after the Cold War. This is followed by an analysis of the domestic acceptance of neutrality. This essay concludes by highlighting the role of neutrality for small states within or outside the EU.

Neutrality as a Small State's Security Policy Instrument

Our understanding of smallness is both dynamic and relational. Rather than considering small states on the basis of the power they possess, the focus is on the actual power they exercise towards other states or organisations (Chapter 1 in this volume; Mouritzen and Wivel 2005: 3).[3]

Small states' security is therefore characterised by a profound dilemma, which originates from the need to compensate for their power deficit (Goetschel 1998: 19). Due to their lack of resources, small states must prioritise whether they want to prevent other states from influencing them or whether they should instead try to directly influence other states (Fendius Elman 1995: 171). In other words, small states must choose between favouring influence or autonomy (Mouritzen 1997: 101-6). This leaves small states with two basic security options: they can either choose to maximise their influence by adopting a cooperative strategy or favour to protect their autonomy through the adoption of a defensive posture (Rickli 2008: 309). While the former option corresponds to joining an alliance the latter translates into opting for neutrality.

Neutrality can be defined as a foreign policy principle whose purpose is the preservation of the independence and sovereignty of small states through non-participation and impartiality in international conflicts. The measure of its effectiveness relies on the degree to which it can keep the neutrals out of the wars of others. Neutrality has been codified in the conventions of Paris (1856), London (1909) and the Hague (1907). The Hague Conventions of 1907 (War on Land and

---

3   The literature on small states argues that small states have a deficit of power due to their weak ability to mobilise resources, which could be material, relational or normative (e.g. Goetschel 1998; Wivel 2005). See Chapter 1 of this volume for a discussion of the concept of small states.

War at Sea) define neutral states' rights and obligations and they have remained the basis of the codified law of neutrality.

The law of neutrality recognises certain obligations for the neutral state solely during wartime and only in case of interstate conflicts. Neutral states must not provide military support either directly or indirectly to the belligerents. The indirect support provision is however limited to the duty of non-discrimination (regarding export restrictions on certain goods) as well as the prohibition of territorial and personnel support for military operations (Interdepartmental 2000: 13). Thus neutral states must treat the belligerents impartially. The neutrals are also obliged to maintain their territorial integrity and defend their sovereignty by any means at their disposal. Finally, they must tolerate inspection of their properties in the context of naval warfare.

Since the legal basis was drawn up at the beginning of the twentieth century, many developments pertaining to the conduct of war (e.g. aerial warfare) or to the development of international law (e.g. UN system of collective security or the recognition of the universality of fundamental human rights) are not covered by the Hague Conventions. Their effects on the law of neutrality have been incorporated by international customary law[4] such as for example in the case of coercive measures decided by the United Nations. As a matter of fact, international customary law is now regarded as the decisive source of law for the contemporary law of neutrality (Interdepartmental 2000: 11).

The law of neutrality is restricted to international armed conflicts. In case of intra-state war the law of neutrality does not apply and therefore the neutral state's scope of action is unhindered and left to its own discretion. The law of neutrality also only applies during wartime. However, a state can opt for neutrality also in peacetime. In this case, a state that pursues a policy, which makes certain preparations in peacetime that aim at bolstering neutrality in wartime, acquires the status of permanent neutral (Bindschedler 1976). Unlike the neutral wartime requirements, the Hague Conventions do not regulate the status of permanent neutral states in times of peace. Customary law, however, has developed an additional duty, which is the impossibility of joining a military alliance.

During the Cold War, a neutral security policy was determined by the requirements of establishing a credible neutrality policy that would not threaten other states so as to avoid a security dilemma as well as draw the neutral state into war. To this end the neutral states adopted an independent and comprehensive conception of defence: total defence. This refers to a 'security and defence policy, which combines military forces with, usually, a well-developed civil defence structure and an attempt to "link" the civilian economy and political infrastructure explicitly in defence planning'[5] (Stein 1990: 17).

---

4 International customary law is determined by state's practice and in the case of the law of neutrality mainly by Austria and Switzerland.

5 During the Cold war, Austria, Finland, Sweden, Switzerland and Yugoslavia, adopted some variant of total defence.

The military policy of the neutral states relied on a two-tier military doctrine composed of dissuasion and territorial defence (Rickli 2008: 312). Dissuasion entails a weaker dimension than deterrence because it is not based on threats of retaliation but on increasing the costs of invasion (Däniker 1992: 8). This was best achieved by the adoption of a comprehensive territorial defence posture that focused on defence in depth or on frontal defence so as to most effectively thwart any belligerent's design.

The non-aggressive posture of the neutral states was bolstered by an active foreign policy. The latter was underpinned by a moral dimension, which considered that the pursuit of neutrality represented a contribution towards international peace (Palme 1984). To this purpose, the neutral states developed a strategic culture that relied on an aversion to project military power except in cases of peacekeeping operations. Through the adoption of a reactive defence policy and pro-active foreign policy, the neutral states tried to bolster their credibility so as to be recognised as trustworthy partner in international security.

The next section looks at the way the Austrian and Swiss governments used the principle deriving from neutrality to conduct their security policy after the Cold War.

Austrian Neutrality Policy After the Cold War

By the end of the 1980s, the reforms initiated by Mikhaïl Gorbachev in the Soviet Union and the resulting détente in East/West relations allowed the Austrian government to see an opportunity to get more involved in European affairs. In 1989, Austria formally applied to the European Community (EC). The government considered this perfectly compatible with Austria's neutrality. Unlike the other neutral states (Sweden and Finland), Austria's EC application contained a formal neutrality proviso. This clause was to ensure the ability of the Austrian state to fulfil 'its legal obligation arising out of its status as a permanently neutral state' even as a member of the EC and 'to continue its policy of neutrality as a specific contribution to the maintenance of peace and security in Europe' (Luif 2001: 142). The inclusion of this clause resulted both from the pressure of the Social-Democrat Party (SPÖ)[6] to preserve Austria's permanent neutrality and from the continuing opposition from the Soviet Union.

The neutrality clause however was an impediment to Austria's accession to the EC because its member states feared that Austria's neutral status might prevent it from undertaking obligations entailed by the future Common Foreign and Security Policy (CFSP) (European Commission 1992a: 18; Reiter 1993: 346-9). Similarly, the European Commission was concerned by the fact that Austria could 'oppose systematically certain measures which in its view clashed with its policy of neutrality, notably in the framework of a future common foreign and security

---

6 Which formed a government coalition with the People's Party (ÖVP) since 1983.

policy' (European Commission 1992a: 16). The Commission made it then clear that future member states would have to subscribe fully to the implementation of the CFSP and the eventual framing of a common defence policy (European Commission 1992b). In response to these conditions for membership, the Austrian government began to de-emphasise the importance of neutrality.

Unlike Switzerland, Austria participated in UN peacekeeping operations during the Cold War because the Austrian government had considered that the UN Security Council (UNSC) 'would be required to respect Austrian neutrality and would not ask Austria to participate in any measures under Chapter VII' of the UN Charter (Krüger 2003: 9). In 1991, Austria granted overflight and transit rights to the UN coalition forces during the Gulf War. Since this operation was conducted under chapter VII of the UN Charter, the law of neutrality was adapted accordingly by giving priority to implementing UNSC resolutions under Chapter VII and article 25 of the UN Charter rather than to the obligations under the neutrality act (Austrian Ministry of Defence 2001: 37). This new understanding was based on the premise that actions taken by the UN against an aggressor did not constitute a war and therefore did not call for the application of the law of neutrality. The obligations under the UN Charter took precedence over Austria's status of neutrality. The Cabinet reduced the definition of neutrality to its military core, that is no participation in wars and military alliances as well as no establishment on Austrian soil of foreign countries' military bases.

This new interpretation was followed by Austria supporting the entire responsibilities and duties of the Maastricht Treaty without reservations once it became an EU member in 1995. This included the provision of the CFSP as mentioned in Art J.4 of the Treaty (European Community 1992). To avoid incompatibilities of Austria's participation in the CFSP with the law of neutrality, provision 23f was added to the Austrian Constitution (Bundespressedienst 2000). This amendment allowed Austria to participate in the CFSP and also in the implementation of economic sanctions decided by the EU. It guaranteed that the Neutrality Act would not impede Austria's participation in the CFSP. The Austrian position aimed at dampening the EU member states' hesitation about Austria's membership by demonstrating that its assessment of security policy issues corresponded closely with those of the EU and that its foreign policy positions were in line with the development of the CFSP (Österreich 1994: V 2.3–V 2.4).

With the ratification of the Amsterdam Treaty in 1998, Austria was obliged to adopt a new constitutional amendment of article 23f enabling it to participate in the entire spectrum of the Petersberg tasks irrespective of the law of neutrality (Austrian Ministry of Defence 2001: 38). These tasks comprise the whole spectrum of crisis management missions, including peace enforcement. With the constitutional amendment on 'cooperation and solidarity in sending units or individual persons abroad', Austria's participation in international operations became no longer dependent on neutrality but on the conformity to UN and CFSP principles (Niederberger 2001: 83). With the entry into force of the Amsterdam Treaty, on May 1, 1999, Austria was then no longer compelled 'to observe neutrality stipulation with respect to the CFSP' (Gustenau 1999: 10). Austria could now participate in all operations in which the EU or the UN were involved. As a result, the residual neutrality restricted Austria's participation only in common defence situation or NATO-led peace support operation not mandated by the UN (Gustenau 1999: 12).

In 1999, the NATO campaign in Kosovo stirred fierce domestic opposition against the Alliance and was electorally exploited by the SPÖ. Neutrality became more popular than ever in Austria. As the NATO campaign against Serbia was not approved by a UN Resolution, the Austrian government did not grant transit rights to NATO aircrafts, forcing them to bypass the country.[7] Yet at the same time, Chancellor Viktor Klima endorsed NATO operations by supporting an EU statement of the Head of States stating their determination not to tolerate the killings and indicating their support to military action (see EU 1999: point 2). Kosovo demonstrated the inconsistencies of Austria's policy by exposing the contradictions of the policy conducted by a neutral state member of the EU when massive force must be used in peace enforcement operations.

Domestically, the two governmental parties clashed over the issue of NATO membership when it came to elaborate a new security policy doctrine – the Option Report – in 1998 (Austrian Ministry of Defence 1998).[8] While the ÖVP supported a rapid accession to NATO, the SPÖ refused to accept a report hinting at rapid membership of NATO, which would be in contradiction with Austrian neutrality. The failure of the Option Report and the ensuing conflict over neutrality was one of the reasons for the disbandment of the ÖVP-SPÖ coalition after the 1999 parliamentary elections.

The new ÖVP-FPÖ coalition government was the first Austrian government to officially question the relevance of Austria's neutrality. The government program stated that Austria would commit itself to active participation in the development of the ESDP including a possible mutual military assistance guarantee (*Beistandpflicht*) in case of armed aggression against an EU member state.[9] It also added that Austrian neutrality would have no effect on this and warned that, should progress on ESDP within the EU not materialise, then other

---

7 It is worth noting that similar decisions were taken by Austria in two other instances. In September 1998, Austria denied a transfer on the Danube of French tanks for an exercise in Slovakia. In March 1999, the transit of Czech, Polish and Hungarian military units that went to Italy for a military exercise was also refused. The Austrian behaviour was obviously harshly criticised (Luif 2001: 151).

8 From 1970 to 1982 Austria was governed by the Social Democratic Party (SPÖ). Then, the SPÖ entered into coalition with the rightwing Christian-Conservative Party (ÖVP) in order to offset its steady decline. This coalition converted the traditionally euro-sceptical SPÖ into a supporter of the European agenda. In 2000, the ÖVP made a coalition with the nationalist Freedom Party (FPÖ) of Jörg Haider. Since 2006, the traditional SPÖ–ÖVP coalition has returned to power.

9 In May 2001 this idea was formally expressed by Chancellor Schüssel (Höll 2002: 302, fn 43).

security policy alternatives would be sought (Austrian Government 2000: 96). This meant to develop Austria's relationship with NATO beyond its membership of the Partnership for Peace (PfP) to consider its full membership to NATO (Austrian Government 2000: 97).

On December 12, 2001 the Lower House of the Austrian Parliament (*Nationalrat*) adopted a new security policy doctrine: the *Austrian Security and Defence Doctrine* (Austrian National Parliament 2002: 1). This doctrine marked a fundamental paradigm shift from a reactive to a preventive security policy based on strong European cooperation and solidarity (Scheibner 2001: 17). The main assumption was that Austria's security interests were best served through its integration in the European security architecture. To this purpose, Austria would support any initiative to strengthen a common European defence in the future (Austrian National Parliament 2002: 11). That was a major breakthrough because it meant that the Austrian government would support the inclusion of a security guarantee in the EU which would de facto transform the EU into a military alliance (Neuhold 2003: 16). Neutrality was no longer deemed a serious security policy instrument. This view was formally expressed by Chancellor Wolfgang Schüssel during the celebration of the national day – which represents the day on which the law of neutrality was enacted in 1955 – on 26 October 2001, when he said: 'the old template – Lippizaner,[10] Mozartkugeln [chocolate balls], or neutrality no longer subscribe to the reality of the twenty-first century' (Schüssel 2001). By this he meant that neutrality had become a cliché that the Austrians should forget.

The 2001 Doctrine defined Austria's status as non-allied and demonstrated a political willingness to move away from neutrality. However, neutrality was still constitutionally anchored and 'was rediscovered' during the American invasion of Iraq in 2003 (Neuhold 2003: 17). Austria prohibited the overflight of military aircrafts from members of the US coalition, and justified its decision by its neutral status (Rees 2006). Then, during the negotiations on the European Constitution Austria supported the inclusion of the 'Irish clause' which prevents from subscribing to alliance obligation contrary to the status of neutrality.

After the Heads of States and Government could not agree on the draft Constitutional Treaty in Rome in December 2003, the idea of a 'core Europe' composed of member states that would be ready to move faster in the integration process re-emerged. Chancellor Schüssel reaffirmed at this occasion the European commitment of his country and came up with the formula 'solidarity within Europe, neutrality in wars outside Europe' (quoted in Neuhold 2004b: 14). This formula implies that in theory Austria considered the obligation of a collective defence system in Europe to be compatible with its neutral status. As Neuhold rightly observed, this position obviously turns the concept of neutrality on its head (Neuhold 2004a). This approach was supported by Austria's ratification of the Lisbon Treaty in 2008.

---

10   Horses of the Spanish Riding School in Vienna.

The review of Austrian neutrality demonstrates that neutrality has become very marginal in terms of security policy principle. With the 2001 doctrine, Austria has replaced neutrality with solidarity especially within the EU. This move away from neutrality was confirmed by the 2004 defence reform which aimed at transforming the Austrian Armed Forces into expeditionary forces capable of participating in the entire spectrum of the Petersberg tasks (Bundesheerreformkommission 2004).

Swiss Security Policy After the Cold War

When the Eastern threat collapsed, the Swiss government was quick to reassess its strategic position through the publication of a new security policy report (Report 90) in October 1990 (Conseil Fédéral 1990). Report 90 extended the goals of security policy by including the promotion of peace and the contribution to international stability. Yet, Switzerland very quickly faced a dilemma between maintaining security through armed neutrality, or through cooperation in a new European security architecture (Däniker and Spillmann 1992: 604).

During the 1991 Gulf War, Switzerland took part in UN economic sanctions against Iraq but unlike Austria, denied the coalition's aircraft the right to fly over its territory.[11] This decision was a strong departure from the Swiss doctrine of not taking part in any sanctions.[12] The head of the Department for Foreign Affairs (DFAE), René Felber, justified it by the fact that:

> The adoption of economic sanctions is not contrary to the law of neutrality. This law does not impose on the neutral state the obligation to maintain economic relations with a party involved in a conflict. The decision by a permanently neutral state on whether or not to adopt economic sanctions must be appreciated from the point of view of its policy of neutrality the implementation of which is left to its discretion (quoted in Schindler 1992: 109).

This change of practice[13] signalled the readiness of the Swiss government to enforce Security Council Resolutions on non-military sanctions and demonstrated that Switzerland had returned to the policy of differential neutrality (i.e. participation in economic but not in military sanctions) which it had followed as a member of the League of Nations until 1938 (Schindler 1992: 111).

---

11   Exceptions were made for flights of humanitarian character.
12   This doctrine was a consequence of Switzerland's unfortunate experience with economic sanctions during the Abyssinian War of 1935–1936 that subsequently led Bern to ask the League of Nations to exempt it from the duty to participate in sanctions (Schindler 1992: 109).
13   Similar decisions were then taken in the case of the UN arms embargo and air traffic against Libya and with regard to the UN economic sanctions against Yugoslavia.

The ambiguous behaviour of Switzerland during the Gulf War forced the government to reassess the relevance of neutrality. In 1993, the Federal Council published a report on neutrality based on the recommendations of a study group which had proposed to reduce neutrality to its military core, i.e. to military non-participation in interstate wars. However, it introduced an important caveat, namely that the law of neutrality was not applicable to UN sanctions decided under Chapter VII (Studiengruppe 1992: 20). Therefore economic neutrality should be abandoned as well as the anticipated effects of neutrality introduced in the 1950s.[14] When it comes to military sanctions Switzerland should abstain from actively supporting military operations but should also not impede them through the granting of overflight and transit rights. This led the report to affirm that in the military field, neutrality had lost much of its relevance: 'the necessity of our neutrality – originally conditioned by Switzerland's geographic situation between rival powers – no longer exists except to a very limited extent' (Studiengruppe 1992: 15).

These recommendations were implemented in the 1993 Foreign Policy Report (Report 93), which initiated a paradigm change in Swiss foreign and security policy (Conseil Fédéral 1994). The 'traditional concept of "security through neutrality and independence" was to be supplemented with "*security through cooperation*" [original]' (Federal Council 1993: 15). Swiss security policy would rely on two pillars: a national conception based on permanent neutrality through national defence and an international dimension based on solidarity through peace promotion (Federal Council 1993: 28).

The continuity of Swiss foreign policy was demonstrated through the maintenance of permanent neutrality, which was justified by the fact that during this time of transition and uncertainty characterised by the emergence of new dangers the armed forces and neutrality were the best-proven guarantors of Switzerland's security (Federal Council 1993: 12). Yet, the government acknowledged that 'neutrality needs to be interpreted in light of the requirements of international solidarity and should be used to serve the international community and world peace' (Federal Council 1993: 11). To this purpose, Switzerland committed itself to abide by non-military sanctions imposed by the UN but also those of the EU. The rationale behind it was that such measures would serve 'to re-establish order and thereby serve the peace' and that was 'in accordance with the spirit of neutrality' (Federal Council 1993: 28). The solidarity with the EU was justified by the fact that the CFSP goals were 'fully compatible with the spirit of [Swiss] neutrality' that is the elimination of the prospect of war from Europe (Federal Council 1993: 26). The new understanding of the application of neutrality was thus reduced in the sole case of interstate wars that occur outside Chapter VII of the UN Charter. In all, Report 93 re-focused Swiss foreign and security policy on the promotion of

---

14 These stem from the view that Switzerland had an obligation to abstain from anything that could draw the country into a war in peacetime.

peace and humanitarian assistance and restricted the applicability of neutrality to the requirements of solidarity (Federal Council 1993: 11).

This new interpretation of neutrality was applied immediately after the publication of Report 93. The Swiss Government granted transit right to NATO AWACS airplanes for their UN observation mission in Bosnia-Herzegovina on 23 December 1993. However, the creation of a peacekeeping contingent, which should have bolstered the new security policy orientation, was refused by the Swiss population in a referendum in 1994. Consequently any prospect for a Swiss military engagement to bolster international stability was frozen.[15]

The year 1996 represented a milestone for Swiss security policy because Switzerland held the OSCE presidency and joined NATO PfP. Fearful of domestic reactions, the government prefaced the presentation document with a declaration that it did not intend to renounce neutrality and should the PfP take a defensive alliance character, Switzerland would relinquish its membership (Federal Council 1997: 119). Similarly, Switzerland would refuse to take part in art. 5 type exercises because they pertain to collective defence. Within its OSCE mandate, Switzerland had to monitor the Dayton Accord. Since, military participation in the NATO IFOR was excluded, the Swiss government deployed a logistical support unit (Yellow Beret) to assist the OSCE in Bosnia-Herzegovina. It is worth noting that unlike 1991, Switzerland agreed to grant ground and air transit rights to NATO IFOR units.

The unanswered questions regarding the conduct of a policy of neutrality became very acute with NATO Operation Allied Force in Kosovo in 1999. Similar to Austria, Switzerland conducted an ambiguous policy partly aligned with European states' policy and partly deviated from the other states, using neutrality as its justification (Goetschel 2005: 91). In 1998, the Federal Council decided to take part in the EU's coercive measures against Yugoslavia (e.g. embargo on goods of repression, prohibition of new investments, freezing of assets, visa restrictions) because it was permitted by international law, it safeguarded Swiss interests but also because it showed solidarity with the EU (Interdepartmental 2000: 6). Switzerland adopted economic sanctions for the first time without a corresponding UN Security Council resolution. In April 1999, the DFAE declared that Switzerland would take part in the UN war-materials embargo against former Yugoslavia. A month later however, the Federal Council decided against complete support of intensified EU sanctions[16] although Switzerland was participating in the first series of EU economic sanctions against the Federal Republic of Yugoslavia. By participating in the oil embargo the law of neutrality's principle of non-discrimination would have to be observed against all parties including all NATO

---

15 Two years earlier, the Swiss population had already notified the government that it was against an internationalisation of Swiss foreign policy by rejecting the membership of the EEA.

16 These concerned EU ban on oil transactions as well as EU's sanction against the Yugoslav airline JAT.

states. In order to avoid this, the Federal Council declined to impose an export ban on oil to Yugoslavia (Interdepartmental 2000: 8). Swiss contradictions were further exposed when the government granted overflight rights for humanitarian purposes but not for NATO aircrafts involved in combat. After the cessation of hostilities and the adoption of UN resolution 1244, the Federal Council approved the overflights and transit of NATO KFOR troops as well as Swiss participation in this force with a company sized unit.

A governmental commission tasked to analyse the relevance of neutrality after the Kosovo experience concluded that Switzerland complied consistently with the law of neutrality and that the credibility and predictability of Swiss neutrality had not been jeopardised (Interdepartmental 2000: 20). These conclusions however were dubious because the manoeuvring between a political and a legal interpretation of neutrality were confusing for outsider observers. This highlighted firstly that the Swiss government had not come to grip with the new international setting. The principles of solidarity and multilateralism were inconsistently applied especially regarding the support of the EU's sanction because the government still partly relied on the application of neutrality under the old rationale (Borchert 2001: 179).

Secondly, Switzerland's ambiguous policy also demonstrated the irrelevance of neutrality as a security policy principle based on cooperation since political issues could not be answered via purely legal approaches (Goetschel 2005: 91). The issue of sanctions perfectly illustrated Switzerland's new security policy dilemma by highlighting the clash of its two antithetical concepts: neutrality and the new philosophy of human security. To be consistent with the latter requires an assertive policy against those states that represent a threat to their own people. This however is contrary to the policy of neutrality (Tanner 2003: 58-9). Although Switzerland adjusted its policy of conditionality and sanctions to the policies of the UN and the EU, the Kosovo example demonstrated the limits of the approach combining neutrality and denunciation of human rights abuses. Austria was caught in a similar dilemma but its EU membership overruled the requirements of neutrality.

Following a reflection on the orientations of Swiss security policy that had started in 1996, the government published a new security report in 1999 (Report 2000), which shifted from an autonomous and reactive stance towards prevention and cooperation. It noted that during the Kosovo experience the law of neutrality had prevented Switzerland from supporting the measures taken by other states even if they were compatible with the objectives of Swiss foreign policy. The report therefore openly questioned the relevance of permanent neutrality for safeguarding Swiss foreign and security interests and alluded to Switzerland adopting the status of an ad hoc neutral state similar to that of Sweden or Ireland. This would give Switzerland more room to manoeuvre in the conduct of its security policy. The report cautiously concluded by stating that alliance membership was part of preserving Switzerland's freedom of action but rejected NATO membership (Conseil Fédéral 1999: 44, 47). The new underlying assumption of Swiss security policy was that 'participation, rather than neutrality or an independent national defence strategy, [would] safeguard the government's freedom of action' (Wenger 2003: 38). The armed forces reform launched in 2004 built upon this assumption and made interoperability the key principle of the structure of the Swiss armed forces.

Similar to Austria, the war in Iraq provided Switzerland with another opportunity to apply neutrality since the military operations against Saddam Hussein could not be based on a UN resolution. On 21 February 2003, the Federal Council declined a request from the United States to grant overflight rights for military purposes to its aircrafts.[17] When the war broke out, the government banned allied aircrafts, including reconnaissance and surveillances flights, from transiting over Swiss territory. The only exception was regarding overflights for humanitarian and medical purposes (DFAE 2005: 12). When the war between Israel and Hezbolah in Lebanon broke out in 2006, the limits of neutrality in contemporary conflicts were exposed. Since this war opposed a state to a non-state actor, the Swiss government did not act because it could not agree on the application of neutrality.

These confusing interpretations of neutrality led to a reorientation of Swiss foreign policy in the 2000s. The Swiss government realised that '*[Switzerland's] influence in the sphere of foreign affairs ha[d] undoubtedly diminished over the past decades* [original]' (Federal Council 2000: annex 1). Swiss membership of the UN in 2002 was a first step. Another was to replace the passive conception of neutrality policy of the Cold War with an active dimension: peace policy (Calmy-Rey 2004). The adoption of peace policy was conceived as a modern form of good offices and aimed at getting international influence (Calmy-Rey 2005, 2006). In line with the neutral ethos, the objective of this policy was to promote peace by 'facilitating the non-violent resolution of existing problems' through the promotion of human rights (Federal Council 2000: 28). Multilateral cooperation became a key principle of Swiss security policy because remaining politically absent risked isolating Switzerland and making it defenceless against decisions taken abroad (Federal Council 2000: 25). The peace policy demonstrated that neutrality was no longer considered as a viable guide for security and foreign policy for Switzerland because its lack of influence could no longer be offset by the maximisation of its autonomy. Yet, in order to get domestic approval for peace policy, the latter relied on the ethos of neutrality which was still strongly supported by the population.

The Current Function of Neutrality

The evolution of the understanding of neutrality demonstrates that it has become a marginal security policy instrument justifiable only in situations where the UN and the EU bodies of law do not apply (Gabriel 1995: 173). However, Austria and Switzerland still legally retain this concept. This can be explained by the fact that neutrality has provided these countries with a specific identity, which is strongly supported by the population and prevents the governments from abandoning it.

---

17 Surveillance and reconnaissance flights were however permitted.

This is because the population tends to have 'nostalgic and exaggerated views on the value of non-alignment and neutrality' (Herolf 2006: 70). As the Swiss government concluded 'the *perception* by the Swiss population over a very long period that neutrality conveyed with it *security* has thus become *deceptive* [original]' (Conseil Fédéral 1999: 42). This, in turn, creates a gap between the functional understanding of neutrality by the elite and the normative attachment of the population. This is confirmed by surveys analysis of different issues pertaining to neutrality.

In Switzerland, neutrality approval scored around 80 percent in the 1990s and around 90 percent in the 2000s peaking at 92 percent in 2008 while it has ranged between 60 percent and 70 percent in Austria (Haltiner et al. 2008; Reiter 1999; SWS 1992a, 1995, 1999). A closer examination demonstrates that it is the normative dimension of neutrality which people are attached to. For the Austrian population, neutrality has purely an identity function while the original security policy function has become increasingly irrelevant. Indeed, 63 percent support participation in a combined European force but only 28 percent are in favor of relinquishing neutrality in case of participation (Schaller 2003: 16). Also, 58 percent disagree that Austria avoids the threat of terrorism because of its neutrality (Schaller 2003: 12). In 1991, in comparison, only 6 percent thought that neutrality was a liability for security and 49 percent thought that neutrality was the best guarantor of Austrian neutrality followed by participation in a European security system (27 percent) (SWS 1991, 1992b). Until 1995, neutrality was considered as a protection against military conflict by 53 percent of Austrians (SWS 1995). This demonstrates that the population has developed a normative attachment to neutrality but its security policy function is no longer recognised.

In Switzerland, there are also differences between the different functions of neutrality. Thus, the solidarity function[18] scored between 85 percent and 90 percent in the 2000s and the identity function[19] rose from 70 percent to 80 percent by 2007 (Haltiner et al. 2007: 117, 119). These figures demonstrate that the Swiss population has an even stronger normative attachment to neutrality than the Austrians. The security policy function of neutrality gathers less support however. In 2008, 55 percent believed that armed neutrality was a contribution to European stability and security but 48 percent doubted that neutrality could still be defended and therefore less than half (49 percent) favoured military autonomy (Haltiner et al. 2008: 94). From these figures it can be stated that similar to Austria, neutrality has primarily an identity function for the Swiss population. The security policy function has also become increasingly irrelevant though it is still supported by about half of the population.

For the Austrian and Swiss populations, the legacy of neutrality after the Cold War is mainly normative. Neutrality is related to national identity; is part of statehood. The security policy function of neutrality has become obsolete for

---

18   This function consists of seeing neutrality as enabler of good offices.
19   Here, people consider neutrality inseparable of statehood.

the Austrian population because by becoming member of the EU, the sense of belonging to a security community has diminished traditional security threats and therefore the relevance of neutrality. In Switzerland, a similar trend can be observed though it is less important because the country is not a member of the EU (Rickli forthcoming).

Conclusions

With the end of the Cold War, the security policy function of neutrality in Austria and Switzerland has been increasingly questioned. The application of neutrality has become marginal, limited to interstate wars such as the 1991 Gulf War, the 1999 Kosovo War and the 2003 American-led coalition against Iraq. Yet, the security discussions in these states are still framed in reference to neutrality. This is because neutrality has acquired a normative function that relates to statehood. This normative attachment to neutrality, which stems from the Cold War, translates into a strong domestic support of the traditional pillars of the neutral strategic culture: military non-alliance and the non-offensive use of force. This has impacted the strategic choices of Austria and Switzerland. Austria, being a member of the EU, has been compelled to move beyond neutrality and adopted solidarity as a principle of its security policy. Neutrality in Austria has been de-emphasised so as to be in line with the European Security and Defence Policy, yet the bottom line has remained the non-participation in a military alliance. In Switzerland, the passive conception of neutrality of the Cold War has been replaced by a more active and cooperative security policy, peace policy. The latter favours non-belligerency and a civilian approach to peace promotion. In both countries, the security policy function of neutrality has become marginal but the legacy of the principles of neutrality has determined the shape of their new security policy orientation.

References

Austrian Government, 2000. *Regierungsprogramm*, 4 February. Vienna.
Austrian Ministry of Defence, 1998. *Bericht über alle weiterführenden Optionen Österreichs im Bereich der Sicherheitspolitik (Option Bericht)*. Vienna: Ministry of Defence.
Austrian Ministry of Defence, 2001. *Security and Defence Doctrine, Analysis, Draft Expert Report*, 23 May. Vienna.
Austrian National Parliament, 2002. *Austrian Security and Defence Doctrine*. Vienna.
Bächler, G. 1994. *Beitreten oder Trittbrettfahren? Die Zukunft der Neutralität in Europa*. Chur/Zürich: Rüegger.
Bindschedler, R.L. 1976. Neutralitätspolitik und Sicherheitspolitik. *Österreichische Zeitschrift für Aussenpolitik*, 6, 339-54.

Borchert, H. 2001. Switzerland and Europe's Security Architecture: The Rocky Road from Isolation to Cooperation, in *Small States and Alliances*, edited by E. Reiter and H. Gärtner. Heidelberg: Physica-Verlag, 161-82.

Braillard, P., Djalili M.-R. and Tanner, F. 1990. *La Politique de sécurité des Etats européens neutres ou non alignés: les défis d'une adaptation à une Europe en profonde mutation.* Berne: Office central de la défense.

Bundesheerreformkommission, 2004. *Bericht der Bundesheerreformkommission Bundesheer 2010.* Wien.

Bundespressedienst, 2000. *Austrian Federal Constitutional Laws (Selection).* Vienna. Available at: http://www.ris.bka.gv.at/info/bvg_eng.pdf [accessed: 18 November 2004].

Calmy-Rey, M. 2004. *Die Friedenspolitik der Schweiz*, Vortrag gehalten von Frau Bundesrätin Micheline Calmy-Rey, Offiziersgesellschaft Zürichsee rechtes Ufer.

Calmy-Rey, M. 2005. *Die Friedenspolitik als integraler Teil der Schweizerischen Aussenpolitik*, Vortrag gehalten von Frau Bundesrätin Micheline Calmy-Rey, Neue Helvetische Gesellschaft, Sektion Basel, 3 November.

Calmy-Rey, M. 2006. *Politique de puissance – politique d'influence: opportunités et limites d'une politique d'influence*, Conférence des Ambassadeurs, Berne, 21 August.

Conseil Fédéral, 1990. *La politique de sécurité de la Suisse dans un monde en mutation, Rapport 90 du Conseil Fédéral à l'Assemblée Fédérale sur la politique de sécurité de la Suisse du 1er octobre 1990.* Berne.

Conseil Fédéral, 1994. Rapport sur la politique extérieure de la Suisse dans les années 90 du 29 novembre 1993. *Feuille Fédérale*, 146(I), 150-237.

Conseil Fédéral, 1999. *Sécurité par la coopération*. Rapport du Conseil Fédéral à l'Assemblée Fédérale sur la politique de sécurité de la Suisse, (RAPOLSEC 2000), 7 June 1999. Berne. Available at: http://www.vbs.admin.ch/internet/vbs/fr/home/documentation/publication/p_security.parsys.0009.downloadList.00091.DownloadFile.tmp/sipol2000f.pdf [accessed: 15 July 2009].

Däniker, G. 1992. Swiss Security Policy in a Changing Strategic Environment, in *The European Neutrals in the 1990s*, edited by H. Neuhold. Boulder: Westview Press, 3-16.

Däniker, G. and Spillmann, K.R. 1992. Die Konzeption der Schweizerischen Sicherheitspolitik, in *Neues Handbuch der Schweizerischen Aussenpolitik*, edited by A. Riklin, H. Haug and R. Probst. Bern: Haupt, 591-605.

DFAE, 2005. *Neutrality under scrutiny in the Iraq Conflict: Summary of Switzerland's Neutrality Policy during the Iraq Conflict in response to the Reimann Postulate (03.3066) and to the motion by the SVP Parliamentary Group (03.3050)*. 2 December. Bern.

Dulles, J.F. 1956. The Cost of Peace. *Department of State Bulletin*, 34, 999-1000.

EU, Press release, 1999. *Chairman's Summary of the Deliberation on Kosovo at the Informal Meeting of the Heads of States and Government of the European Union in Brussels*, 14 April.

European Commission, 1992a. The Challenge of Enlargement: Commission Opinion on Austria's Application Membership. *Bulletin of the European Communities*, Supplement 4/92, 15-18.
European Commission, 1992b. Europe and the Challenge of the Enlargement. *Bulletin of the European Communities*, Supplement 3/92.
European Community, 1992. *The Maastricht Treaty, Treaty on European Union, Maastricht, 7 February 1992*. Luxembourg: Office for Official Publications of the European Communities.
Federal Council, 1993. *White Paper on Neutrality: Annex to the Report on Swiss Foreign Policy for the Nineties of 20 November 1993*. Bern.
Federal Council, 1997. *Präsentationsdokument der Schweiz für die Partnerschaft für den Frieden vom 30. 10. 1996*. Zurich.
Federal Council, 2000. *Foreign Policy Report 2000; Presence and Cooperation: Safeguarding Switzerland's Interests in an Integrating World*, 15 November 2000. Bern.
Fendius Elman, M. 1995. The Foreign Policies of Small States: Challenging Neorealism in Its Own Backyard. *British Journal of Political Science*, 25(2), 171-217.
Gabriel, J.M. 1995. Neutralität für den Notfall: der Bericht des Bundesrats zur Aussenpolitik der Schweiz in den 90er Jahren. *Swiss Political Science Review*, 1(2-3), 163-91.
Goetschel, L. 1998. The Foreign and Security Policy Interests of Small States in Today's Europe, in *Small States Inside and Outside the European Union*, edited by L. Goetschel. Dordrecht: Kluwer Academic Publishers, 13-31.
Goetschel, L. 2005. *Swiss Foreign Policy: Foundations and Possibilities*. London: Routledge.
Gustenau, G. 1999. *Towards a Common European Policy on Security and Defence: An Austrian View of Challenges for the 'Post-Neutrals'*. Paris: Institute for Security Studies.
Haltiner, K.W., Wenger, A., Würmli S. and Lipowiscz, A. 2008. *Sicherheit 2008: Aussen-, sicherheits- und verteidigungspolitische Meinungsbildung im Trend*. Zürich: Forschungsstelle für Sicherheitspolitik der ETH Zürich und Militärakademie an der ETH Zürich.
Haltiner, K.W., Wenger, A, Würmli, S. and Wenger, U. 2007. *Sicherheit 2007: Aussen-, sicherheits- und verteidigungspolitische Meinungsbildung im Trend*. Zürich: Forschungsstelle für Sicherheitspolitik der ETH Zürich und Militärakademie an der ETH Zürich.
Herolf, G. 2006. The Nordic Countries and the EU-NATO Relationship: Further Comments, in *The Nordic Countries and the European Security and Defence Policy*, edited by A.J.K. Bailes, G. Herolf and B. Sundelius. Oxford: SIPRI/Oxford University Press, 67-76.
Höll, O. 2002. Aussen- und Sicherheitspolitik, in *Europäisierung der österreichischen Politik*, edited by H. Neisser and S. Puntscher Riekmann. Wien: WUV-Universitätsverlag, 369-95.

Interdepartmental Working Group, 2000. *Swiss Neutrality in Practise – Current Aspects. Report of the Interdepartmental Working Group of 30 August 2000.* Bern.
Joenniemi, P. 1993. Neutrality Beyond the Cold War. *Review of International Studies*, 289-304.
Karsh, E. 1988. *Neutrality and Small States.* London: Routledge.
Krüger, M. 2003. Austria, in *Neutrality and Non-Alignment in Europe Today*, edited by H. Ojanen. Helsinki: Finnish Institute of International Affairs, 9-13.
Kruzel, J. 1989. The Future of European Neutrality, in *Between the Blocs: Problems and Prospects for Europe's Neutral and Nonaligned States*, edited by M.H. Haltzel and J. Kruzel. Cambridge: Cambridge University Press, 295-311.
Kux, S. 1994. *Zukunft Neutralität? Die Schweizerische Aussen- und Sicherheitspolitik im Umbruch*, Bern: Haupt.
Luif, P. 2001. Austria's Permanent Neutrality – Its Origins, Development, and Demise, in *Neutrality in Austria*, edited by G. Bischof, A. Pelinka and R. Wodak. New Brunswick and London: Transaction Publishers, 129-59.
Mouritzen, H. 1997. *External Danger and Democracy: Old Nordic Lessons and New European Challenges.* Aldershot: Ashgate.
Mouritzen, H. and Wivel, A. 2005. *The Geopolitics of Euro-Atlantic Integration.* London: Routledge.
Neuhold, H. 2003. Comments on the Austrian Positions, in *Neutrality and Non-Alignment in Europe Today*, edited by H. Ojanen. Helsinki: Finnish Institute of International Affairs, 14-18.
Neuhold, H. 2004a. Aussenpolitik und Demokratie: 'Immerwährende' Neutralität durch juristische Mutation, in *Demokratie und sozialer Rechtsstaat in Europa, Festschrift für Theo Öhlinger*, edited by S. Hammer, A. Somek, M. Stelzer and B. Weichselbaum. Wien: WUV-Universitätsverlag, 68-91.
Neuhold, H. 2004b. Comments on the Austrian Position, in *Challenges to Neutral and Non-Aligned Countries in Europe and Beyond*, edited by E. Munro. Geneva: Geneva Center for Security Policy, 13-17.
Niederberger, J. 2001. Österreichische Sicherheitspolitik zwischen Solidarität und Neutralität, in *Bulletin 2001 zur Schweizerischen Sicherheitspolitik*, edited by K. Spillman and A. Wenger. Zürich: Forschungsstelle für Sicherheitspolitik und Konfliktanalyse, 69-94.
Österreich, Bundesregierung, 1994. *Weissbuch der Bundesregierung.* Wien: Bundesregierung.
Palme, O. 1984. *Sveriges Utrikespolitik.* Stockholm: Tidens förlag.
Rees, N. 2006. The Neutral States and the Challenge of ESDP: Kosovo, Iraq and the Transatlantic Divide, in *The Transatlantic Divide*, edited by O. Croci and A. Verdun. Manchester: Manchester University Press, 173-89.
Reiter, E. 1993. *Österreichische Sicherheits- und Verteidigungspolitik.* Frankfurt am Main: Peter Land.
Reiter, E. 1999. *Die Meinungen der Österreicher zu Neutralität, Sicherheit und Nato.* Wien: Landesverteidigungsakademie/Militärwissenschaftliches Büro.

Rickli, J.-M. 2008. European Small States' Military Policies after the Cold War: From Territorial to Niche Strategies. *Cambridge Review of International Affairs*, 21, 307-25.

Rickli, J.-M. Forthcoming. *The Military Policies of European Neutral and Non-Allied States after the Cold War*, (PhD thesis). Oxford: University of Oxford.

Schaller, S. 2003. *25 'Armies' Or Just One? Austrian Attitude Towards a Combined European Force*. Vienna: Austrian Society for European Politics.

Scheibner, H. 2001. Eine neue Verteidigungspolitik für Österreich. *Österreichische Militärische Zeitschrift*, XXXIX (1), 17-24.

Schindler, D. 1992. Changing Conceptions of Neutrality in Switzerland. *Austrian Journal of Public and International Law*, 44, 105-16.

Schüssel, W. 2001. *Rede anlässlich des Nationalfeiertags*, Oktober 26, Wien. Available at: http://www.presseportal.at/meldung.php?schluessel=OTS_200 41019_OTS0085&ch=politik [accessed: 18 November 2004].

Stein, G.J. 1990. Total Defence: A Comparative Overview of the Security Policies of Switzerland and Austria. *Defence Analysis*, 6(1), 17-33.

Studiengruppe zu Fragen der schweizerischen Neutralität, 1992. *Schweizerische Neutralität auf dem Prüfstand – Schweizerische Aussenpolitik zwischen Kontinuität und Wandel. Bericht.* Bern.

SWS. 1991. *Fragebogen 274*, March. Wien: Sozialwissenschaftliche Studiengesellschaft.

SWS. 1992a. *Fragebogen 281*, January. Wien: Sozialwissenschaftliche Studiengesellschaft.

SWS. 1992b. *Fragebogen 286*, September. Wien: Sozialwissenschaftliche Studiengesellschaft.

SWS. 1995. *Fragebogen 304*, March/April. Wien: Sozialwissenschaftliche Studien-gesellschaft.

SWS. 1999. *Fragebogen 327*, May/June. Wien: Sozialwissenschaftliche Studien-gesellschaft.

Tanner, F. 2003. Swiss Foreign Policy, Peace Promotion and the New International Security Agenda: 'Il faut faire quelque chose'. *Nouveaux Mondes*, 13, 47-63.

Thürer, D. 1995. Sicherheitspolitik und Neutralität, in *Die Schweizerische Sicherheitspolitik im internationalen Umfeld*, edited by R. Rhinow. Basel: Helbling and Lichtenbach, 121-36.

Wenger, A. 2003. Swiss Security Policy: From Autonomy to Co-Operation, in *Swiss Foreign Policy, 1945–2002*, edited by J.M. Gabriel. Basingstoke: Palgrave MacMillan, 23-45.

Wivel, A. 2005. The Security Challenge of Small EU Member States: Interests, Identity and the Development of the EU as a Security Actor. *Journal of Common Market Studies*, 43(2), 393-412.

Chapter 13
The Icelandic Crash and its Consequences: A Small State without Economic and Political Shelter

Baldur Thorhallsson

The Icelandic economic miracle that began in the mid-1990s is over. The volatility of the small economy is once again evident. The collapse of the Icelandic financial sector and the króna (ISK) resulted in a swift turn from a blooming economy to an economic crash in early October 2008. The Icelandic government was defenceless against the economic turmoil that ensued when the small economy was hit by the international financial crisis. It had been unable to seek substantial external assistance from neighbouring countries and international organisations prior to the crisis in order to strengthen the foundation of the economy, particularly the overgrown financial sector.

Moreover, the government had severe difficulties in guaranteeing external assistance when the financial crisis hit the country with full force. Iceland's economy came to a standstill and the Icelandic Central Bank only provided foreign currency for the import of food, medicine and petrol (The Central Bank of Iceland 2008a). The British government used its anti-terrorist rules to take control of assets held in Britain by the beleaguered Icelandic banks (Donaldson and Vina 2008) and demanded full payback from the Icelandic government to British account holders. The tense relations that followed between the two countries, where to Iceland's dismay all member states of the European Union (EU), including the Nordic states, stood by Britain, delaying much-needed external assistance (Morgunblaðið 2008). Iceland faced challenges on all fronts since the governments of Germany, the Netherlands and Luxembourg also demanded full guarantees of their citizen's savings, 'lost' in the branches of the Icelandic banks in these states, from the Icelandic government.

The International Monetary Fund (IMF) finally came to the rescue a few weeks into the crisis – after Iceland had accepted preconditions for settling the dispute with Britain, i.e. given in to Britain's demands. In May 2009, a new government put forward a bill to the Icelandic parliament, the Althingi, proposing that Iceland apply for membership of the European Union.

These events raise the question of whether the Icelandic government failed to guarantee its small economy and society sufficient economic and political shelter. This chapter examines Iceland's past shelters, particularly in the twentieth century, why Iceland has not followed its Nordic neighbours and applied for EU membership until now and whether, as has happened before, any powerful neighbour, or the EU, is likely to provide Iceland with shelter in order to cope with international economic downturns and guarantee its interests. The chapter also examines the consequences the economic crash has had on the views of political parties towards closer engagement in the European project.

Vulnerability of Small Economies

The economies of small states are considerably different from those of large states. Small states rely to a much greater extent on imports and exports than large states do due to the smallness of their domestic markets. This makes their economies more open and vulnerable to international economic fluctuations. Moreover, small states seek specialisation and economies of scale in export markets in order to be competitive internationally and thus often rely on one or two export products. Their exports are also more concentrated than large states' since most of their trade relies on a particular state or a specific market. Hence, small states are often the first to experience international economic crises: economic downturns may hit swiftly and can become deeper than in large states, particularly if the narrow-based export industry is badly hit (Katzenstein 1985; Handel 1981; Ólafsson 1998). Thus, in economic affairs – as in security affairs (cf. Jervis 1978: 172-3) – small states tend to have less influence over international events and a smaller margin of trial and error. This is one of the most important consequences of being the weaker part in an asymmetric relationship (cf. Chapter 1 in this volume).

The case of Iceland fits perfectly into this picture: the economy having undergone distinct cycles depending on the success of the fishing industry at any given time (Jónsson 2002). Moreover, the dramatic rise of the banking sector in the first decade of the twenty-first century – which had assets valued at eight times Iceland's GDP in 2007 (Gros 2008) and, for the first time, contributed more to GDP than the fishing industry in 2007 (Hagstofa Íslands 2009a) – made Iceland even more exposed to the fortunes of the international economy. Early in October 2008, *The New York Times* reported that Iceland was the first sovereign state to fall victim to the credit squeeze (Pfanner 2008).

On the other hand, small states can be the first states to recover from international economic crises. This is because their small bureaucracies, with short distances between decision-makers and speedy decision-making, make them quicker to adapt to new circumstances. Thus, they may be faster and better able to adjust to global competition and other challenges (Kautto et al. 2001). In order to compensate for their economic vulnerability, small states seek protection from large neighbours and international organisations (Handel 1981). In the second half of the twentieth century, most small states sought multilateral economic shelter in international organisations, such as the EU, the IMF, the World Bank, the World Trade Organisation (WTO) and the Nordic Council rather than shelter provided by a large neighbour under a bilateral agreement. However, the case of the smallest states in Europe indicates that not all small states conform to a single pattern in this respect. Iceland, despite being a member of most of the international organisations created after the Second World War, and receiving some direct economic benefit from membership, particularly from the IMF, the World Bank and the Nordic Council, was mainly protected economically by its largest neighbour, the United States. This was also the case of the smallest states in Europe – Andorra, Monaco, Liechtenstein and San Marino – which turned to their larger neighbours for economic and political shelter. All other European small states have sought full participation in European integration, though some of them have been held back by their electorates. The literature generally claims that small states have a stronger negotiating position within multilateral organisations than in bilateral negotiations with a large state (Vital 1967; Neumann and Gstöhl 2004; Chapter 1 in this volume). Small states benefit from clear procedures, rules and regulations within international organisations – making it more difficult for large states to use their greater power resources, such as a larger administration, economic and military power, to press their interests single-handedly (see, for instance, Vital 1967; Keohane 1969). Accordingly, international organisations provide small states with political shelter. The recent negotiations between Iceland and the US about the closure of the military base in Iceland, on the one hand, and between Iceland and Britain about British savers' deposits in the Icelandic banks, on the other, clearly demonstrate the superior position of the larger state (see, for instance, Ingimundarson 2008a; *The Economist* 2008a). While the small states (Latvia, Hungary and Romania) of the EU that were worst hit by the banking crisis were provided with rescue packs by the Union and given immediate help with arranging loans from the IMF (BBC 2009), Iceland was left defenceless and had to struggle to obtain IMF assistance.

Where has Iceland Sought Shelter?

One could argue that Iceland enjoyed shelter provided by its more powerful neighbours from the late thirteenth century down to the late twentieth century/early twenty-first century. Iceland became part of the Norwegian kingdom in 1262, one reason for this being the king's promise to guarantee annual supplies to the country (Lindal and Thorsteinsson 1978). In the following centuries, Iceland had some economic shelter from European sailors and merchants, which provided important trade links with Europe in times of a limited or non-existence of a domestic fleet. However, Iceland was part of the Danish Kingdom until the mid-twentieth century (after a merger of the Norwegian and Danish Kingdom in 1387). Iceland became a sovereign state in 1918 but still enjoyed a measure of cover by the Danish government. For instance, the Danish Foreign Service handled Iceland's external relations until 1940 – despite foreign affairs being in the hands of the Icelandic government – due to the non-existence of a foreign service in Iceland.

The US government took over from the Danes early in the Second World War and provided not only defence in the form of a military presence in the country but also substantial economic and trade shelter until the late 1960s. This was not only a relief to Icelandic policy-makers due to the threat of a German invasion during the War, but also because some of them found it appealing that Iceland was not any longer on its own on the British North-Atlantic territory (Ingimundarson 2002). This later became evident in the Cod Wars with Britain (Confrontations in 1950s and 1970s regarding fishing rights). The US government, from the beginning, provided Iceland with considerable aid (much higher than other European states received, per capita), beneficial loans, monetary donations and favourable trade (best terms) deals with US companies and guaranteed Iceland's exports by buying up unsold fish stockpiles. Moreover, the US built up Iceland's infrastructure, such as Keflavík International Airport, paying the cost of running it and paying for the expensive military and civil radar surveillance systems until 2006. Its military presence also contributed considerably to Iceland's GDP and provided much-needed foreign currency earnings (Thorhallsson and Vignisson 2004a).

The political shelter provided by the US was also a decisive factor in Iceland's successes in extending its exclusive economic zone to 200 nautical miles. Britain and other European fishing nations hesitated to use their full force against Iceland's rigorous extensions of its economic zone due to the US government's and NATO's concerns about the future of the military base in the country (Ingimundarson 2003). The visible political/military shelter provided by the United States lasted until 2006 when it closed the military base, to the indignation of the Icelandic government. However, the bilateral defence agreement between the two countries is still in place, providing Iceland with US protection in the event of a security crisis.

Iceland sought shelter in the European integration process in 1970 when it joined EFTA, ten years after its creation, as a policy response to an economic downturn (the collapse of its important herring stock) and due to the fact its economy was better prepared for membership than before (having been undeveloped and heavily held back by trade barriers). In addition, it was clear that the US government would no longer provide the country with direct economic assistance. EFTA membership also paved the way for a bilateral free trade agreement with the European Economic Community (EEC), signed in 1972. Already in the late 1950s, Iceland had taken part in negotiations, which came to nothing, on a free-trade area in Western Europe, and had considered EFTA membership but was not invited to the EFTA talks because at the time it was involved in a fishing dispute with Britain. In the early 1960s, the Icelandic government seriously considered applying for EEC membership, at the same time as some of its neighbouring states were seeking to join the EEC, in order to guarantee its future exports to the European market. In the end, the government decided to apply for associate membership – without knowing what exactly this would involve. The government concluded that its economy was not prepared for membership and was afraid of the consequences membership would have for its extensive trade with the Soviet

Bloc. That said, all this came to nothing when Britain was denied entry into the EEC – Britain being Iceland's most important single trading partner (Thorhallsson and Vignisson 2004b).

Iceland sought further economic shelter within the EU framework through its joining the European Economic Area (EEA in 1994) – having encountered considerably higher import duties against its fish exports to Spain and Portugal after those countries joined the EEC (1986). EEA membership provided Iceland with tariff-free access for over 96 percent of its fish exports to the Common Market (Thorhallsson and Vignisson 2004c). The Icelandic government still did not consider EU membership as did the other EFTA states, the reason being that EEA membership was seen as being highly beneficial to the economy and, in fact, more beneficial than outright EU membership. EU membership was seen, by nearly all politicians, as entailing considerable strain on the fishing and agricultural sectors. The leadership of the Independence Party (Icelandic conservative party), which had taken the decision not to apply for EU membership in 1992, also disapproved of transferring decision-making concerning monetary policy and free-trade agreements from Reykjavik to Brussels. The EEA Agreement had already been very controversial in the country – the political discourse being on the transfer of sovereignty that the agreement entailed. The Independence Party, the largest party leading all governments from 1991 until 2004, was split on the EEA, and its leadership stifled all discussion of a possible application for EU membership in order to prevent an outright split of the party (Thorhallsson 2008a).

However, Iceland joined the Schengen scheme (2001), along with Norway, after the Nordic EU member states made it a precondition for keeping the Nordic Passport Union functioning. Membership of Schengen has provided Iceland with a more important shelter than was anticipated at the beginning due to the importance of police collaboration as increased international crime has affected the country. Schengen accession was less controversial than the two previous European steps, though the Left-Greens opposed it, as did a few MPs of the Independence Party. The long-serving Prime Minister, David Oddsson (1991–2004), was also not enthusiastic about the membership and stated that Iceland was only taking part in Schengen in order to guarantee the continued free movement of Icelanders to the other Nordic states (Thorhallsson 2008a).

The Financial Crisis Hits

Iceland takes part in the four freedoms of the EU under the EEA Agreement. The Icelandic financial sector, after privatisation (the most decisive steps where taken in 2002 and 2003 when two State banks were privatised), made full use of the liberalisation of the sector and free movement of capital within the EEA. The sector rapidly outgrew the state's capacity to back it up and stabilise the free-floating Icelandic currency. In early 2008, the banking system had assets valued at eight times Iceland's GDP. Icelandic banks had massively borrowed abroad in order to buy foreign banking assets, leveraging their capital base several times over. Also, Iceland's extremely high net foreign debt ratio added to its vulnerability (Gros 2008). The rise of the financial sector resulted in a multiplication of inward and outward FDI. In 1990 to 2000, average annual FDI flows were US$ 64 million inward and US$ 75 million outward. In 2007, these figures had become US$ 3,078 million and US$ 12,127 million respectively (UNCTAD 2008). As a percentage of Iceland's GDP, inward FDI flows in 1990 were 2.3 percent of GDP and outward flows 1.2 percent of GDP. In 2007, FDI flows were 61.5 percent inward and 127.3 percent outward. In total, outward Iceland's FDI flows accounted for 0.6 percent of world total FDI flows in 2007. For a small country like Iceland, that was a relatively large share[1] and further accentuated the vulnerability of the small economy (Hagstofa Íslands 2008a and b).

In the first half of 2008, the vulnerability of the Icelandic financial sector and the inability of the State, as the lender of last resort, to save the banks, should write-downs in the value of foreign assets place them in difficulty, became more evident (The Central Bank of Iceland 2008b). Underestimated risk of foreign currency shortage and later lack of access to foreign currency significantly contributed to the financial crisis in Iceland. This was further enhanced by a much too narrow focus on the risk involved in operations of individual banks, rather than a much wider attention which should have been given to the risk involved in the operation of the financial sector as a whole (Guðmundsson 2009). However, the Icelandic Central Bank sought assistance from the European Central Bank and the member states' central banks, but found their doors closed (The Central Bank of Iceland 2008c). Also, to Icelandic decision-makers' surprise, the US government and its Central Bank was not willing to help out – despite providing the other Nordic states with swap facility arrangements that they could draw upon if necessary (The Central Bank of Iceland 2008d). In other words, the US no longer provided Iceland with economic shelter. This should have already been clear to the Icelandic decision-makers, since the US government had for decades been scaling down its assistance and operations in Iceland. In addition, the changed world order after the end of the Cold War and the 11 September 2001 terrorist attacks had fundamentally altered the strategic importance of Iceland. The Bush administration did not consider it of any importance to provide Iceland with political and economic shelter (see, for instance, the discussion in Ingimundarson 2008b). Therefore, the Americans simply expressed relief when the Russian government hinted that it was willing to bail Iceland out with a substantial loan after the crisis hit (Information from the US embassy in Reykjavik 2009). This finally struck Icelandic decision-makers, most coming from within the Independence Party, both within the government and the Central Bank, that the Americans had left Iceland on its own in the middle of the North Atlantic. However, many European states were very concerned about

---

1   Outward FDI flows per country in percent of world FDI flow in 2007: Luxembourg accounted for 2.6 percent, Sweden 1.8 percent, Belgium 2.5 percent and Malta for 0.0009 percent; see more on www.unctad.org.

the potential Russian loan (Information from the British and French Embassies in Reykjavik 2009), particularly the other Nordic states, which promised further assistance – having been the only states that provided Iceland bilateral swap facility arrangements (*The Economist* 2008b). Poland also offered Iceland a considerable loan with the wish that Iceland would not accept the Russian loan (Rozhnov 2008).

The collapse of the banking system was severe. The Icelandic currency, the króna, depreciated more than most small states' currencies. The depreciation has substantially increased the debt burden borne by those households and firms – many of which were already bankrupt – that had borrowed in foreign currency. The depreciation had substantial inflationary effects, with inflation peaking at nearly 19 percent in January 2008. Consumption and investment fell by almost one-fourth, year-on-year in the fourth quarter of 2008. A contraction of close to 50 percent in imports of goods and services, however, implied a much smaller reduction in total output, or 1.5 percent. The surplus on external trade has not provided the króna with the expected support, which has made it more difficult for monetary policy to facilitate the reconstruction of private sector balance sheets (The Central Bank of Iceland 2009a). Accordingly, unemployment rose to its highest level ever (since registration started in 1957) to over 9 percent in spring 2009 (Hagstofa Íslands 1997 and 2009b). The outlook remains grim, according to the Central Bank: 'As long as there is substantial uncertainty about the country's external debt, the status of public sector finances and the restructuring of the financial system, capital controls will remain a prerequisite for significant easing of monetary policy. … Consequently, unemployment will remain high. …The disinflation already underway will continue unabated' (The Central Bank of Iceland 2009b). In January 2009, the government announced that the Treasury's total liabilities would rise by just over ISK 400 billion in 2009. In addition, the Treasury guarantees the debt due to 'lost' savings in the Icelandic banks abroad and the loans from the IMF and others to the Central Bank of Iceland, in the amount of almost ISK 1,300 billion. It is estimated that the Treasury's debt will approach ISK 1,100 billion by the end of 2009. According to the National Budget for 2009, the Treasury deficit for 2009 will be ISK 150 billion (The Ministry of Finance 2009).

In November 2008, the IMF had approved a two-year Stand-By Arrangement for Iceland to support the country's programme to restore economic stability. According to the plan, Iceland will receive a loan of US$ 2.1 billion from the IMF, and supplementary loans totalling some US$ 3 billion from Denmark, Finland, Norway, Sweden, Russia, and Poland. In addition, the Faroese Government offered Iceland a loan of approximately US$ 50 million (International Monetary Fund 2008).

As stated above, Iceland did not seek EU membership at the same time as the other EFTA states in the early 1990s. The negotiations on the EEA, between the EFTA states, on the one hand, and the EU member states, on the other, were at their height when the Cold War ended and the Soviet Union collapsed, and the EFTA states started to look at the EEA Agreement as a temporary solution. They all sought full political and economic integration with the European Union – though the electorates in Norway and Switzerland prevented their political elite from joining the Union. Iceland, Norway and Switzerland and Liechtenstein became stranded within the EFTA and EEA (Switzerland did not join the EEA since the electorate refused to ratify the agreement and consequently the Swiss government froze its EU application). Accordingly, the Swiss government found it necessary to conclude a series of bilateral agreements with the EU and join the Schengen scheme. This can be explained by a combination of a pressure from the ongoing European integration process on a small state, a quest to benefit from it and a longing for a partial shelter in the European project. The decision by the Icelandic government not to apply for EU membership had, in fact, been a deliberate decision. This decision was repeated by all subsequent coalition governments until the spring of 2009. When the financial crisis hit the country – despite partial engagement in the European integration and having been protected economically by the American eagle for decades – the country was suddenly on its own without a proper American or European shelter.

Searching for Shelter

In spring 2008, the rapid fall of the króna had already sparked a heated debate about the feasibility of EU membership and adopting the euro. The entire business community demanded a currency change – the fishing industry insisting on a currency change without joining the EU. Employers' associations, except for the fisheries and agricultural organisations, requested an immediate EU application, as did the main labour union (Thorhallsson 2008b). All political parties started to examine in greater depth the pros and cons of EU membership. The Progressive Party (the central agrarian party) adopted a pro-European policy, i.e. that Iceland should apply for membership under rigid conditions (Framsóknarflokkurinn 2009). The Social Democratic Alliance (SDP) emphasised, for the first time, strongly its pro-European stance in the election campaign in spring 2009 – focusing mainly on the potential economic benefits of membership and the euro. The EU and the euro became the main election issues, and the SDP gained ground in the election and got 29.8 percent of the vote, even though it had been in government at the time of the crash (since 2007) and was partly blamed for it. The SDP made a EU application a pre-condition for forming a government with the Left-Green Movement despite the outright opposition of the Left-Greens towards EU membership (Vinstrihreyfingin-Grænt framboð 2009). The SDP and the Left-Greens were bound to form a government after the election since, for the first time in Icelandic history, the left had a majority in parliament – after having been in a minority government for three months. The general election had been called at the beginning of the year after the collapse of the coalition government (Independence Party and the SDP), after weeks of violent protests (the most severe in Iceland's history) and disputes within the government about how to tackle the economic crisis and political unrest.

The leadership of the Independence Party had initiated a detailed examination of the pros and cons of EU membership within the party after considerable pressure from the employers' wing (service and industrial sector) of the party and its coalition partner in government. However, at the special party conference, convened to review its EU policy, the EU opponents, rallied by the powerful forces of the fisheries and agrarian sectors, within the party managed to prevent a policy change. According to the party policy, a 'EU membership does not serve Icelandic interests', referring mainly to the fisheries and agricultural sectors and to the opposition to the transfer of sovereignty and to being bound by the 'flood' of regulations from Brussels (Sjálfstæðisflokkurinn 2009a and b). The firm opposition of the party to EU membership contributed to its election defeat – the worst defeat in its history – when it received only 23.7 percent of the vote, down from 36.6 percent two years earlier. The party remains split on the issue and faces a serious challenge every time it will try to find a common policy towards further European involvement (see discussion in details about the policy of the Independence Party in Thorhallsson 2008b).

The general election unexpectedly provided a majority for a EU application in parliament. The four new MPs of the Citizens' Movement, an offspring of the winter protests, announced that they would support a EU application in order to see what an accession agreement would entail. Thus, the SDP had a strong negotiating position for putting the EU issue on the agenda and for forming a coalition government with the Left Greens, who had won a decisive election victory, receiving 21.7 percent of the votes, up from 14.3 percent. The Progressive Party also advocated for EU membership. Together, the three pro-EU parties received 33 out of 63 seats in parliament. However, to complicate things, it is a known fact that a few of the Progressive MPs are not at all keen on a EU application, and few of the 16 Independence Party's MPs are in favour of an application.

The economic crisis clearly sparked the current debate on possible EU accession. Supporters of closer engagement in the European project have, in fact, always advocated and won approval by emphasising the economic benefits. This was the case for both EFTA and EEA membership. On the other hand, Eurosceptics have mainly emphasised the negative consequences of transferring sovereignty from Iceland to 'supranational' institutions and the negative effects which membership might have for the fisheries and agricultural sectors. Moreover, closer European engagement has been said to threaten the Icelandic way of life and limit Iceland's international room for manoeuvre, e.g. as regards entering into other free-trade agreements and adopting its own negotiating position within international organisations such as the WTO and regarding the Kyoto Protocol on climate change. Eurosceptics have also raised concerns about the costs involved in membership. Furthermore, Iceland's small size, combined with its lack of power resources to influence EU decisions, has been prominent in the arguments used by opponents of closer European integration. The small size of the Icelandic market and its profound reliance on marine exports, leading to substantial volatility of the economy, has also frequently been used as an argument for protectionism: all decisions concerning the economic and monetary policy must be taken in the country itself in order to respond speedily to economic swings. Retaining the Icelandic króna was seen as important in order to have a currency which would fluctuate according to the economy (see, for instance, Thorhallsson 2004d and 2008c).

However, the economic collapse led to a swift change of attitude towards the vulnerability of the economy and its small currency. The volatility of a small economy in the new globalised arena could not be illustrated more clearly. The collapse of the overgrown financial sector, which had sought expansion abroad within the EEA framework, led to economic downsizing on a scale rarely seen before. Iceland had liberalised its economy – particularly its financial sector – without securing the necessary economic and political shelter, e.g. from the European Central Bank and other EU institutes. Iceland, instead of being sheltered by the EU, encountered outright hindrance by its member states in its attempt to seek international assistance, due to the damage the Icelandic financial sector was causing within the Union.

Conclusion

Icelandic governments have reluctantly sought shelter within the framework of European integration in order to guarantee access to the European market and to respond to economic downturns. This was particularly the case in the heydays of Iceland's EFTA and EEA membership. Later, Iceland joined the Schengen scheme to assure the continuation of free movement to the other Nordic states and to enjoy the shelter of European police collaboration. Once again, the government is considering the European alternative, i.e. to join the EU and adopt the euro. A question mark has been put against the chances that Iceland could succeed in nurturing a sustainable economy without the shelter of the formal EU institutional framework and a more stable and reliable euro.

Icelandic governments have preferred the bilateral approach, which proved to be successful when gaining independence from Denmark and was portrayed as the successful method in the Cod Wars with Great Britain over fishing rights in the North Atlantic. The bilateral approach was also the base for the Nordic cooperation and Iceland's relations with the US (see the detailed study by Thorhallsson 2005 and 2006). The failure of this bilateral approach in the economic crash has altered the view of many politicians and interest groups on the feasibility of joining the supranational institutions of the EU. Iceland was left without any suitable bilateral relations or multilateral framework to help out. 'The American century' is clearly over – a period during which Iceland enjoyed the economic and political protection granted by its neighbouring superpower for over half a century. The Nordic cooperation, or Iceland's long-standing bi-lateral relations with its Nordic neighbours, did also not provide such a refuge: the Nordic states simply did not have the resources to come to Iceland's rescue on their own and, in fact, took a stance with their EU partners instead. The assistance provided by the IMF, after the economy came to a standstill, was restricted by British conditions. Thus, Icelanders are seriously considering to what extent the EU and its single currency can offer the country political and economic shelter.

The focus on the concept of sovereignty, the supremacy of fisheries and agricultural interests, an undeveloped economy and the shelter provided by America contributed to the continuation of Euroscepticism in Iceland. As a result, Icelandic policy-makers have neither sought the institutional shelter of the European Union, despite benefiting enormously from access to the common market. Nor have Icelandic politicians wanted to participate in EU policy-making, even though the EU's regulations are implemented in Iceland under the EEA. Although Icelandic governments have responded to the reality that the only way for a small state to have a say about international rules is to become actively engaged in international organisations, such as the WTO, the World Bank and the IMF, they have not taken up the option of becoming an active member of the EU. Thus, they were not able to influence EU regulations (e.g. in the financial sector), nor could they seek protection against domestic and international turmoil under the EU institutional framework. Iceland took full part in the liberalisation of its financial sector though the EEA Agreement, but failed to seek the shelter needed to protect the foundation of the sector itself in time of crisis, and so, in fact, the foundation of its own economy.

Regional and international organisations such as the EU, the WTO and the IMF provide small states with an opportunity to become actively engaged in a dialogue with larger powers. Were it not for the existence of these and other multilateral organisations, larger states would simply make rules and regulations on their own – and others would have to follow these due to the larger states' greater administrative, economic, political and military resources. For this reason, international organisations are of fundamental importance for small states. The fact that all small states in Europe have sought EU membership, except for the smallest four which have substantial defence and/or economic co-operation agreements with their larger neighbours (including authorisation to use the euro), indicates the importance of the Union. The EU not only provides access to the largest world market; it provides small states with shelter from economic downturns and a seat at the negotiating table. Access to the decision-making procedure may be as vital as the provided protection shield. This could be seen during Iceland's financial crises: a lack of access to the EU decision-making and contact network. Britain used its anti-terrorist legislation against Icelandic banks and was supported by all the EU member states, delaying the much-needed IMF assistance. Iceland was stuck in bilateral negotiations with Britain, and then later the EU itself, without the comfort of a multilateral framework.

The new globalised economy, particularly the globalised financial sector, makes small states more vulnerable than before to international economic crises, as was illustrated by the events of 2008. All states – including the large powers – sought first and foremost to save their own financial sectors and economies. The only actors that were willing to help individual countries with substantial loans were international organisations such as the EU, the IMF and the World Bank. These institutions rely, of course, on their members' willingness to give assistance, but they provide the framework for backing up the states that were worst hit by the crisis. The countries, which in the end, were willing to lend Iceland money did so under the conditions that the loans would be provided through the IMF framework (Jolly 2008). The EU is the only organisation that provides access to a single currency, support for it, in times of trouble and substantial aid to members in need in the short run as well as in the long run.

On the other side one has to see that European integration also poses several constraints on independent European small states. The common European market and the powerful euro may restrict small states' room of economic manoeuvre. They may find it increasingly more difficult to stand on their own, e.g. conducting their own economic and monetary policy. Thus, they may be pressured into taking full part in the project. On the other hand, small states do have a choice whether or not they want to join the EU as is indicated by the cases of Norway, Switzerland, Iceland, San Marino, Liechtenstein and Andorra. But, the decision not to take part in the European project requires arranging other forms of shelter, such as that provided by a large neighbour, or to be willing to pay the cost of staying out of the Union. The four smallest states have a neighbouring shelter; Norway and Switzerland could afford to stay outside. Iceland could not and paid the price.

References

BBC News, 2009. *Romania gets IMF Emergency Loan,* 25 March. Available at: http://news.bbc.co.uk/2/hi/business/7962897.stm [accessed: 27 May 2009].

British Embassy in Reykjavik, 2009. *Discussion about the Russian Bailout Loan and the Concern of European States.* (Personal communication, 10 March).

The Central Bank of Iceland, 2008a. *Tímabundin temprun á útflæði gjaldeyris.* Available at: http://sedlabanki.is/lisalib/getfile.aspx?itemid=6491 [accessed: 28 May 2009].

The Central Bank of Iceland, 2008b. An Assessment in London about the Financial System in Iceland. February 2008. (In-house personal notes).

The Central Bank of Iceland, 2008c. *Gjaldeyrisskiptasamningar og viðleitni til eflingar gjaldeyrisforða.* Available at: http://www.sedlabanki.is/?PageID=13&News ID=1888 [accessed: 29 May 2009].

The Central Bank of Iceland, 2008d. *Norrænir seðlabankar framlengja gjaldmiðlaskiptasamninga.* Available at: http://www.sedlabanki.is/?PageID=13&NewsID=1970 [accessed: 29 May 2009].

The Central Bank of Iceland, 2009a. *Monetary Bulletin 2009*, Vol. 12, 2 May, 6. Available at: http://www.sedlabanki.is/lisalib/getfile.aspx?itemid=7031 [accessed: 29 May 2009].
The Central Bank of Iceland, 2009b. *Monetary Bulletin 2009,* Vol. 12, 2 May, 5. Available at: http://www.sedlabanki.is/lisalib/getfile.aspx?itemid=7031 [accessed: 29 May 2009].
Donaldson, K. and Vina, G. 2008. UK Used Anti-Terrorism Law to Seize Icelandic Bank Assets. *Bloomberg*, 9 October. Available at: http://www.bloomberg.com/apps/news?pid=20601102&sid=aXjIA5NzyM5c [accessed: 26 May 2009].
The Economist, 2008a. *Cold Comfort for Iceland.* Intelligence Unit, 21 November. Available at: http://www.economist.com/agenda/displaystory.cfm?story_id=12666594 [accessed: 26 May 2009].
The Economist, 2008b. *Cool Aid?* Intelligence Unit, 28 October. Available at: http://www.economist.com/agenda/displaystory.cfm?story_id=12500312 [accessed: 28 May 2009].
Framsóknarflokkurinn (The Progressive Party), 2009. *Kosningastefnuskrá 2009.* Available at: http://www.framsokn.is/files/4540-0.pdf [accessed: 2 June 2009].
French Embassy in Reykjavik, 2009. *Discussion about the Russian Bailout Loan and the Concern of European States.* (Personal communication, 10 March).
Government Offices of Iceland, 2009. *Utanríkis og Evrópumál.* Available at: http://www.stjornarrad.is/Stefnuyfirlysing/#Utanrikis-_og_Evropumal [accessed: 1 June 2009].
Gros, D. 2008. Iceland on the Brink? Options for a Small, Financially Active Economy in the Current Financial Crisis Environment. *CEPS Policy Briefs*, 7 April. Available at: http://shop.ceps.eu/BookDetail.php?item_id=1635 [accessed: 25 August 2008].
Guðmundsson, M. 2009. Hin alþjóðlega fjármálakreppa, in *Skírnir: Tímarit hins íslenska bókmenntafélags*, edited by H. Guðmundsson. Reykjavík: Hið íslenska bókmenntafélag, 35-51.
Hagstofa Íslands (Statistics Iceland), 1997. Atvinnuskipting og vinnuafl, in *Hagskinna: Sögulegar hagtölur um Ísland (Icelandic Historical Statistics)*, edited by G. Jónsson and M. S. Magnússon. Reykjavík: Hagstofa Íslands, 243-46.
Hagstofa Íslands (Statistics Iceland), 2008a. *Fjöldi starfandi eftir atvinnugreinum, kyni og landssvæði 1991–2007.* Available at: http://hagstofa.is/temp/temp/VIN0110220892434382820.jpg [accessed: 24 September 2008].
Hagstofa Íslands. (Statistics Iceland), 2008b. *Laun fullvinnandi á almennum vinnumarkaði eftir atvinnugrein og kyni 1998–2007.* Available at: http://hagstofa.is/temp/temp/VIN02013200892438598124.jpg [accessed: 24 September 2008].
Hagstofa Íslands (Statistics Iceland), 2009a. *Framleiðsluuppgjör.* Available at: http://hagstofan.is/?PageID=758&src=/temp/Dialog/varval.asp?ma=THJ08101%26ti=Hlutur+atvinnugreina+%ED+landsframlei%F0slu+1973%

2D2008+%26path=../Database/thjodhagsreikningar/framluppgj_ISAT01/ %26lang=3%26units=Hlutfall [accessed: 2 June 2009].
Hagstofa Íslands (Statistics Iceland), 2009b. *Vinnumarkaðurinn.* Available at: http://hagstofan.is/?PageID=637&src=/temp/Dialog/varval.asp?ma=VIN042 04%26ti=Skr%E1%F0ir+atvinnulausir+og+hlutfall+%FEeirra+af+mannafla+ eftir+m%E1nu%F0um+1980%2D2009%26path=../Database/vinnumarkadur/ atvinnuleysi/%26lang=3%26units=Fj%F6ldi/hlutfall [accessed: 1 June 2009].
Handel, M. 1981. *Weak States in the International System.* London: Frank Cass.
Ingimundarson, V. 2002. Viðhorf Bandaríkjanna til íslenskrar hagstjórnar á 5. og 6. áratugnum, in *Frá kreppu til viðreisnar, þættir um hagstjórn á Íslandi á árunum 1930–1960*, edited by J.H. Haralz. Reykjavík: Hið íslenska bókmenntafélag, 327-44.
Ingimundarson, V. 2003. Fighting the Cod War in the Cold War: Iceland's Challenge to the Western Alliance in the 1970s. *The RUSI Journal*, 148, (3 June), 91-2.
Ingimundarson, V. 2008a. Frá óvissu til upplausnar: 'Öryggissamfélag' Ísland og Bandaríkjanna, 1991–2006, in *Uppbrot hugmyndakerfis, Endurmótun íslenskrar utanríkisstefnu, 1991–2007*, edited by V. Ingimundarson. Reykjavík: Hið íslenska bókmenntafélag, Chapter 1.
Ingimundarson, V. 2008b. Frá óvissu til upplausnar: 'Öryggissamfélag' Ísland og Bandaríkjanna, 1991–2006, in *Uppbrot hugmyndakerfis, Endurmótun íslenskrar utanríkisstefnu, 1991–2007*, edited by V. Ingimundarson. Reykjavík: Hið íslenska bókmenntafélag, 12-20.
International Monetary Fund (IMF), 2008. *IMF Executive Board Approves US$2.1 Billion Stand-By Arrangement for Iceland.* Available at: http://www.imf.org/ external/np/sec/pr/2008/pr08296.htm [accessed: 29 May 2009].
Jervis, R. 1978. Cooperation Under the Security Dilemma. *World Politics*, 30, 167-214.
Jolly, D. 2008. $2.5 Billion Is Added to Bailout for Iceland. *The New York Times*, 20 November. Available at: http://www.nytimes.com/2008/11/21/business/ world business/21icebank.html?scp=3&sq=imf%20loan%20to%20iceland&s t=cse [accessed: 2 June 2009].
Jónsson, G. 2002. Hagþróun og hagvöxtur á Ísland 1914–1960, in *Frá kreppu til viðreisnar: Þættir um hagstjórn á Íslandi á árunum 1930–1960*, edited by J.H. Haralz. Reykjavík: Hið íslenska bókmenntafélag, 9-39.
Katzenstein, P. 1985. *Small States in World Markets: Industrial Policy in Europe.* Ithaca and London: Cornell University Press.
Kautto, M. (ed.) 2001. *Nordic Welfare States in the European Context.* London and New York: Routledge.
Keohane, R.O. 1969. Lilliputians' Dilemmas: Small States in International Politics. *International Organization*, 23(2), 291-310.
Líndal, S. and Thorsteinsson, B. 1978. Lögfesting konungsvalds, in *Saga Íslands III*, edited by S. Líndal. Reykjavik: Hið íslenzka bókmenntafélag, 34-40.

The Ministry of Finance, 2009. *The Treasury's Asset and Liability Statement.* Available at: http://www.ministryoffinance.is/news/2009/01/29/nr/11710 [accessed: 29 May 2009].
Morgunblaðið (*The Daily Paper*), 2008. *Nefndi ekki ábyrgð Íslands: Morgunblaðið*, 13 November, 6a.
Neumann, I.B. and Gstöhl, S. 2004. *Lilliputians in Gulliver's World? Small States in International Relations.* Available at: http://www3.hi.is/solofile/1008303 [accessed: 26 May 2009].
Ólafsson, B. G. 1998. *Small States in the Global System: Analysis and Illustrations from the Case of Iceland.* Aldershot: Ashgate.
Pfanner, E. 2008. Iceland, in Financial Collapse, is Likely to Need IMF Help, *The New York Times*, 10 October. Available at: http://www.nytimes.com/2008/10/10/business/worldbusiness/10icebank.html?pagewanted=print [accessed: 14 July 2009].
Rozhnov, K. 2008. Russia's role in rescuing Iceland. BBC, 13 November. Available at: http://news.bbc.co.uk/2/hi/business/7720614.stm [accessed: 29 May 2009].
Sjálfstæðisflokkurinn (The Independence Party), 2009a. *Ályktun um utanríkismál.* Available at: http://xd.is/?action=landsfundur_2009_nanar&id=917 [accessed: 2 June 2009].
Sjálfstæðisflokkurinn (The Independence Party), 2009b. *Ályktun um Evrópumál.* Available at: http://xd.is/?action=landsfundur_2009_nanar&id=1007 [accessed: 2 June 2009].
Stjórnarráðið, 2009. *Samstarfsyfirlýsing ríkisstjórnar Samfylkingarinnar og Vinstrihreyfingarinnar græns framboðs: Utanríkis- og Evrópumál.* Available at: http://www.stjornarrad.is/Stefnuyfirlysing/#Utanrikis-_og_Evropumal [accessed: 2 June 2009].
Thorhallsson, B. (ed.) 2004d. *Iceland and European Integration: On the Edge.* London: Routledge.
Thorhallsson, B. 2005. *What Features Determine Small States Activities in the International Arena?* Available at: http://stjornmalogstjornsysla.is/index.php?option=com_content&task=view&id=68&Itemid=47 [accessed: 29 May 2009].
Thorhallsson, B. 2006. *Iceland's Involvement in Global Affairs Since the Mid-1990s: What Features Determine the Size of a State?* Available at: http://stjornmalog stjornsysla.is/images/stories/fg2006h/baldur.pdf [accessed: 29 May 2009].
Thorhallson, B. 2008a. Evrópustefna íslenskra stjórnvalda: Stefnumótun, átök og afleiðingar, in *Uppbrot hugmyndakerfis: Endurmótun íslenskrar utanríkisstefnu 1991–2007*, edited by V. Ingimundarson. Reykjavik: Hið íslenska bókmenntafélag, 83-101.
Thorhallsson, B. 2008b. The Influence of Ideology on the European Policy of the Independence Party, in *Rannsóknir í félagsvísindum IX*, edited by G.Th.

Johannesson and H. Björnsdóttir. Reykjavik: The Social Science Research Institute, 15-26.

Thorhallsson, B. and Vignisson, H.Th. 2004a. The Special Relationship Between Iceland and the United States of America, in *Iceland and European Integration: On the Edge*, edited by B. Thorhallsson. London: Routledge, 119-21.

Thorhallsson, B. and Vignisson, H.Th. 2004b. The First Steps: Iceland's Policy on European Integration from the Foundation of the Republic to 1972, in *Iceland and European Integration: On the Edge*, edited by B. Thorhallsson. London: Routledge, 28-33.

Thorhallsson, B. and Vignisson, H.Th. 2004c. A Controversial Step: Membership of the EEA, in *Iceland and European Integration: On the Edge*, edited by B. Thorhallsson. London: Routledge, 39-41.

UNCTAD, 2008. *World Investment Report 2008*. Available at: http://www.unctad.org/ sections/dite_dir/docs/wir08_fs_is_en.pdf [accessed: 19 September 2008].

US Embassy in Reykjavik, 2009. *Discussion about the possible Russian bailout loan*. (Personal communication, 10 March).

Vinstrihreyfingin-Grænt framboð (Left-Green Movement), 2009. *Sjálfstæð utanríkisstefna, félagsleg alþjóðahyggja*. Available at: http://www.vg.is/stefna/utanrikisstefna/ [accessed: 29 May 2009].

Vital, D. 1967. *The Inequality of States: A Study of the Small Power in International Relations*. Oxford: Clarendon Press.

PART IV
Conclusion

Chapter 14
Conclusion

Robert Steinmetz and Anders Wivel

'During World War II it was widely asserted that the day of the small power was over. Not only could such a state have no security under modern conditions of war; it could have no future in the peace that presumably one day would follow', writes Annette Baker Fox in her classic study of the power of small states (Baker Fox 2006 [1959]: 39). As the chapters of this volume show, the death of the small state was widely exaggerated. In fact, since the end of the Second World War, the geopolitical landscape of the Euro-Atlantic area transformed in such a way that much more room for manoeuvre in small state foreign policy was created, facilitating the influence of small states on the future of the region (cf. Løvold 2004). Power politics remains, but it is no longer exercised by military means. Diplomacy, economic pressure and institutional design have become the weapons of choice of the region's great powers, at least when acting inside Europe (cf. Mouritzen and Wivel 2005).

This transformation has had a profound impact on the challenges and opportunities of small European states. The end of the Cold War radically changed the geopolitical conditions for foreign policy-making in Europe. For the first time since the birth of the modern state system in 1648, small states in the region do not face conventional military threats to their security and survival. The most important consequence for small states is that they can now pursue offensive foreign policy strategies without putting their survival at risk. The continuing deepening and widening of the European Union (EU) gives small member states particularly good opportunities to do this, because of its decentralised and highly institutionalised nature. As summed up by Hey, '[s]mall states today enjoy more international prestige and visibility than at any other time in history' (Hey 2003: 1).

Still challenges remain. The most recent enlargements of the EU, combined with a transformed security environment after the Cold War, 9/11 and the Iraq War have fundamentally changed the political and institutional structures in the EU. This transformation has profound implications for the opportunities and challenges of small states inside and outside the EU. However, analyses of the EU tend to focus on the role of the larger members of the EU, in particular Germany, France and the United Kingdom, and powerful EU outsiders, most importantly the United States and Russia, whereas much less attention is paid to the role of smaller European states. Although it is only natural that most studies focus on those actors that are able to affect the integration process the most, this focus has the unfortunate side effect of leaving out the vast majority of European states.

The need for analyses and discussions of the problems shared by small European states as a consequence of the development of the EU, is only exacerbated by the significant growth in the proportion of small EU member states over the years and in particular since the end of the Cold War.[1]

This volume has aspired to fill that void by analysing the behaviour of small states towards the EU. Through a diverse compilation of contributions by authors across Europe, the book has endeavoured to provide an up-to-date and accessible overview and analysis of foreign policy opportunities and challenges faced by small states in Europe. More specifically, the institutional changes at the European level were studied closely in order to illustrate the impact of the EU on the policy choices of small states.

The introduction of the book formulated four fundamental questions: first, what are the major opportunities and challenges facing small states in Europe today? Second, how have Europe's small states responded to these opportunities and challenges? Third, why did small states respond in the way they did? Fourth, what are the costs and benefits of the most important small state strategies in Europe today?

The Challenges and Opportunities of Small European States

No state wishes to carry the label of being 'small' or 'weak' in an international system based on the principle that all states are equal and where 'the international legal system legitimises political units without regard to size' (Knudsen 1996: xv). In contrast to nineteenth century Europe, when the great powers met in concert in order to decide the rules of the game in the region (Neumann and Gstöhl 2006: 5), the authors of the present volume show that small states now have the opportunity to make a significant impact on European policy-making, at the same time as they point to the challenge that some states continue to be more equal than others.

Opportunities: European Integration, Niches and Smart Choices

In many ways, the book emphasises the main opportunities offered by the European integration process. Considering the attempts by numerous small states, which still find themselves on the frontiers of the EU, to be welcomed into the European family, it seems clear that one first lesson could be formulated as follows: by closely cooperating with larger states, and doing so within a fairly rigid framework of rules, small states have a very good chance of successfully pursuing their own

---

1 In 1957, the European Economic Community was created, when three big states (Germany, France and Italy) and three small states (the Netherlands, Belgium and Luxembourg) signed the Treaty of Rome. Today, 21 out of the 27 European Union members are generally considered small states. For a discussion of the concept of small states, see Chapter 1.

foreign policy goals. Hence, small states ought to be keen on further and, more particularly, deeper European integration. Especially, considering the reluctance of larger states to follow this process, small states should take full advantage of so-called 'enhanced cooperation' and deepen cooperation in key policy areas. One area is cross-border integration in sub-regions. As argued by Criekemans and Duran in Chapter 3, sub-national entities may be useful partners for small states in a complex international environment, not least with regard to the creation of cross border regions, which offers many advantages, both economically and politically. Another area is European Security and Defence Policy (ESDP), where small states have proved to be particularly effective actors. As shown by Clive Archer in Chapter 4, small EU member states have made an important contribution to the ESDP by actively contributing to the policy, in particular its civilian side, by making distinct niche contributions to a number of operations and by providing significant troop contributions.[2] Small states have the potential to play a more active role as contributors to the development of the EU's soft power potential as called for by Plamen Pantev in Chapter 7. Toms Rostoks' analysis of the changing nature of power in Chapter 6 shows that larger international developments may facilitate this process: the relative importance of different types of power resources changes over time. Military power is less important in Europe today than in the past, whereas economic power and transnational relations have increased in importance.

Several chapters underline the crucial need for small states to carefully rationalise their interests and narrowly define their specific foreign policy goals, if they want to be successful at the European level as well as in the wider international arena. Especially at a time of economic turmoil, global struggle against climate change and an ever more difficult battle against terrorism and extremism, small states have the opportunity to raise their profiles, provide leadership on the global stage, in particular by acting as mediators, building bridges between competing views. The quest for so-called policy niches represents a key to success for small states in the pursuit of their policy goals. Even if one would assume that larger states would take the lead in certain key policy issues, paradoxically it is often the case that on precisely these issues progress is minimal. Hence, small states should dare to make their voices heard on these issues and put forward alternative, bolder and more effective policy options.

One prerequisite for doing this is to recognise the multidimensional nature of the EU as an organisation. As argued by Anders Wivel in Chapter 2, small states are affected in different ways by the organisational aspects of the EU (which entail a combination of formal EU institutions and rules, a shared consensus culture and the complex and loosely coupled aspects associated with 'stakeholder Europe'). In order to maximise influence in this institutional environment, small states would benefit from acting as 'smart states' by pursuing a strategy, which focuses resources

---

2   For a particular interesting contribution to this debate, see Jakobsen's study of the Nordic influence on the civilian aspects of the ESDP (Jakobsen 2009).

on carving out political niches where the small state may make a difference by acting as a mediator. Small states may do this by focusing their efforts on issues where traditional material power capabilities play only a secondary role for success. These issues include intercultural dialogue, climate change and offering expertise in areas such as judicial reform and the establishment of the rule of law. They also include non-violent military actions, such as peacekeeping missions and the training of foreign police forces. Through such choices, small states can directly enhance their status as legitimate and reliable partners to the extent that they become indispensible 'pieces of the puzzle'. Their expertise and actions will become increasingly relied upon in the future.

Challenges: Crises, Directoire and Democracy

At the European level, institutional reform and the revision of the Nice Treaty represent crucial challenges to small states. The jury is still out on who will effectively gain from the various reforms, but there seems to be a tendency favouring larger member states. The Lisbon Treaty reduces the power of small states in a number of ways (to name a few: weighted votes in the Council, extended use of qualified majority voting, fewer seats in the European Parliament and less representation within the European Commission, first, by the reduction of portfolios, and second, by the rotating representation of member states). Even though, because of the informal aspects of EU policy-making and successful coping strategies of small states,[3] the political effect of these institutional changes may be less important than they appear at first sight it remains to be seen how small states can continue to maintain their visibility, defend their interests and influence the agenda. Although obviously all member states remain equal, small states can no longer profit from their overrepresentation in the institutional architecture.

Moreover, considering recent procedures adopted by certain Council presidencies, most specifically the French Presidency, which – under the leadership of President Sarkozy – called for more regular high level summits, big EU member states have recently seemed more eager to control the agenda than in the past. Some small states were quick to react, stressing that such procedures would jeopardise the EU's traditional institutional 'habits', undermine the so-called 'community method' and threaten solidarity between member states. Unofficial communication and negotiation among the European great powers have always played important roles in the history of the European integration project, where Franco-German cooperation has at times resembled a 'cooperative hegemony' (Pedersen 1998), and in EU security policy, where the 'big member states are especially known to negotiate amongst themselves before going to the Council table' (Gegout 2002: 331-2; cf. Keukeleire 2001). However, in recent years, concert-like negotiations among the big member states taking place outside the formal EU institutions have become even more common (cf. Wivel 2005).

---

3   Cf. Anders Wivel's analysis in Chapter 2.

This increased use of intergovernmental methods – often in closed, informal fora – penalises small states, as they simply lack the means and policy instruments that large states possess.

What is more, some large EU member states are also represented in larger fora outside the EU, which are considered as 'exclusive clubs' by small states, (for instance the formation of the 'G8' or 'G20' groups of industrialised and developed nations). Decisions taken in these fora can have a major impact on the fates of small European states, which have few means to influence the members of these fora. Hence, it can be argued that there exists a tendency towards the establishment of a 'Directoire' of large states. This can be particularly threatening for small states, especially as this 'Directoire' seems to be forming outside of the structure of the EU, is taking shape without a legal framework of sorts, and yet impacts upon all EU member states – including those that are not represented at the negotiation table.

In the EU context, a 'Directoire', which would be running the Union's business on a day-to-day basis, would clearly relegate small states to the 'backbenches' of decision-making at the European level. Therefore, small states have stressed that the principle of equality must be respected and they have resisted attempts by some capitals to weaken the culture of consensus of the Union. This tendency, in combination with a weaker EU Commission, which has traditionally been perceived as a natural ally of small states, represents an important challenge to small states' interests.

The pertinence of this challenge is illustrated in several chapters. For instance, as noted by Jan Rood in Chapter 8, having access to the big EU member states – France and Germany in particular – and cultivating a good relationship with these states is pivotal for small states aiming to maximise their influence in the EU. Therefore, a big member state directorate is considered a serious threat to Dutch influence. Also, to Luxembourg, as is noted in Chapter 9 by Jean-Marie Frentz, a strong European Commission is the best bulwark against dominance by great powers. To both of these founding members, the recent enlargements of the EU present new opportunities for influence, but at the same time bring with them the threat of losing their traditionally strong positions within the EU and becoming marginalised. However, for small member states, which have only entered the EU in recent years, the challenge is even bigger: they have limited past experience in navigating the complex institutional landscape of the EU and thus no past positions or privileges which they can rely on. Mats Braun's analysis of the different EU approaches of Slovakia and the Czech Republic in Chapter 10 illustrates that this challenge can be handled in very different ways, even by states that share a number of characteristics. The situation may be particularly difficult to tackle for small states if the relation to the EU involves issues perceived as central to national security. As shown by Costas Melakopides in Chapter 11, the unique security situation of Cyprus has had important effects on its position in Europe and its relation to the EU and still remains unresolved. In Austria, as argued by Jean-Marc Rickli in Chapter 12, neutrality – which was traditionally fundamental to

Austrian security policy – has been de-emphasised in order to comply with ESDP, even though non-participation in a military alliance remains central.

Explaining the Foreign Policy of Small European States

How have small states responded to these challenges and opportunities and why have they responded in the way they did? The contributors to this book show that small states' approaches to cooperation with great powers may be placed along a continuum from reactive and strictly intergovernmental relations to proactive full integration. Among the countries analysed in this book, Switzerland and Iceland are positioned close to the reactive intergovernmental end of the continuum, whereas the Netherlands and, in particular, Luxembourg are close to the proactive full integration end of the continuum. For both groups, the EU may be seen as an opportunity. For Iceland, as Baldur Thorhallsson's analysis in Chapter 13 shows, the EU represents a potential for political and economic shelter in a time of turmoil. For Luxembourg, the EU represents a unique opportunity for punching above its weight and to influence some of the major actors in its geopolitical vicinity. Thus, in Chapter 9, Jean-Marie Frentz argues that Luxembourg has compensated for a small bureaucracy by relying on EU bureaucracy to do much of the diplomacy it would otherwise have had to do itself. At the same time, Luxembourg has carefully cultivated its role as honest broker and negotiator by working closely with the European Commission and being open to alliances with other member states.

Whether they use the EU as a shelter or as a platform for increased influence, the cost of giving up some of their sovereignty is a price, which the vast majority of European small states is willing to pay. Small states that choose to stay outside the EU (such as Norway and Switzerland) usually have both (i) special interests which are difficult to reconcile with the policies of the EU and (ii) the economic assets necessary to back up a position as EU outsider.

The contributions to this volume illustrate that the approaches of small states do not simply depend on whether they are members of the EU. Even though small states outside the EU typically pursue strategies that are more intergovernmental and reactive than those adopted by small states within the EU, the analyses by Thorhallsson and Rickli show that even Iceland and Switzerland are – in different ways – becoming more inclined to adopt institutional strategies than they were in the past. Also, within the EU, there are considerable variations in small state approaches. Luxembourg is proactive and institutionalist, while the Netherlands are proactive but guarded against great power dominance, Slovakia is keenly adapting to EU policies, while the Czech Republic is more hesitant, Cyprus seems to be caught between an attempt to pursue its national interests and the interests of the great powers to whom Cyprus matters only little as compared to other, more powerful actors.

How can we explain that small European states are almost uniformly pursuing foreign policies that strengthen international institutions, including the EU, while pursuing very different policies within these institutions? Based on the contributions to this volume, we can point to a number of factors explaining this puzzle.

Factors at the global and European level have created strong incentives for small states to favour European integration. Most importantly, the end of the Cold War and the ensuing collapse of the Soviet Union dramatically changed the geopolitical landscape in Europe. The most important consequence for the region's small states was that, for the first time in centuries, they no longer needed to fear a conventional military attack by any of the region's great powers. Combined with the regulation of interstate relations through EU rules and institutions, this left small states with more freedom of manoeuvre in their foreign policy, allowing them to focus more on maximising their influence and less on guarding their territorial integrity against the threat of invasion.

A second consequence of the end of the Cold War was that the collapse of the Soviet Union left the United States as the only superpower. This poses both an opportunity and a challenge to the region's small states. On the one hand, the American order – now expanded to include most of the international system – creates a stable international environment allowing small European states to thrive without fearing for their survival. Even though European small states are not always in agreement with the United States on global climate policy, the importance of the United Nations or policies on the Middle East, they remain strong supporters of the basic values of the American world order: liberal democracy, the rule of law and market economy. On the other hand, to the extent that the United States chose to 'go-it-alone', unchecked American power in itself poses a threat to a rule-governed international society and therefore small state influence. Strengthening the EU as an international actor represents the most important opportunity for small states to balance American power and to influence the United States in a way which preserves those important aspects of the American world order conducive to small states interests.

Small state reliance on European integration also increased due to globalisation. Challenges to small state security no longer primarily originate from neighbouring great powers, but from indirect and unpredictable threats in the international system including terrorism, pandemics and financial and environmental instability. Whereas the absence of threats from neighbouring great powers creates new opportunities for pursuing national ideas and interests internationally without the fear of invasion, the new security environment increases small states' reliance on great powers and international organisations with sufficient surveillance resources. At the same time, globalisation increases complexity of international relations by increasing the number of governmental and non-governmental actors trying to influence politics globally, regionally and nationally. For small states this presents both an opportunity and a challenge. The increased number of actors increases the chance of forging viable coalitions. Yet, at the same time, increased complexity challenges the limited political and administrative resources of small states. In this situation, European integration represents an opportunity for small states, both to seek shelter against what are perceived as the negative consequences of globalisation and to use the EU as a tool for pursuing small state interests in a globalised world. As is argued by Kattel, Kalvet and Randma-Liiv in Chapter 5, the new global challenges create strong incentives for regional collaboration in the future, not least in relation to innovation policy.

Despite its many benefits for small European states, participating in the European integration process has costs as well. Most importantly, the integration process presents small states with an 'integration dilemma' between, on the one hand, preserving national autonomy and, on the other hand, seeking to influence European affairs through active participation in European integration (Kelstrup 1993; Petersen 1998; cf. Goetschel 1998). This integration dilemma has intensified over the past decades as the EU has consolidated its 'monopoly' as the only supplier of regional integration and the pivotal platform for economic and political negotiations over Europe's future. However, at the same time, a number of institutional developments, in particular the increasingly contested authority of the European Commission and the presence of great power directorates in EU policy-making, threaten the influence of small EU member states. For small states, the costs of lost autonomy and the benefits of influence both continue to rise as EU integration deepens and widens.

The contributors to this volume show that small European states ascribe different values to autonomy and influence when trying to handle this dilemma. But how do we explain the variations in EU approaches among small European states? One hypothesis could be that the better small states can afford the luxury of autonomy, the more likely they are to act with reservation or even choose to stay outside the European integration process. This might explain why rich countries such as Norway and Switzerland stay outside the EU, but it does not explain why Luxembourg is one of the most active small state participants in the Union.

However, a number of contributors to this volume point to an alternative explanation: small states are heavily influenced by the 'shadow of the past', often past security challenges. The lessons learned from these experiences may be viewed by the outside observer as either imagined or real, but nonetheless 'exert a restrictive influence on future state behaviour, including foreign policy. Most importantly, the lessons of the past influence the priority given to national autonomy' (Mouritzen and Wivel 2005: 38-9). Lessons learned during the Cold War and the early post-Cold War years continue to mark most small states' policies in Europe. For instance, as shown by Jean-Marc Rickli in Chapter 12, the large sections of the Austrian and Swiss political elites and populations consider neutrality as being tied to eras of comparative security and growth that contributed to the establishment of modern societies. Thus, even though the meaning of neutrality today is very different to the meaning of neutrality when the concept first gained importance in the foreign policy of these countries, elites and populations still perceive 'neutrality' to be a central concept. Also, according to Mats Braun in Chapter 10, the shadow of the past – in the form of perceptions of the state as a continuation of the Czechoslovak state or as a newly independent state – explain the different EU approaches of Slovakia and the Czech Republic respectively. Also, Jan Rood in Chapter 8, points out that the relatively ambitious foreign policy of the Netherlands may be explained by recalling that in the past the Netherlands was one of Europe's leading powers. Thus, whereas a large majority of small states consider further European integration beneficial, they continue to strike the compromise between the cost of lost autonomy and the benefits of increased influence in different ways.

The Future of Small States in Europe

Small states in Europe are simultaneously challenged and privileged. Challenges abound. Institutional reforms undermine some of the traditional channels of small state influence in the EU. Big EU member states often prefer to negotiate some of the fundamental issues related to Europe's future development on their own and to further their interests in great power fora, at which small European states are not even represented. At the same time, small states are challenged by globalisation and the increasing number of non-state and sub-state actors aiming to influence regional and global politics.

However, these challenges should not overshadow the many opportunities of small European states. In the Euro-Atlantic area, territorial conquest is ruled out as a great power policy, and even though the region's great powers have entered international institutions in order to pursue their national interests and regularly attempt to use the institutions as their own instruments, these institutions still help to regulate the actions of all their member states, both formally and informally. For these reasons, small states are in a better position than ever to pursue their own interests and maximise influence on international affairs. Even though their position as the weaker part in an asymmetric relationship by definition excludes small states from agenda-setting on most policy areas at the same time as their lack of resources prevents them from implementing any larger international initiatives on their own, the contributors to this book have shown that small states often succeed in pursuing their own interests. Small states may even increase their influence on international affairs by optimising their strategies.

In a world grappling to establish some kind of a new global order, small states may take advantage of the opportunity to play a more prominent role on the world stage. With the United States struggling for supremacy; Russia re-asserting itself; China, Brazil and India rising as economic competitors to the EU; the African continent struggling to develop; and free-riders Iran and North Korea striving for power, small European states cannot and need not accept marginalisation. They not only represent the 'glue' that holds the puzzle together, but also an alternative. By their very existence, they prove that alternatives to military muscle politics exist, and that alternative solutions can be found.

References

Baker Fox, A. 2006 [1959]. The Power of Small States: Diplomacy in World War II, in *Small States in International Relations*, edited by C. Ingebritsen, I.B. Neumann, S. Gstöhl and J. Beyer. Seattle: University of Washington Press, 39-54.

Gegout, C. 2002. The Quint: Acknowledging the Existence of a Big Four-US Directoire at the Heart of the EU's Foreign Policy Decision-Making Process. *Journal of Common Market Studies*, 40(2), 331-44.

Goetschel, L. 1998. The Foreign and Security Policy Interests of Small States in Today's Europe, in *Small States Inside and Outside the European Union*, edited by L. Goetschel. Dordrecht: Kluwer Academic Publishers, 13-31.

Hey, J.A.K. 2003. Introducing Small State Foreign Policy, in *Small States in World Politics*, edited by J.A.K. Hey. Boulder: Lynne Rienner, 1-11.

Jakobsen, P.V. 2009. Small States, Big Influence: The Overlooked Nordic Influence on the Civilian ESDP. *Journal of Common Market Studies*, 47(1), 81-102.

Kelstrup, M. 1993. Small States and European Political Integration: Reflections on Theory and Strategy, in *The Nordic Countries and the EC*, edited by I.D. Petersen and T. Tiilikainen. Copenhagen: Copenhagen Political Studies Press, 136-62.

Keukeleire, S. 2001. Directorates in the CFSP/CESDP of the European Union: A Plea for 'Restricted Crisis Management Groups'. *European Foreign Affairs Review*, 6, 75-101.

Knudsen, O.F. 1996. Introduction, in *Small States and the Security Challenge in the New Europe*, edited by W. Bauwens, A. Clesse and O.F. Knudsen. London: Brassey's, xv-xxiii.

Løvold, A. 2004. Småstatsproblematikken i internasjonal politikk. *Internasjonal Politikk*, 62(1), 7-31.

Mouritzen, H. and Wivel, A. 2005. *The Geopolitics of Euro-Atlantic Integration*. London: Routledge.

Neumann, I.B. and Gstöhl, S. 2006. Introduction: Lilliputians in Gulliver's World?, in *Small States in International Relations*, edited by C. Ingebritsen, I.B. Neumann, S. Gstöhl and J. Beyer. Seattle: University of Washington Press, 3-36.

Pedersen, T. 1998. *Germany, France and the Integration of Europe: A Realist Interpretation*. London: Pinter Publishers.

Petersen, N. 1998. National Strategies in the Integration Dilemma: An Adaptation Approach. *Journal of Common Market Studies*, 36(1), 33-54.

Wivel, A. 2005. The Security Challenge of Small EU Member States: Interests, Identity and the Development of the EU as a Security Actor. *Journal of Common Market Studies*, 43(2), 393-412.

Index

Amsterdam Treaty 47, 52, 185
Annan Plan 162, 166-7, 168, 172, 175
asymmetric relationship 6-8, 15-16, 31, 32, 49, 50, 59, 66, 104, 110, 119, 125, 147, 148, 158, 161, 166, 225
Austria
   Common Foreign and Security Policy (CFSP) 185-6
   ESDP 186, 222
   Lisbon Treaty 187
   NATO 186-7
   neutrality after the Cold War 184-8
   perception by citizens 193-4
   Soviet Union 181, 184
   United Nations 185
autonomy 9-10, 25, 53, 54, 182, 192, 193, 224-5

Baltic States
   economy 74-5
   foreign and security policy 52, 54, 58, 59
banking crisis 155, *see also* Iceland
bandwagoning 32, 53, 55, 59, 88, 127
Benelux xii, 10, 16, 118, 126, 131, 133, 134, 141
Bretton Woods international financial system 74

Central and Eastern Europe 3, 11, 48, 50, 72
   accession into EU 77-8
Cod Wars 202, 208
Council of Europe 133, 165-7
Cyprus
   economy 172-3, 176
   European Union 53, 167-70, 172-3
   historical background 162-4
   public opinion 171-2
   Turkey 161, 164, 168-9, 174, 175-8, *see also* Annan Plan, Turkey

Turkish Republic of Northern Cyprus TRNC 164, 165, 175
United Nations 163, 164-6, 170, *see also* Annan Plan, Laakso Report
United States 163, 165
Czech Republic 41, *see also* Czechoslovakia
   European Union 148-51, 155-7, 221, 222, 224
   European Security and Defence Policy (ESDP) 51, 55, 57
   Lisbon Treaty 147, 149, 151, 154, 156
   NATO 154
   presidency 156
Czechoslovakia 3, 148, 151, 152, 155, 157

Denmark 10, 47, 48, 52, 55, 57-8, 59, 205, 208
diplomacy, *see also* bandwagoning
   of small states 31-4, 29-42, 104, *see also* Luxembourg, Netherlands
   of sub-states 34-41

Estonia
   electronic industry 70, 72
   security and defence 49, 51, 52, 57
EUREGION 36, 38, 41, *see also* Luxembourg
European Council 121, 126, 127, 134, 220, *see also* European Union decision-making, Lisbon Treaty
   of Brussels (2004) 48
   of Copenhagen (2002) 168
   of Laeken (2001) 48
   of Luxembourg (1997) 148, 153
   of Luxembourg (2005) 135, 138, 140
   of Santa Maria da Feira (2000) xiii

presidency xii, 16, 19, 20-21, 23, 123-4, 149, 220, *see also* Czech Republic, Finland, Luxembourg, United Kingdom
European Economic Area (EEA), *see* Iceland
European Free Trade Association (EFTA), *see* Iceland
European Security and Defence Policy (ESDP) 47-59, 109, 122, 219, *see also* Austria
  Constructivist explanation 56-7
  Neo-Liberal Institutionalist explanation 55-6
  Realist explanation 53-5
European Union
  decision-making, *see also* European Council presidency
    consensus 20, 21, 23, 124, 136, 139, 219, 221
    veto 20, 127, 156-7, 170, *see also* Luxembourg veto
    voting system 18-21, 23, 125, 134, 220, *see also* Lisbon treaty
  fiscal matters xiii-xv, 73, 78, 140, *see also* taxes
  founding members xi, 10, 117, 118, 133, 221, *see also* Benelux

Flanders 31, 35, 37, 38, *see also* sub-state diplomacy
Finland, *see also* bandwagoning
  European Union 10, 47, 49, 51, 52, 54, 57, 59
  Iceland 205
  industry 65, 67, 70, 72
  NATO 54-5, 59
  presidency 56
  Russia 97
  and size 96

GDP (Gross Domestic Product)
  Iceland economy 200, 204
  Luxembourg economy xiii, 132
Geopolitics xi, xvi, 21, 97, 132-3, 143
Gilpin, Robert 88-9, 92-4

hard power 97, 106, 108, 111
honest broker xii, 25, 128, 222, *see also* mediator

Iceland, *see also* Cod Wars
  Denmark 201-2, 208
  economy 200
  European Economic Area (EEA) 202-3, 205-8
  European Free Trade Association (EFTA) 202, 205-8
  European Union 206-8, 209-10
    Schengen Agreement 203, 206, 208
  financial crisis 199, 203-6
  IMF 199, 201, 205, 209-10
  Nordic Countries 199-200, 203, 208, 209
  Russia 204-5
  United States 201, 202, 204, 208
IMF (International Monetary Fund) xv, 199, *see also* Iceland
Information and Communication Technologies (ICT) 69-71, 75, 79-80
innovation 24, 65-80, 224
International Relations (IR) theory of xvi, 7-8, 12, 17, 32, 53, *see also* ESDP, Gilpin
  uncertainty 87, 89, 94, 95-100

Juncker, Jean-Claude xi, xv, 138, 141

Katzenstein, Peter 77, 136

Laakso Report on Cyprus 166-7
lessons of the past 48, 105, 120, 147, 151-7, 153, 162-4, 192-3, 224-5
Lisbon Treaty 16, 18-20, 142, 220, *see also* Austria, Czech Republic, Luxembourg, Netherlands, Slovakia, European Union voting system
Luxembourg xi-xvi, *see also* Benelux, EU fiscal matters
  economy 132, 133, 140, 142
  and enlargement 134
  ESDP 51, 52, 135, 141
  foreign policy 132-43, 222, 224
  Grande region 41

Lisbon Treaty 142, 221
NATO 52, 132
presidency xi, 135, 137, 138, 139-40
United Nations 135
veto xii-xiii, 140

Maastricht Treaty xi, 47, 48, 140, 157, 185
mass production or Fordist paradigm 68, 70, 74, 75, 77, 79-80
mediator 25, 26, 110, 138, 139, 140-41, 219-20

National Innovative Systems (NIS) 78-9
NATO 7, 10, 47-50, 52, 52, 54-5, 56-9, 106-7, *see also* Austria, Czech Republic, Finland, Luxembourg, Netherlands, Slovakia
    enlargement 48, 50, 154
    Kosovo campaign 52, 54, 186, 190, 191
Netherlands
    diplomacy 120
    European Union 117-18, 121-2, 125-6, 222, *see also* EU decision-making
    ESDP 51, 52
    Lisbon Treaty 117, 123-5, 128
    foreign and security policy 41, 119-20, 122, 141, 149, 225
        bilateral relations 128
            size 50-51, 118-21, 127, 128, 169
    NATO 47, 120, 122
    United States 122
neutrality 10, 182-4, 224, *see also* Austria, Switzerland
Netherlands 120
New Public Management (NPM) 76-7
Nice Treaty 52, 120, 134, 220
Nordic countries 10, 24, 55, 68-9, 74, 151, *see also* Iceland
Norway 10, 50, 107, 203, 206, 210, 224
Nye, Joseph, 89-90, 162, *see also* soft power

peace-keeping 47-8, 56, 134, 135, 163, 184, 190, 220
    Austria 185
power, concept of 88-92
Pralinengipfel 141

Russia 15, 54-5, 58-9, 98, 153, 173, 175, 225, *see also* Finland, Iceland, Soviet Union

Slovakia, *see also* Czechoslovakia
    European Union 148-51, 152-5, 222
    ESDP 51, 55
    Lisbon Treaty 147, 149, 154
    NATO 154
Schüssel, Wolfgang 187
Slovenia 39, 49, 51, 52, 107, 155
small states, smallness
    definition 4-7, 66, 87, 104-5, 131, 169
    and innovation 67-71, 79-80, *see also* ICT
    strategy xii, 9-11, 15-6, 23-6, 96, 99-100, 137, 218-20
smart state 15, 17, 23-6, 96, 104, 137, 219
soft power 24, 31-2, 38, 48, 90, 98, 99, 106, 108-11, 139, 169-70, 219, *see also* Joseph Nye
Stability and Growth Pact 138, 141, 142
Sweden 10, 47, 50, 52, 54-5, 56, 59, 110, 151, 184, 191
Switzerland
    and banking xiii-xv, 140
    EFTA 206
    European Union 204, 206, 222
        CFSP 189
        Schengen Agreement 206
    NATO 190-91
    neutrality 181, 182-4
        perception by citizens 193-4
    United Nations 185, 188-9
    United States 192

taxes xiii-xv, 70, 73, 74, 75, 80, 133, 137, 140, 149, *see also* fiscal matters
Thucydides 15, 88
Turkey
    accession to the European Union 161, 167, 170, 174, 177
    regional power 50

United Nations, *see also* Annan Plan, Austria, Cyprus, Luxembourg

UN Charter 106, 164, 170, 185, 189
United States of America xiii, xiv, 223, 225, *see also* Cyprus, Iceland, Netherlands, Switzerland
European Union 23, 217
United Kingdom
　Cyprus 162
　ESDP 49, 51
　military power 23, 49, 55
　NATO 50, 55
　presidency 168
　United Nations 162

Väyrynen, Raimo 6, 31
Vital, David 6, 201

Wallonia 31, 37, *see also* sub-state diplomacy
Waltz, Kenneth 53, 57, 88-9, 95
Washington Consensus 69, 71-3, 74, 75, 76, 79
welfare state 68-9, 74, 79
Werner, Pierre xi-xii

Yugoslavia 3, 47-8, 135, 190-91, *see also* peace-keeping